DESIRE

Love Stories in Western Culture

Catherine Belsey

BLACKWELL
Oxford UK & Cambridge USA

Copyright © Catherine Belsey 1994

The right of Catherine Belsey to be identified as author of this work has been asserted in accordance with the Copyright, Designs and Patents Act 1988.

First published 1994

Blackwell Publishers
108 Cowley Road
Oxford OX4 1JF
UK

238 Main Street
Cambridge, Massachusetts 02142
USA

British Library Cataloguing in Publication Data
A CIP catalogue record for this book is available from the British Library.

Library of Congress Cataloging-in-Publication Data
Belsey, Catherine.
    Desire : love stories in Western culture / Catherine Belsey.
        p.   cm.
    Includes bibliographical references and index.
    ISBN 0-631-16813-3 (acid-free paper).—ISBN
0-631-16814-1 (pbk : acid-free paper)
    1. English literature—History and criticism—Theory, etc.
2. Love stories, English—History and criticism.   3. Arthurian
romances—History and criticism.   4. Love stories—History and
criticism.   5. Desire in literature.   6. Love in literature.
I. Title.
PR149.L6B45   1994
809'.93354—dc20

94-14118
CIP

Typeset in 11½/13½ pt Garamond 3
by Best-set Typesetter Ltd., Hong Kong
Printed in Great Britain by Hartnolls Ltd, Bodmin

This book is printed on acid-free paper

*To the memory of my mother
who would have gone along with some of it*

Contents

Illustrations

Preface

'Perfect love,' affirms the narrator of Colette's *Bella-Vista*, 'tells its story in three lines: *He* loved me, I loved *Him*, His presence effaced all other presences; we were happy, then *He* stopped loving me and I suffered.'

To be in love is to be the protagonist of a story, even when the story is as brief and as sceptical as the one Colette tells here. Desire in Western culture is inextricably intertwined with narrative, just as the tradition of Western fiction is threaded through with desire. Though sometimes only incidentally, the great majority of stories are love stories. It seems, therefore, that people like reading about desire. At the same time, desire presses to be written, to be narrated: people find it exhilarating to tell their stories.

This book is about desire, but it is also about desire's inscription, the pleasures of reading and the problems of writing. Moreover, to the extent that the second half also represents an essay in cultural history, the book itself tells a succession of stories, recounts the ways of desire at different times. And if the stories it tells are not as laconic as Colette's, they are short, all the same. Part II comprises a series of discontinuous narratives of historical change: tales of love, not a single, unfolding, comprehensive story of its development.

In this field everyone is an expert. I am grateful to the many people who have allowed me to profit from their expertise by telling me stories, as well as to those who have been generous with their scholarly knowledge. Since it is impossible to name them all, I single out Philip Armstrong, John Astington, Julia Briggs, Linda Charnes, Martin Coyle, Jim Dale, Alan Dessen, Antony Easthope, Terence Hawkes, Harriett Hawkins, Elaine Jordan, Duncan Large, Ann Lecercle, Kate McGowan, Nickianne Moody, Barbara Mowat, John

Peck, John Percival, Mike Peterson, Elizabeth Schmitt and Susan Zimmerman. Stephan Chambers helped me invent the book in the first place. I am grateful to Andrew Belsey for William Morris and the copula, and to Louise Tucker for Colette. Balz Engler and Bernd Richter explained Freud's German. I learned from discussing Donne with Cécile le Bigot, Sabine Heer, Roland Heinmüller, Alex Kendall, Emma Lewis, David McCalden, Jane Morfitt, Elisabeth Palser and Andrew Stott. David Lee Miller commented on an earlier version of Chapter 6. John Hines was kind but firm about medieval adultery. I could not have written the book without Charles Shepherdson's indispensable and detailed commentary on the theory chapter. David Skilton supplied *The Belton Estate* and unremitting support.

Above all, for an endless readiness to discuss the issues, as well as for books, references, and incisive comments on parts of the text, I am forever indebted to Peter Alldridge, Fred Botting, Cynthia Dessen, Jane Moore and Lena Cowen Orlin.

I thank the staff of the Folger Shakespeare Library for their kindness, and the Folger Institute for a great deal of intellectual stimulus while I directed a seminar there. The staff of the Arts and Social Studies Library, University of Wales, Cardiff were patient, sympathetic and always willing to enter into the quest for sources.

Earlier versions of chapters 1, 2, 3 and 4 have appeared in *The Glasgow Review*, *Women: A Cultural Review*, *Textual Practice*, and *New Literary History*. Figure 1 is reproduced by permission of The Tennyson Collection, University of Wales, Cardiff Library.

Part I

Desire now

I

Prologue: Writing about Desire

I

Desire: a kind of madness, an enchantment, exaltation, anguish . . .
perhaps the foundation of a lifetime of happiness. Writing about desire: compulsive, a challenge, self-indulgence, anxiety . . . above all, a
project that defies completion.

This is a book about desire in Western culture. It sets out to analyze
the textual presentation of what must surely be the commonest and
yet the most singular condition we know. At once shared with a
whole culture, but intimate and personal, hopelessly banal and yet
unique: if these are not exactly paradoxes of desire, they are perhaps
undecidabilities, instances of the difficulty of fixing, delimiting, de-
lineating a state of mind which is also a state of body, or which perhaps deconstructs the opposition between the two, throwing into
relief in the process the inadequacy of a Western tradition that divides
human beings along an axis crossed daily by this most familiar of
emotions.

Writing about desire. It has, of course, been done before – by poets,
dramatists, novelists, sexologists, moralists, psychoanalysts, socio-
biologists . . . But something seems to remain unsaid. And it is primarily this that motivates still more writing. Desire eludes final
definition, with the result that its character, its nature, its meaning,
becomes itself an object of desire for the writer. I want to know
about desire; I want to pry into its secrets and have access to its holy
places; and I want these things with a special kind of intensity which
perhaps bears witness to the peculiar privilege Western culture accords
to desire.

3

II

There is, of course, in addition to the personal engagement, a politics of writing about desire. First, a sexual politics – by which I mean not so much a politics of gender in this case, as a politics of sexuality. Western culture's current understanding of desire is the location of norms, proprieties and taxonomies, which constitute a form of constraint. God's Enlightenment surrogate, Nature, polices modern Western sexuality to deeply coercive effect. Most obviously, Nature forbids transgressive sexual practices, though the result of this, as Michel Foucault has so persuasively argued in *The History of Sexuality Volume One*, is not the elimination but on the contrary the *construction* of perversion, as Nature's differentiating, demonized other. The 'unnatural' defines by its difference what is acceptable, and in the process either brings into line or outlaws sexual subjects.

Transgression, and gay and lesbian sexuality in particular, is at last beginning to elicit the political attention it deserves. But there is another sexual constraint, more insidious, less commonly detected, but possibly no less coercive in its consequences. The sexual relation, Enlightened common sense insists, in its acceptable, heterosexual mode, is natural, healthy, wholesome and organic. Sex, so the story goes, is ultimately reproductive and therefore useful: it has survival value for the species. According to this teleological, functionalist account of sexuality, if we get our sexual relations wrong, if they do not work out for us, that is in one way or another the result of a failure of adjustment.

We know, of course, that it can be difficult, that there is a question beyond the mechanics of sex. Sex education in schools has become elaborate and complex, often involving role-play so that children can enact the problems in a safe context: a monologue on the life and times of the rabbit is no longer thought to be enough. But the explanation of any given problem is always specific to the situation. Does Othello strangle his wife in their wedding sheets? It must be, according to current Shakespeare criticism, because he is an outsider, and thus a prey to all kinds of anxieties, especially sexual anxieties. Do the hard, phallic heroes of popular romances resist true love and the eternity of domestic happiness that it entails? It must be because they are damaged, often deprived of real affection, and in need of the repair that can be brought

4

about only by the love of a good woman. Scarlett O'Hara can't get it together with Ashley Wilkes? An incompatibility of minds and bodies. Scarlett O'Hara and Rhett Butler? A collapse of communication in a society that keeps women infantile . . . One way or another, the problem is commonly seen as either individual or cultural. If sexuality is natural, the failure of the sexual relation, disappointment in love, the implicit argument goes, is our failure, the consequence of an afflicted personality or a repressive culture, or both, and the cure must be a return to nature, which cannot get it wrong, even though, it is worth noting, nature is what has to be *taught* – in sex education classes and popular handbooks.

But what if sexuality precisely calls into question that opposition between nature and culture? What if there is no human sexual relation outside culture, outside the regime of the signifier? What if we can never be uncontaminated organisms, wholesomely getting out from under the burden of the cultural order that identifies us precisely as *human* animals? Desire, I believe, is the location of the contradictory imperative that motivates the signifying body which is a human being in love. Desire is in excess of the organism; conversely, it is what remains unspoken in the utterance. In consequence it has no settled place to be. And moreover, at the level of the unconscious its objects are no more than a succession of substitutes for an imagined originary presence, a half-remembered 'oceanic' pleasure in the lost real,[1] a completeness which is desire's final, unattainable object. Perhaps, therefore, desire itself, the restlessness of it, and not our inadequacy, is the heart of the problem. Perhaps the sexual relation has no more to do with nature than granary bread or herb shampoo. And possibly by naturalizing it we construct exclusions and make failures.

Meanwhile, the struggle to measure up, to establish a happy and wholesome sexual relation, to satisfy what might possibly be an insatiable desire, keeps us quite literally off the streets. Modern Western culture privileges private life and personal experience over every other kind of satisfaction. Indeed, since Freud other activities are very often seen as a substitute for sex, a way of making do when the sexual impulse is frustrated or denied. Public affairs, by contrast, rate very low in the scale of values, and political intervention is hardly to be imagined as a source of happiness. Social stability thus depends in more ways than one on the profoundly anti-social couple, cultivating their relationship, tending it, agonizing over its moments of crisis, anxiously watching it grow.

Part of my project in writing about desire is to redress the balance a little. Not to reverse it, *not* to invert the hierarchy, privileging the public over the private, or the political over the personal. All poststructuralists know that to reverse the values of a binary opposition is to leave the terms of the opposition in place. In drawing attention to the politics of desire, I want to question not merely the privilege we accord the personal, but its autonomy, its isolation from affairs of state. Of course, a moment's reflection makes clear that private experience is not the independent, untroubled realm that pop songs and romances promise, a garden of Eden, just made for two. In practice, partnerships inhabit a world of rents and food prices and bus fares, though they transcend them too. But true love, the heart of a heartless world, is often the reason why the world stays heartless, and prices keep on going up. More effectively even than Christianity in the nineteenth century, true love in the twentieth acts as the solvent of class struggle.

Meanwhile, family values, cemented by true love, legitimize oppressive state policies and inadequate social expenditure. All those who repudiate, lose, or simply never track down the ideal happiness that nature is supposed to have intended for them are seen by the right as deviant and culpable, betraying society by rejecting the promise it holds out of nuclear cosiness for life. Single parents are held to be irresponsible and penalized accordingly; working mothers are blamed for neglecting their children and fostering crime; and in both cases the provision of adequate child-care facilities would solve most of the problems and generate a good deal of employment in the process.

At the same time, desire is also the location of resistances to the norms, proprieties and taxonomies of the cultural order. I have mentioned transgressive sexualities in this context and the important work that goes on in that field. I do not especially want to make that a central issue in this book, though I shall have some things to say about it. But I am not so much concerned at this stage with sexually-defined identities, or with specific object-choices. It is not self-evident that we can isolate a unitary homoeroticism, whether for men or women, or that there is a single, undifferentiated, distinguishable female desire. Desire, I am convinced, can go anywhere, and I would support all efforts to legitimate sexual dissidence. But I am also interested in the common ground. In her novel *Written on the Body*, Jeanette Winterson tells a love story without revealing the gender of the narrator. The object of the narrator's desire is a woman, but there have been others, some of them men. Winterson's story is compelling, passionate, lyrical. What matter, it seems to say, who is speaking, when desire is always derivative, conventional, already *written*. Of course love is also intensely individual, so that what is written is repeated with a difference, including the difference of sexual preference. But it is also important to emphasize the way desire in all its forms, including heterosexual desire, commonly repudiates legality; at the level of the unconscious its imperatives are absolute; and in consequence it readily overflows, in a whole range of ways, the institutions designed to contain it. The heterosexuality that oppressively 'founds society', as Monique Wittig puts it,[2] has its own tendency to repudiate the social arrangements in which it passes for nature. Desire in Western culture thus demonstrates the inability of the cultural order to fulfil its own ordering project, and reveals the difficulty with which societies control the energies desire liberates.

Moreover, desire imagines a utopian world, envisaging a transformation and transfiguration of the quotidian which throws into relief the drabness we too easily take for granted. Madame Bovary's degraded romanticism, no less a product of the culture she inhabits, as Flaubert's novel makes clear, nevertheless has the effect of focusing attention on the triviality and the complacency of bourgeois provincial life. Desire, even when it is profoundly conventional, is at the same time the location of a resistance to convention. It demonstrates that people want something more.

But I have another project, too, in writing about desire, and this is to contribute to the production of a differentiated cultural history. Just as desire has claimed a grounding in nature, so it has also affirmed its universality. This most intimate of conditions is commonly held to transcend cultural boundaries and historical difference, to be shared across time and space. However much sexual practices and preferences are known to differ culturally, the desire that motivates them is tacitly understood to be the same throughout history. It is for this reason that the book is about desire and not sexuality. And it begins to seem to me that there *are* historical distinctions to be made. The problem is difficult. In order for there to be difference, there has to be continuity, to the extent that it is necessary to be able to use the term *desire* at all for what happened in Greece or Rome or early modern Europe. But there are also discontinuities, which indicate that human experience is neither eternal nor immutable. Things change.

A representative Silhouette romance defines the protagonist's erotic dilemma in these terms: 'Her body wanted what he was doing. There was no question about that. But, a warning voice from within her scolded, did she?'[3] That question, however naively formulated, is surely intelligible, recognizable, indeed, to most twentieth-century Western readers. I am not convinced that it would have been intelligible to Ovid or to the anonymous author of *Sir Gawain and the Green Knight*, though they would both have acknowledged that desire might conflict with morality. It is not self-evident that the distinction the modern narrative makes between the body and *identity* ('Her body wanted what he was doing . . . But . . . did *she?*') would have been intelligible to Plato, though he certainly perceived the possibility of a conflict in the soul between temperance and excess.[4] Cartesian dualism, locating identity in consciousness, reconstructs not just our theory but our experience of desire.

Things change. The political implications of that analysis are considerable. We are not at the end of history. On the contrary, history goes on, at least if the world survives our present drive to self-destruction, and human experience will not always be as it is now. Things will change again, and we can choose to intervene or not, to determine the direction of change or to leave it to chance, which is to say to the cultural logic of late capitalism. Desire constitutes a test case for the possibility of change in an area which seems most personal, most private, most independent of history.

In other words, part of my project is to interrogate the metaphysics of desire, to call into question the widespread notion that desire, however differently conceptualized by fiction, sexology or psychoanalysis, remains a fundamental and constitutive category of human experience, indifferent to the signifier, and the common assumption that this condition, because it is simply given, needs no analysis. It is curious how little attention literary criticism has paid to the desire which features so commonly in the texts it analyzes. Conventionally Shakespeare's comedies, for instance, are dissected in quest of their moral message, not their accounts of desire. In the 1980s a whole school of American criticism insisted that love in Elizabethan poetry is not love but politics in disguise.[5] The desire in these texts somehow *goes without saying*.

This metaphysical desire has no history. I want to furnish desire with a history, which is not another grand narrative, but a record of difference, of change. Jean-François Lyotard has taught us to distrust the seamless metanarratives of progress or emancipation, which legitimate oppressive regimes, whether based on consent or terror. My aim is more modest: to trace the constraints and resistances of desire in their historical discontinuity. The book therefore tells stor*ies*. It begins not in the past but in the present, with desire now. And when it goes on to consider desire at other times, it opts explicitly and deliberately for a sequence of local and differentially constituted narratives, comparative accounts of marriage, adultery and demonic love at distinct historical moments, each with its own beginning, its own imperatives. There are advances and retreats. The emphasis is on change, not chronological development: I have not set out to produce a totalizing, explanatory, diachronic history of desire. On the contrary, I seek to repeat in another register some of desire's unpredictability, and its indifference to temporal regularity.

The stories the book tells are thus in one sense fables. They attempt to characterize desire, to exemplify its modes of address and behaviour. But this does not mean that I have felt entitled to make them up. Scepticism towards the grand narratives of Western culture does not exempt the postmodern narrator from a scholarly obligation to the documents of social history or from fidelity to the specificity of fictional works. We have surely let go of the notion that there is a single, correct interpretation, but it does not follow that there is no possibility of misreading. Most misreading is simply inattentive to the text. To the degree that these fables are inattentive or ill-informed, they are open to criticism or correction.

Besides producing a speculative, discontinuous history, I have also wanted to look into the future – not with a programme (heaven forbid!), but with a view to giving an account of the ways in which people have imagined the alternative modes of desire, particularly in utopian writing. And if all this seems ethnocentric, as it is, I want to draw attention to the dangers of imperialism inscribed in anthropology. Just as feminists want men to take us seriously, but not to speak on our behalf, so it is not for me to speak for other existing cultures, whether Third-World or African-American. My job here, I believe, is to listen.

III

So much for the motives and the project. What are the materials of this study? Experience? Perish the thought! Texts, then. But *which* texts? Second, what is to be my theoretical framework? Does the kind of scepticism I have gestured towards allow me authority figures (Foucault, Jacques Derrida, Jacques Lacan, Julia Kristeva, for choice), or am I obliged to treat their work as texts too? And third, how is desire to be represented? How is it possible to write about desire? What kind of writing would do it justice?

First, the materials. I do not believe that we have access to other people's experience. I am not even sure that we have access to our own. But more important, experience, like sexuality, surely does not exist in the raw, in its natural state, outside the order of language and culture. Experience is lived as differential, and difference is the mark of the signifier. Experience inhabits the symbolic order, whether in a state of submission or resistance to it. That it also exceeds the symbolic does not justify a metaphysics of experience, investing experience with a presence anterior to signification. On the contrary, experience simply participates in the differance (with an *a*), the distancing and the displacement, which is the condition of all signifying practice.[6] Its presence, similarly, is an illusion.

To deal in texts, then, is to come clean about differance. It is to surrender the authority of experience (which is not, after all, open to discussion), and to stage the debate in the arena of textuality, which is available to anyone. But which texts? Psychoanalysis, of course, and histories of sexuality, naturally. But also fiction. (I use the term in its broadest sense, to include poetry, drama and opera, as well as film . . .) And especially popular fiction. It is surely ironic that the most detailed investigation of the privileged category of desire should take place in the least privileged modes of writing, the texts produced by the entertainment industry.

Or perhaps not. In the Middle Ages love tended to be relegated to fiction because fiction was appropriately trivial. The Church con-

cerned itself with lechery, but love was mainly a matter for vernacular romances and lyric poetry. When in the Enlightenment period reason and science supplant theology, serious writing requires plain prose to transmit clear, sharply defined analysis of the concepts which are held to constitute knowledge. Meanwhile, all that is excluded by these values, the irrational, arbitrary, inexplicable residue which exceeds or defies the category of the knowable, becomes the theme of fiction (in the broad sense), which is entitled to be figurative, paradoxical and elusive.

Desire is thus not repressed. On the contrary, as Foucault has argued, it is extensively represented and explored, but the exploration takes place behind the back of the Enlightenment, so to speak, not in secret, but in a region which can remain unacknowledged in the hard, rational, analytical world whose hero is 'man'. This region is private, marginal and in a sense feminine. Women were the first writers and readers of the novel in the eighteenth century; women were permitted to be experts on desire.

But in a patriarchal culture men rapidly appropriate whatever women invent. No sooner had Richardson, Fielding and Sterne commandeered the novel, than at the end of the eighteenth century Romanticism began to idealize fiction as 'art'. 'Literature', as a repository of moral truth, rapidly came into being, along with Grand Opera and Family Values, with the result that love became a serious matter. By the end of the century Freud on the one hand and the sexologists on the other were ready to subject desire to scrutiny as a worthy object of scientific knowledge. The position had apparently been reversed.

And yet in the process of scientific analysis something slipped away. What is arbitrary, paradoxical and elusive, subjected to explanation and measurement, becomes drab and clinical. Fiction, meanwhile, entitled to be figurative, evasive, contradictory, sustained the mystery. To my mind, fiction remains the supreme location of writing about desire.

Fiction, then, constitutes the primary material for analysis. But which fiction? In view of the suspicion which now quite rightly attaches to the literary canon, its narrowness, its exclusions, I began, resolutely, with popular romances. They are easy to read; they are eminently familiar, even to people who have never read one before; and they throw into relief all the problems of desire that Cartesian dualism both poses and offers to solve: mind and body apparently reconciled, in practice driven further apart in the cataclysmic rapture of true love. I engaged in depth with *Gone With the Wind*, probably the best-selling love story of all time, and I found it more revealing for my purposes than most of the canonical literary texts of the twentieth century, with the possible exception of Toni Morrison, whose brilliant and initially non-canonical fiction has recently been snapped up for the syllabus, and is even now being chewed over and digested in progressive literature departments all over the English-speaking world. (A similar fate probably awaits Jeanette Winterson in due course. It is not obvious that expanding the canon without changing the practice of reading is necessarily a radical move.)

I have learnt a great deal from popular romance, but one striking feature of many of the Harlequin or Mills & Boon romances I have read is the frequency with which they feature governesses or nannies far from home, who fall in love with their dark, Byronic, brooding employers. Indeed, dark Byronic heroes with a secret are extraordinarily common in romantic fiction, as are heroines who do not consider themselves beautiful and who have to make a living. We have been here before – in *Jane Eyre*, for instance. The canonical nineteenth-century novel returns to haunt twentieth-century popular fiction in ways which suggest that cultural studies cannot get out from under English Literature with quite the abandon that we once hoped. Harriett Hawkins has written a witty book about the imbrication of Literature and popular culture. In *Classics and Trash* she draws attention to the relationships between *Phantom of the Opera* and *The Bostonians*, Robin Hood and Shakespeare's *Henry V*, *Gone With the Wind* and *Daniel Deronda*. Sam Spade quotes Prospero to haunting effect at the end of *The Maltese Falcon*. The inference Hawkins draws is not exactly that popular culture is parasitic on the canon, but that culture in general is not so easily divided between classics on the one hand and trash on the other.[7] It is possible that at this historical moment we cannot choose to discard the canon. While the right foresees the fall of Western civilization with the decline of the old ethnocentric Great Books courses, and the ultra-left imagines a synchronic world of wall-to-wall cultural studies, perhaps we need to perceive culture itself as more complex, more densely determined than either of these opposed positions allows.

When it comes to the past, to an engagement with historical difference, my anti-canonical impulses are still more severely tested. The work of Chrétien de Troyes, Edmund Spenser and John Donne, if not

exactly popular, was offered as entertainment in its own day. Since my
interest is not only in what can be written, but also in forms which
enlist the desire of the reader, I have opted primarily for texts which
have been widely read. Keats, Tennyson and Edgar Allan Poe have all
been read for pleasure. It is we who have canonized them; to refuse to
take account of them, on the grounds that they now represent elite
culture, is simply to cut ourselves off from some of the most important
locations of the meanings in circulation in earlier periods.

The question what we should read seems to me now relatively easily
answered: everything. What matters, I increasingly believe, is that we
read it *other*wise: not, that is to say, looking for the organic unity of the
work; not looking for the author behind the text; and not, above all, in
order to evaluate, to assess merit on a scale from one to ten, to allocate
a judgement that issues in little more than self-congratulation at our
own discernment. I think we could afford to read better than we have.
The reaction against New Criticism led to a certain contempt for close
analysis of the text, and some forms of radical criticism have earned
themselves a bad name by their lack of attention to textual detail. But
this tendency is not legitimated by poststructuralist theory or practice.
Roland Barthes in *S/Z* dissects Balzac's short story more minutely than
any New Critic had time for. Derrida pores over the textual details,
often apparently marginal, of Saussure, Rousseau and Nietzsche. And
Foucault reads trial records, and prisons themselves, as if they were
poetry.

The implication is that if we are to learn from them, we should treat
texts – all texts – with almost infinite respect. This might sound
surprising, since much recent interpretative practice precisely unpicks
the seams of the text, dwells on the uncertainties, seeks out the in-
stability of meaning. But it could be argued that the kind of traditional criticism which claimed to show a proper deference to the text,
in practice often treated it with inadvertent contempt. It is not in the
end respectful to regard the text as the implementation of a prior,
unifying thematic agenda; it is not respectful to see the text as the slave
of an organizing authorial intention; and it is certainly not respectful to
allocate it a critical grade which implies in almost all cases that it could
have been better than it is.

A text might be seen as a delicate ensemble of signifying practices
which bears witness to the undecidability, the polyphony, the hetero-

geneity of meaning at a specific historical moment. That heterogeneity is the evidence that the signified is always unstable, subject to change. It demonstrates that the meaning of wife, or mistress, say, meanings lived out by people's bodies, in people's experience, is not fixed by nature, or even by culture, but is always a potential site of struggle, which is a struggle simultaneously for meanings and bodies and experience. Resistance is both a political act and a textual characteristic. The difficulty with which the text makes its meanings stick puts on display the pressure points for change; the precariousness of its propositions makes imaginable the possibility of alternatives.

IV

So much for the material. What about the theory? There is surely no practice without theory, whether the theory is explicit or not. It follows that the theory had better be explicit if we are to have the least idea what we're doing. The problem, however, is that there seems no absolute reason to opt for one theory rather than another. If truth is no longer an available option, since there can be no extra-linguistic verification procedure, since, in other words, we can only *know* in language, which is culturally relative, then there are no guarantees of the accuracy, or even the sophistication of one theory as opposed to another. The choice, since we do choose our theoretical frameworks, owes *something* to an element as unreliable as personal taste, of course. I find sociobiology, for example, deeply distasteful, crude, as well politically reactionary. And politics, come to that, is important too: I am drawn to theories that permit the kind of analysis that seems to me politically productive.

But there is, perhaps, both more and less than personal preference at stake. Can we, for example, talk seriously about desire without taking account of psychoanalysis? It might not be much, but it is probably the only theory we have that focuses on desire without ignoring the signifier. It is not necessary to adopt it uncritically. Freud, for instance, wonderfully isolated the ungendered, polymorphously perverse, infinitely desiring infant that inhabits the unconscious and refuses to grow up, but in other ways Freud carries too much nineteenth-century baggage for us simply to take over some of his 'scientific' categories, not to mention his antifeminism. There is, moreover, a naive, reductive, post-Freudian Freud, who reproduces the conventional duality of nature and culture, and conceives of sexuality as a powerful natural impulse which civilization consistently inhibits. But there is also to be found in Freud's texts an understanding of desire as always caught up with prohibition and loss, and the resolution of the Oedipus complex as the reluctant and always incomplete renunciation of a forbidden love. Meanwhile, Jacques Lacan remakes this version of psychoanalysis for a world of sliding signifiers and subjects constructed outside themselves, in the Other, the locus of the deployment of speech. Lacan's work, in turn, is deeply phallocentric, but it is also, and elsewhere, subtle and seductive in its elegiac lyricism. Here is an instance from 'The Direction of the Treatment and the Principles of its Power':

> Desire is produced in the beyond of the demand, in that, in articulating the life of the subject according to its conditions, demand cuts off the need from that life. But desire is also hollowed within the demand, in that, as an unconditional demand of presence and absence, demand evokes the want-to-be under the three figures of the nothing that constitutes the basis of the demand for love, of the hate that even denies the other's being, and of the unspeakable element in that which is ignored in its request. In this embodied aporia, of which one might say that it borrows, as it were, its heavy soul from the hardy shoots of the wounded drive, and its subtle body from the death actualized in the signifying sequence, desire is affirmed as the absolute condition.
>
> Even less than the nothing that passes into the round of significations that act upon men, desire is the furrow inscribed in the course; it is, as it were, the mark of the iron of the signifier on the shoulder of the speaking subject.[8]

Psychoanalysis is often invoked to explain the characters in the text or the symptoms of the author, as if to diagnose a pathology. I want to use it to read cultural history, but not on the assumption that cultures are sick. In Freud, and even more emphatically in Lacan, desire is not a disease but a structural inevitability; in consequence, it is neither good nor bad. I can put Lacan's account to work — to identify in texts by authors who had never dreamt of Lacan, absence as desire's recurring figure, as it is in Renaissance lyric poetry,[9] or the trace of antipathy which inhabits desire in *Antony and Cleopatra* and *The Golden Bowl*, not to mention *Casablanca*. But if Lacan explains, he does not explain away:

15

in the light of his work desire remains elusive and contradictory. His prose, difficult and tantalizing and infuriating, re-enacts the modes of speech of unconscious desire itself in its figurative plurality.[10] The project is not so much to systematize as to specify, and to specify as problematic.

And that, perhaps, is the attraction of poststructuralist theory at this historical moment. It problematizes. Far from providing a theoretical grid that can be brought to bear mechanically on any text, poststructuralism makes difficulties, and so calls into question the clichés and complacencies of common sense, the taxonomies of Enlightenment culture, which neatly polarize love and hate, wanting and possessing. Derrida's account of language, by analogy, does not dismiss metaphysics, still less reason and truth, but his work makes it impossible to invoke them as guarantees that the familiar answers to our questions are final.

It was (is) perhaps imperative that we should doubt the certainties of the past. The theories I invoke will be supplanted in due course. In the mean time they make it possible to reopen issues that seemed closed, and to reread texts that appeared transparent. The authority I claim for them tentatively, hesitantly, is in the end no more than that. And if Lacan and Derrida seem to me to be right, to tell it like it is, that proves nothing, except that I am an effect of a specific cultural and historical moment.

V

Finally, and this is the really difficult question, how is it possible to write about desire? Not (and this is not open to negotiation), *not* in the coy, quasi-objective and actually coercive formulae of professionalized literary criticism: 'As we have seen . . .', 'As we shall see . . .' What is this imagined 'we' whose consensus is so effortlessly assumed? And not with the affected authority of subjectless 'scientific' neutrality: 'impartially' described from a distance, desire retains all of its absurdity and none of its charm. Should I, then, by contrast, simply allow desire to speak for itself? Here it is in Barbara Cartland's version:

> As he drew near to her he knew that she quivered and he was almost sure it was not with fear.

He stood for a moment in silence before he said:

'When I received your letter on Sunday morning and thought I would never find you again, I went to the Library and took down the book of poems we had been reading. I opened it at random, Indira, and read a poem which seemed to me to be the answer to what I was feeling.'

He paused and as if Indira knew she had to make some response to what he had said she raised her eyes slowly and, he thought, a little shyly, and then found it impossible to look away.

Softly the Marquis said:

> 'Kuan Kuan cry the ospreys
> On the islet in the river.
> Lovely is the good lady,
> Fit bride for our lord.'

Indira did not move as he finished speaking but only waited, and he saw a sudden light come into her strange eyes.

Then as the colour rose in her cheeks like the breaking of the dawn she made a little incoherent sound and moved towards him . . .

. . . For a moment she was very still. Then almost like the rhythmic movement of the sea or the sound of music, she lifted her face to his and he found her lips . . .

. . . Only when she felt as if the Marquis had swept her up and they were riding among the stars did he raise his head and ask in a strangely unsteady voice:

'What do you feel about me now?'[11]

Apart from the gender politics of this fairly representative passage, which are unequivocally appalling, what is striking here is that desire hardly speaks at all. The narrative voice draws on the common repertoire of nineteenth- and twentieth-century metaphors for desire: the sea, music, riding among the stars. Desire, we are to understand, is boundless, natural, profound, transfiguring. And like each of the analogies the text invokes, it is wordless. Meanwhile, Indira quivers and makes incoherent sounds; and the Marquis quotes an ancient Chinese poem in his grandfather's translation. Here the regress is almost infinite: as the metaphors themselves also indicate, in order to speak, to ground itself at the level of the signifier, love can only quote, and preferably from a text which is virtually without origin and thus transparent. Desire alludes to texts – but in order to efface its own citationality. It thus draws attention to its elusiveness, its excess over the signifier. Desire is what is *not* said, what is 'hollowed within the demand', as Lacan puts it. The Marquis's desire is not *in* the words of the poem he quotes, though in this passage it is nowhere else. The poem is an oblique proposal of marriage, which means love. Desire is thus *understood* by the reader, recognized as the meaning of a textual gesture which is almost emblematic.

It would be appropriate to write in a way that inhabits the terrain of desire without simply reproducing its self-effacing and ultimately evasive citationality. Roland Barthes achieves something like this in his brilliantly witty and at the same time melancholy exposure of desire's theatricality in the succession of monologues which constitutes *A Lover's Discourse: Fragments*. Barthes here magnificently puts on display desire's anxieties, its torments and tantrums, drawing attention in the process to its citationality by listing his sources in the margin. And he does all this not by description but by simulation, by writing in the first person.[12] The *I* of these utterances is an astute observer of the lover who is held in place within them, so that we perceive desire simultaneously from the inside and the outside. The book is a tour de force, but it is explicitly fragmentary and synchronic. I want to tell stories, even if it is important not to tell the Whole Story.

Foucault tells a story in *The History of Sexuality*, but as the volumes go on it becomes clear that the project is increasingly to treat sexuality as a discipline which constitutes a location for the recruitment of subjects, and not specifically sexual subjects. Substantial and important as it is, *The History of Sexuality* is not really about desire.

Derrida's *The Post Card* is, and the clandestine love letters that fill the first 250 pages of that text are thrilling and disturbing and electrifying. They tantalize the reader with their mixture of 'factual' references and withheld identities; they tease by doing philosophy in this sexy setting; and they thus elude all the oppositional categories that the Enlightenment so rejoices in: fiction and non-fiction; reason and passion; poetry and prose. If there were only one book left in the world, I should want it to be *The Post Card*. But here desire is taken to be the paradigm case of all signifying practice, and the ultimate instance of differance.[13] The case is brilliantly demonstrated, and would certainly bear repeating, but *The Post Card* is not much concerned with historical difference.

Kristeva's *Tales of Love* probably comes nearest to what follows, and I draw on that text a great deal. But Kristeva's book is ultimately about the psychoanalytic project itself, about the transference as a cure for love's anxieties and, though the past is crucial to its argument, *Tales of Love* is perhaps less committed than I am to locating love in cultural history.[14]

There are no models, then. But one feature all these texts have in common, including Lacan's, including Barbara Cartland's, is that by citing, by evading, by teasing, they elicit the desire of the reader, thus demonstrating the degree to which desire is an effect of the signifier. Psychoanalysis proposes that fiction (in my broad sense) is a kind of adventure playground, where grown-ups can imagine that they recover the lost wholeness of childhood, secure from civilization and its discontents.[15] Here conscious and unconscious processes are no longer in conflict, and Kristeva's semiotic sounds and rhythms invest fantasy with pleasure.[16] At the same time, the location of fiction in the symbolic reintroduces absence and death, and by differentiating the fictional, keeps desire in view.

It is important to do that: to write in a way that keeps desire in view for the reader, not just as an object of knowledge (though it is that) but as a lived condition, so that it is possible to see not only *what* but also *how much* is at stake in the stories Western culture tells about desire.

VI

And writing itself, the process, the production of a script? It is a romance, of course, 'an explosion of dreams and desires',[17] by turns painful and euphoric, but both obsessional and utopian either way. Like romance, writing is narcissistic to a degree, at its most elementary level a quest for recognition, the place where the subject appears. But it is also an attempt to reach the beyond of the demand, to transgress the ordering processes of the symbolic or to suspend its prohibitions. And in this sense writing is where, paradoxically, the subject *dis*appears, undergoes the death, precisely, of the author. Nowhere is it more apparent that subjectivity inhabits the field of the Other than in the effort to write something difficult, to formulate an idea which remains either stubbornly elusive or drearily familiar. Moreover, to the degree that to write is to exceed, however momentarily, the space allotted to the subject in the signifying chain, to break the symbolic Law, it is also to know for sure, at least from time to time, that the Cartesian *Cogito* is neither in control nor an origin. In that respect, you might choose to say, why, it's almost like being in love . . .

2

Reading Love Stories

I

She is young, though not as young as she used to be. She is also beautiful, sensuous and witty. She is likely to have remarkable hair, frequently intractable, springy and full of a vitality which can be read as evidence of sensuality. Her eyes are often an unusual colour (green, like Scarlett O'Hara's, or tawny or violet, for instance). She is not necessarily a virgin, and these days she commonly has an absorbing career. She is, of course, the heroine of a romance.

The hero, meanwhile, is probably dark, certainly striking, frequently rugged. He is hard, muscular and powerful. Since height signifies authority in Western culture, he is also tall. The hero normally has a career which entitles him to slightly higher social status or prestige than the heroine's, though that is beginning to change. He has impeccable taste. Although he appears indifferent, even ruthless, he is often at the mercy of a passion he is unable or unwilling to acknowledge. He is an exceptionally competent lover.

The category romances published by Mills & Boon, Harlequin, Silhouette and others produce dozens of stories in line with this formula every month. By 1982 sixty new series romance titles were being published each month in America alone, in addition to another forty or more mainstream romances.[1] According to the formula, the relationship between the central figures often begins in antagonism. One or both may have been hurt by life, and they resort to attack, we are to understand, as the best means of defence. Their deepening desire for each other, which the reader recognizes long before the characters do, is constantly on the brink of discovery or revelation, as they begin to awaken in one another a new warmth, or maturity, or trust, which is identifiable as the transforming and revitalizing effect of love. But delays and misunderstandings intervene, until in the final chapter circumstances, often in the form of a happy accident, dispel all uncertainty, and the couple know beyond any further shadow of doubt that this really is true love. True love, which is resolutely heterosexual, issues, of course, in marriage.

Individual romances brought out by mainstream publishers may deviate from the formula in detail, sometimes extending it to produce family sagas. But they too generally centre on a reassuring tale of obstacles finally overcome and love ultimately and eternally requited. The story popular romance recounts is most commonly one of triumph, not only over outward impediments but also over merely sensual desire. The heroine finds her identity confirmed, her self-control rewarded or her values realized, as she recognizes the hero's passion and at the same time responds to his attention and care. Romances thus tend to depict a world which, however harsh it may initially appear, is finally shown to be benign. They promise the reader satisfaction, pleasure, fulfilment.

Janice Radway's classic study of the romance includes accounts of detailed discussions with a group of regular romance readers in a midwestern city which she calls Smithton. Radway found that the Smithton women read in quest of happiness. As one of them explained,

> Romances are not depressing and very seldom leave you feeling sad inside. When I read for enjoyment I want to be entertained and feel lifted out of my daily routine. And romances are the best type of reading for this effect. Romances also revive my usually optimistic outlook which is often very strained in day-to-day living.[2]

The inspiriting character of romance was an important ingredient of the Smithton readers' enjoyment: 'Optimistic! That's what I like in a book. An optimistic plot. I get sick of pessimism all the time.'[3] Many of them condemned romances which they found depressing, particularly stories with unhappy endings. Several of the Smithton readers revealed that they often checked the ending before buying the book, in order to make sure that the narrative was satisfactorily resolved.[4] And a satisfactory resolution is synonymous with true love.

Amid the harsh and uncaring public world of politics and the market, true love promises the personal and private happiness of complete reciprocity. In what always appears to be an increasingly materialistic culture, true love proffers a rapture which is freely available to all, because it costs nothing – nothing, that is, but a total commitment for life. And as a guarantee of all this, true love offers to unify mind and body, to overcome the division Western culture has created between two kinds of feeling, caring on the one hand and desire on the other.

When Descartes declared that he must exist since he was capable of reflection, he crystallized the emerging conception of what it was to be a person. The medieval notion of a human being as a mortal body in conflict with an eternal soul gave way in Enlightenment Europe to the more secular and humanist idea of identity as synonymous with consciousness. To be a person was to be a thinking, speaking subject, capable of moral feeling and responsibility. People still had bodies, of course, and the body had its pleasures. But these were held to be transient, trivial or even dangerous, unless they were brought firmly under conscious control. Communication and caring, in contrast, were real, important and enduring values. By the nineteenth century this Enlightenment division of experience had come to seem natural and inevitable.

True love as the romances portray it promises to bring mind and body back into perfect unity, to heal the rift in experience which divides individuals from themselves. Physical sensation, the overwhelming intensity of erotic desire, is to be brought into harmony with rational and moral commitment, a shared life of sympathy and support, freely and confidently chosen. True love, we are to understand, transcends the dualism of passion in conflict with morality. It licenses the release of pleasure, irradiating the vertiginous excitement of erotic activity with an ideal glow. And it undertakes at the same time to unite two subjectivities not only with each other but within themselves. True love apparently joins what the Enlightenment so relentlessly put asunder – the body and its pleasures on the one hand, the mind and its values on the other. Love dissolves the anxiety of division in the subject, and replaces it with a utopian wholeness.

This is the secret of the optimism the Smithton women identify as the effect of reading romances. The stories they most enjoy maintain that the commitment of love is the proper and necessary condition of true sexual fulfilment, and that marriage unites mind and body in 'an emotional bond freely forged'. 'The Smithton women overwhelmingly believe,' Janice Radway explains, 'that sex is a wonderful form of intimate communication that should be explored only by two people who care for each other deeply and intend to formalize their relationship through the contract of marriage.'[5]

II

Love and marriage were ordained, so the story goes, by God – or by his Enlightenment surrogate, nature. Domestic concord, marriage between a couple in sexual and spiritual sympathy with one another, provides the natural context for bringing up happy, normal, loving children. True love is thought of as an essential part of the natural order. And yet, as the romances reveal, there is another nature, another equally fundamental category, and this is the arbitrary, irrational turbulence of sensuality. The body, we are to understand, has a life of its own, independent of the Cartesian *Cogito* which constitutes the person. Over and over again, the story the romances tell is one of struggle against this all-but-irresistible imperative, as the heroine tries desperately to exercise conscious mastery over the unruly body that continually threatens to subject her to a pleasure which is mere sensation. 'The Harlequin heroine is in a constant fever of anti-erotic anxiety, trying to control the flow of sexual passion between herself and the hero', Ann Snitow argues in her excellent essay on 'Mass Market Romance'. In the example she gives, the danger to the protagonist comes not from the hero's power over her, but from her own desire:

> Somehow Charlotte struggled up from the depth of a sexually-induced lethargy. It wasn't easy, when her whole body threatened to betray her, but his words were too similar to the words he had used to her once before, and she remembered only too well what had happened next . . .
>
> She sat up quickly, her fingers fumbling with the zipper, conscious all the while of Logan lying beside her, and the potent attraction of his lean body. God, she thought unsteadily, what am I doing here? And then, more wildly: Why am I leaving him? *I want him.* But not on his terms, the still, small voice of sanity reminded her, and she struggled to her feet.[6]

Here 'sanity' is in conflict with the heroine's own (morally) lethargic body, and the body is treacherously ready to yield to what rationality forbids. In Mills & Boon's *A Secret Understanding* it is only the hero's superior control that saves the protagonists from giving way to an atavistic impulse which is understood to be in an unspecified way prior to reason:

> . . . she realised that she was moving beneath him with a vehement need that was stimulating his own primitive reaction to her. Her whole body was shaking and leaping, heat flaring over her. She was going up in flames and she tried to control her mind, stiffening against him, fighting for breath, only realising that she was sobbing his name aloud when she felt his fingers fastening her dress, his hands firmly moving hers which still clung to him.
>
> She was on her feet, his strength steadying her, before she had really come back to her senses . . .[7]

Two distinct imperatives, two separate metaphysics are here brought into conjunction. The heroine is choosing a husband, and in this critical choice, which is understood to be for life, morality dominates: the hero is required to be gentle, caring, reliable, responsible and likely to prove monogamous, a condition which is conventionally summarized as being 'in love' with her. But desire constantly threatens to betray morality, to subject the heroine to the wrong man. The wrong man is all body: phallic, hard, unromantic. (Or so the narrative would have us believe. Experienced readers know that this hardness is a mask for deep feeling.) His sexuality is felt as almost irresistible. The descriptions are of his body (his mind tends to be an unknown quantity till the end):

> Her first sight of him had shocked her. She had never seen a man so handsome and so hard.
>
> He had been very tanned then, obviously straight back from some overseas assignment. His dark hair was thick and heavy, his cheeks creased as though he laughed a lot, although she had never seen it happen, but those cold, silver eyes had alarmed her.
>
> His hands were powerful, capable, with a sort of hard, masculine grace. He wasn't as tanned now as he had been at first, but he was still a deep golden colour and it showed up those strange eyes vividly.[8]

In romances it is men who are sex objects (no wonder men rarely read them!), and who therefore evoke an illicit response which has to be rigorously controlled:

> His touch burned through the thin silk of her frock and sent a flame of desire shafting through Sarah's body. Her hands clenched so tightly that the nails dug painful crescents into the palms. He sounded sincere, but she wouldn't be swayed all over again by the ardent glow in those dark eyes.[9]

Of course, in these specific instances the reader already has grounds for suspecting that the sexual encounters between the central figures are the prelude to true love, and we know in consequence that the apparent conflict between mind and body, sense and sensuality, will ultimately be revealed in these cases as largely illusory. The gap which is glimpsed between one natural imperative and another is thus not absolute, and is frequently closed off in the utopian ending of the story.

But there seems to be no clear empirical (which is to say, textual) distinction between the physical intensities of desire-as-true-love and its simulacrum, lust, which lacks the moral dimension. In both cases eroticism suspends or submerges the operation of the mind, and once she submits to her own erotic impulse, the heroine is powerless to resist its overwhelming force. Eve Coudert, protagonist of the early chapters of *Till We Meet Again* by Judith Krantz, is a virgin in love for the first time.

> The first wave of pure physical desire she had ever experienced picked her up as if she'd been a swimmer in an unknown sea, and engulfed her, tumbled her over and over into the bottomless deep for silent, shocking minutes until it left her as weak as if she had almost drowned.[10]

Her lover is a practised seducer, a second-rate music-hall singer, shallow and uncaring. Only Eve's innocence impels her to take him seriously, and she learns the truth about him in due course. Sarah Sweet, meanwhile, in Mills & Boon's *Surgeon in Disgrace*, experiences the sexual act itself in much the same metaphoric terms:

She cried out as the surging tumult of his powerful body carried her with him on the tidal wave of his triumph, and the deep, dark waters of sexual fulfilment engulfed her completely.[11]

This time, however, the sexual fulfilment is also the fulfilment of true love.

In Jude Deveraux's *Lost Lady*, when Regan is reunited with Travis Stanford after three years of separation, their bodies meet with the violent intensity of 'a clap of thunder following a burst of brilliant lightning'.[12] Passion in romance is commonly a storm, a flood, a tidal wave, or sometimes flames, a hurricane, a volcano or an earthquake. In all these cases it is elemental, beyond control, majestic, thrilling, dangerous. The helpless protagonist experiences desire as burning, falling through space, submerging, or drowning. Floods have a particularly long pedigree: in Rhoda Broughton's *Not Wisely But Too Well*, published in 1867, Captain Dare Stamer feels passion as a flood 'rising up in him – higher, higher – taking giant steps fiercer than ever it surged and boiled; he *could* not stand it any longer. It was stronger than he.'[13] But the elemental analogy was evidently already a cliché in France ten years earlier, when *Madame Bovary* first appeared:

Love, she believed, had to come suddenly, with a great clap of thunder and a lightning flash, a tempest from heaven that falls upon your life, like a devastation, scatters your ideals like leaves and hurls your very soul into the abyss.[14]

Curiously, the metaphors of desire repeatedly invoke not pleasure, but various kinds of natural disturbance or disaster.

In *The Writing of the Disaster*, Maurice Blanchot calls this sort of catastrophe 'the intense, silent and disastrous affirmation of the outside'.[15] Floods, tempests and earthquakes are always other, external, beyond or out of control, and from the point of view of humanism they represent the return of nature, challenging the sovereignty that the Enlightenment attributes to the rational subject. Disasters mark the limits of human mastery. This is also the character of sexual desire in popular romance. The texts depict sex as an irrational, arbitrary otherness which seems to come from elsewhere, overwhelming the subject from outside, to the extent that it is not under conscious rational control. Sexuality too represents the nature which is not mastered by Enlightenment reason.

The elemental otherness of desire as a constituent of true love is celebrated in romance. But the metaphors, for all their familiarity as clichés, for all their consequent invisibility, are an attempt, whether conscious or not, to acknowledge at the same time its apocalyptic threat. Erotic intensity spells the destruction of the mastering subject, the annihilation of consciousness, the loss of sovereignty and individuality:

> A warm tide of feeling, bewildering, frightening, swept over her, carrying out of her mind the time and place and circumstances.[16]

> He murmured her name against her lips . . . but she was spinning again on the very edge of the world, calling to him in the same far-away voice . . .[17]

> [H]e bent over her and started to kiss her, beginning at her throat and working downwards, evoking delicious sensations that again quickly became so intense that she held onto his shoulders with both hands and felt pleasure spiraling through her body until even her perception of herself was swept away and she felt boundless and pulsing, helpless to stop the tide of feeling that swept over her and left her only after an ecstatic moment that went on unendurably, past all boundaries shattering in its impact.[18]

This last passage shows a protagonist who has lost the awareness of her own identity, all sense that the self has boundaries. In Lacanian terms this is a retreat behind the imaginary, to a condition prior even to the mirror phase, which is the beginning of difference. The heroine experiences undifferentiated polymorphous pleasure, renouncing subjectivity without even knowing that she does so. Sex in these terms is truly apocalyptic ('shattering') for the subject. Indeed, apocalypse itself is the metaphor for Cassandra Preston's climactic encounter with Jordan Preece in *A Secret Understanding*, where, as a result of passion reciprocated, the narrative voice tells us, 'the whole world went up in flames'.[19]

III

True love does not quite keep its promise to unify mind and body. The commonest impediment to happiness in romance is uncertainty about whether the protagonists are really in love or simply subject to an overwhelming erotic imperative, whether, in other words, the whole person is involved. And the engulfing tidal wave of sexual feeling, though it is a necessary condition, is not a sufficient guarantee of true love. In addition the hero is required to speak, to reassert his identity as a subject, to tell the heroine that he loves her and wants to marry her. But erotic intensity, 'bewildering', transporting consciousness, sweeping away all perception of the self, precisely deflects subjectivity and consequently defers the moment of moral commitment. After the world goes up in flames for Jordan and Cassandra, misunderstanding sustains the reader's suspense for another seven pages before the protagonists are sufficiently restored to reveal their love. And only after that is the heroine fully re-established as a knowing subject:

> Cassy smiled happily. She knew she would be smiling for the rest of her life, and as she ate her breakfast Jordan sat opposite, simply looking at her, his chin on his hand, all the love she had ever dreamed of in his eyes.[20]

The conventional gap between the physical demonstration of desire and the declaration of love is exploited to comic effect in Jude Deveraux's *Lost Lady*, where after their tempestuous sexual reunion, Travis Stanford supplies Regan with 742 roses, dozens of notes asking for her hand, a complete travelling circus for their child and a moonlight picnic, and still she hesitates to marry him because he has not told her that he loves her.[21]

Conversely, wise heroines recognize that love declared in the heat of the moment is not to be trusted. Nurse Sarah Sweet is not sure whether to believe her surgeon-lover, until he tells her again at work in the hospital the next morning.[22] Scarlett O'Hara Kennedy, on the other hand, agrees to marry Rhett Butler when her consciousness is suspended by sensuality. Yielding helplessly to the erotic response that his embrace elicits, Scarlett is no longer a thinking, knowing subject, capable of deliberation or decision:

> She whispered 'Yes' before she even thought. It was almost as if he had willed the word and she had spoken it without her own volition . . . She had promised to marry him when she had had no intention of promising. She hardly knew how it had all come about . . .[23]

In consequence, she marries him without knowing that she loves him. Years later, when at last she discovers the truth, it is tragically too late: by this time Rhett notoriously doesn't give a damn.

True love, then, is not so much a union of mind and body, as an alternation of their dominance. The romance protagonists, we are to believe, care deeply for each other *and* want each other sexually. That the one is a condition of the other, however, is a conviction that the texts do not in practice substantiate. On the contrary, the writing of love, its textual crystallization, has the effect of polarizing mind and body. If true love as the romances depict it is a source of happiness, of both reciprocity and rapture, that is the effect not of a unity but merely of a coincidence between affection and sexual attraction.

Passionate sex, as romances define it, is the surrender of control, of subjectivity, of the mind to the body. The body triumphs, but with a corresponding sense of loss, and the metaphors of disaster are a record of that loss. What matters next is the words that are spoken subsequently, independently, once the knowing, willing subject is restored. To the extent that the aim was to dissolve the opposition between mind and body in a story of true love, the project signally fails in these instances. Mind and body remain separate textual entities, and the condition of happiness, it appears, is not in the event the dissolution of their difference, but simply the fact that their distinct imperatives coincide.

Moreover, the happiness of true love itself proves curiously disappointing in relation to the degree of emotional intensity expended in its pursuit. The romances record a struggle. The heroine wants her man, but she wants him on her terms, and her terms are that the relationship between them is true love. This means that he must want *her*, and not merely her body, must recognize her as the *person*, the thinking, feeling consciousness that *she* essentially is. But at the same time the romances also tend to reveal a curious insubstantiality at the heart of this essence. The heroine, when she is not the emotionally damaged figure, is commonly 'caring', supportive, sympathetic – directed, in other words, outward towards her friends, her family and her lover. She repairs the harm done to him, and in the process she feminizes him, teaches him to talk, to acknowledge that he cares, to *resemble* her. But at the core of her identity is not presence but desire, specifically the longing to love and be loved. This constitutes an absence which her lover is to fill – by becoming a reciprocally desiring subject. Two absences do not make a presence. What fills the gap, gives this reciprocal love a being, endowing it with substance, referentiality, is the domestic.

In *Conditional Surrender*, breaking point comes for the pregnant Kate when her husband wants his former mistress to take responsibility for the interior design of their new house. Kate abandons the husband whose love she yearns for but apparently fails to elicit. She leaves their shared apartment for a bungalow in Wales, but once there on her own, she apparently does nothing for the space of five months but 'contemplate their relationship,'[24] clean the bungalow and wait for the telephone to ring. She has already given up her job. Beyond her domestic setting she exists only as an expectant mother: she has no life, no activity, no identity of her own. However, when Greg decorates their home himself, in accordance with the designs she had abandoned in despair, Kate knows that he truly loves her after all. The establishment of the nuclear family in a newly-decorated house seems oddly quotidian as the outcome of a passion which sears, obsesses, torments and finally transforms, and less than absolute as evidence of the integration at long last of mind with body.

IV

Does it matter? Who ever turned to romance in quest of truth? Romances are precisely fiction, and pulp fiction at that. They are mass-produced fantasy, after all, no more than a form of harmless escape. And if in the event the fantasy they offer is a little disappointing, we should not be surprised. Surely it is a mistake to overestimate their importance?

And yet the dualism and its corresponding disappointments are remarkably familiar. What makes romances so *easy* to read, and consequently so easy to despise, is precisely their familiarity. We *know* all this already.

The source of our knowledge is intertextual. Popular romance is clearly rooted in the nineteenth-century novel, with its recurring commitment to the project of disentangling true love from false. The structure of many of the formula romances is already to be found in *Pride and Prejudice* and *Jane Eyre*. *Gone With the Wind* has been compared to *Vanity Fair*, as well as *War and Peace*, and it makes no significant difference that Margaret Mitchell had not read either.[25] She had no need to: the meanings those texts affirm are reproduced endlessly in other works of fiction, other love stories. *Gone With the Wind* certainly resembles *Daniel Deronda* in striking ways, not least in its opening line,[26] but there is no need to assume that this is the effect of direct influence. It goes some way, however, to explain the ready intelligibility of the later work.

The relative sexual explicitness of the twentieth-century romances is, of course, more modern. But here too we can find echoes of canonical fiction, most obviously of D. H. Lawrence, whose writing may also be represented as a struggle to make sense of the relations between mind and body. Lawrence reproduces in the process the dualism that so evidently distressed him. Meanwhile, it was Hemingway who famously invented metaphoric sex-as-earthquake.

The romance is widely held in contempt in Western culture, but it draws its definitions of desire from that culture itself. If the metaphors are overworked until they become virtually invisible, if the ideas are commonplaces, that is because they are commonly recognized. Clichés are clichés precisely to the extent that they are shared. In defining, fixing, specifying the meanings which are their central concern, works of popular fiction draw on the vocabulary that their readers can be expected to recognize, the terms in common circulation in their culture. Many of the affirmations of the romances, much of their understanding of the nature of sexuality, are readily available elsewhere, reiterated in discussions of desire, both public and private, or silently taken for granted in our personal 'experience'.

Carol Thurston in *The Romance Revolution* quotes with evident disapproval an account of an 'experiment' conducted by a man among women.

> I took some women that I know, quite well educated women, and I asked them whether they preferred love – that is, let's say sexuality – with fantasy or without fantasy. In other words, to what extent was their conception of sexuality wrapped up with fantasy, that is, with romantic trappings, with being in love, with being wooed, and so on. And I found that almost uniformly, for whatever reason, it seems that most women prefer to see sexuality in a context of, well, romance.[27]

The experimenter here reveals his own 'impoverished experience of love – that is, let's say sexuality', Thurston comments acidly.

As far as I am concerned, let's say sexuality, by all means, but let us not assume that by doing so we can get back to some sort of basic experience, untrammelled by, well, love, well, culture. What if, after all, there is no stripped-down, basic sexuality, no simple animal or clinical experience outside our culturally induced expectations, hopes, anxieties, values? What if there is no sexuality, in other words, independent of the *meanings* it carries, and these meanings are culturally produced and learned? It would not follow that sex is the same for all of us, since we are not conditioned robots, or the same every time, since desire differentiates infinitely. And, more important, it would not exclude the possibility that the experience might exceed the range of available meanings in unpredictable ways. But it would indicate that we in the West now could not, as an act of will, simply step outside the metaphysics of desire which is our cultural heritage.

Romance insists that sexual fulfilment without love is false, is somehow not *real*. But dualism offers an alternative temptation, as the account of the experiment I have quoted so artlessly demonstrates, and this is the positivist assumption that only the body is real, that appetite is genuine or authentic, and all the rest is self-deception, 'fantasy'.

> The word 'body', its danger, how easily it gives one the illusory impression of being outside of meaning already, free from the contamination of consciousness-unconsciousness. Insidious return of the natural, of Nature.[28]

There is a metaphysics of romance, of love as presence, licensing, legitimating and authorizing sexual pleasure. And there is another metaphysics of the body, of nature as presence, as absolute, as outside culture. Psychoanalysis and sexology, cultural contemporaries of philosophical positivism, can be read as reversing the Cartesian hierarchy, deriving the mind from the body. To the degree that they do so, of course, they simply reaffirm dualism itself. And at approximately the same historical moment, D. H. Lawrence also reverses the hierarchy and sustains the dualism, privileging the body over the mind. But perhaps love, sexuality, desire are not presences; perhaps they are not fundamental categories, given, universal. Nor, possibly, are mind and body, and the difference between them. The alternative is that love, desire, the body are all meanings. As meanings, they are the condition of our experience; and at the same time, as meanings, they are culturally produced and historically limited.[29] It would follow that they are not inevitable, necessary or eternal.

In practice, I want to argue, desire deconstructs the Cartesian opposition between mind and body, radically destabilizing the difference that holds them apart. Desire subsists as an effect of the signifier, in the gap (Derrida would say the differance) that resides within the utterance of an impulse. In this sense it is an effect of absence. But desire is also referential: it inhabits the flesh. Desire is not a property, therefore, or mind or body, still less of mind *and* body. On the contrary, it exceeds the duality of their relationship, and in this excess lies the impossibility of the healing unity the romances promise. There are no *perfectly* happy endings.

V

Radway's Smithton readers claimed that romances made them feel good, reviving their optimism against all external odds. But I have suggested that the romances do not entirely keep their promises, that their happy endings in practice widen the rift they set out to heal. Are the Smithton women, then, simply wrong? Do they fail to notice what academic criticism identifies? Or, more likely, is academic analysis making a fuss about nothing, finding difficulties where none exist for the readers the texts are aimed at?

Possibly. But there need not be any conflict between the two positions. It emerged that the Smithton women were reading a great many romances. Over half of them read between one and four romances every week, more than a third read between five and nine a week, and four claimed to be reading between fifteen and twenty-five.[30] Is it conceivable that this avid reading is an indication that the optimism created by romances is more precarious than it is possible to say? Perhaps the next romance is there to compensate for the disappointments engendered by the last? All we can be sure of is that readers of romance tend to crave more romance. A number of the Smithton women acknowledged an anxiety about whether they might be depressed by their reading, to the point where they checked the endings of the stories before they bought them in order to ensure that the plots would not leave them sad. What if the anxiety is precisely an effect of their extensive reading experience, a silent recognition of unconscious disappointment that the stories have consistently failed to resolve the divisions they depend on?[31]

VI

In an altogether different respect, however, the Smithton readers were surely right all along when they claimed that reading romances made them happy. The ending is not, after all, the whole story. Too often, in my view, commentators on romance isolate the content of the story and look for explanations at the level of the signified, supposing that a satisfying resolution of the plot is the element that ensures a satisfied reader. What they neglect in the process is the pleasure of reading itself, the pleasure, that is, of reading classic realist fiction.[32] Since Roland Barthes has emphatically taught us to renounce classic realism in favour of more disturbing, anarchic, discontinuous and thus *blissful* post-modern writing, there has been a tendency to neglect the erotics of reading *stories*. And yet Barthes himself acknowledges that there is (on certain conditions) the possibility of finding excitement (and not merely contentment) in classical narrative.[33]

Minutes before she permits her lover to carry out a predictably expert seduction, Eve Coudert, the protagonist of the early chapters of *Till We Meet Again*, experiences a feeling which is like falling through space, 'falling in fear, falling in delight, falling faint with curiosity and apprehension'.[34] Breathless with excitement, thrilled, curious and fearful at the same time, the state of mind of a reader fully absorbed in the climactic pages of a classic realist narrative closely resembles Eve's. The reader is transported out of time and place, immersed in the fictional world, and involved with increasing intensity in feelings of increasing tension. He or she is, of course, in the instances when this occurs, in the hands of an exceptionally competent storyteller. The sensation, common among the young, rarer later, is like Eve's, one of delight (the completeness of the absorption ensures it), curiosity (the enigma on which classic realist narrative depends guarantees it) and anxiety (the suspense intensifies it). 'A good read', the experience of those emotions, gave the Smithton readers pleasure.

They might have derived the same effect, of course, from classic realist drama or, more probably, the cinema.[35] This was precisely Brecht's complaint about the 'dramatic theatre', which he so deplored because it wore down the spectator's capacity for thought, analysis and consequent political action. Brecht depicts the audience of classic realist theatre in terms which bear certain resemblances to the erotic experience of romance protagonists. Brecht's spectators too are aroused yet helpless, overwhelmed by sensations, engulfed by the play, their consciousness suspended, as if they were in a trance:

> Looking about us, we see somewhat motionless figures in a peculiar condition: they seem strenuously to be tensing all their muscles, except where these are flabby and exhausted. They scarcely communicate with each other; their relations are those of a lot of sleepers, though of such as dream restlessly because, as is popularly said of those who have nightmares, they are lying on their backs. True, their eyes are open, but they stare rather than see, just as they listen rather than hear. They look at the stage as if in a trance: an expression which comes from the Middle Ages, the days of witches and priests. Seeing and hearing are activities, and can be pleasant ones, but these people seem relieved of activity and like men to whom something is being done. This detached state, where they seem to be given over to vague but profound sensations, grows deeper the better the work of the actors . . .[36]

The anarchism of Roland Barthes has enough in common with Brecht's Marxism to ensure that they share an evaluation and a repudiation of classic realism, but Brecht's account of the reception process seems to me to be more acute than Barthes's. Barthes acknowledges the excitement of suspense, but he insists that in so far as it resembles the erotic, this excitement represents an immature eroticism. In any case, he argues, it is more intellectual than erotic, since it is no more than the desire to *know*, parallel to

> the pleasure of corporeal striptease or of narrative suspense. In these cases, there is no tear, no edges: a gradual unveiling: the entire excitation takes refuge in the *hope* of seeing the sexual organ (schoolboy's dream) or in knowing the end of the story (novelistic satisfaction). Paradoxically (since it is mass-consumed), this is a far more intellectual pleasure than the other: an Oedipal pleasure (to denude, to know, to learn the origin

and the end), if it is true that every narrative (every unveiling of the truth) is a staging of the (absent, hidden, or hypostatized) father . . .[37]

I am not convinced that the wish to know is necessarily either intellectual (if 'intellectual' here is in opposition to 'erotic'), or Oedipal, if 'Oedipal' here is in opposition to 'mature'). Part of the intensity of love is the desire to know the truth of the other's desire, to be *certain*. But, paradoxically, such certainty would be the death of desire. What is missing from Barthes's dismissive account of the childish pleasure classic realism has to offer is the *un*certainty, the fragility, the precariousness of the fictional world itself. The last page of a book which has been a really good read can break hearts, because it compels us to recognize what, of course, we have really known all along (and what the self-reflexive postmodern text triumphantly keeps reminding us), that it wasn't *true*, that the whole experience was a textually induced illusion. The end of the story is desolate, with or without a happy ending, because it reaffirms the textuality of the text. The world we have inhabited *was not real*. Some of the intensity of reading is the longing to make it real, to live it, to possess the world of the fiction by appropriating its absorbing otherness, which was the source of its excitement in the first place. The Smithton readers were happy, but they were also *avid*. The experience of narrative fiction is not just pleasure: it is also pain.

> Reading is anguish, and this is because any text, however important, or amusing, or interesting it may be (and the more engaging it seems to be) is empty – at bottom it doesn't exist; you have to cross an abyss, and if you do not jump, you do not comprehend.[38]

You jump, of course, but the abyss remains, and it is ungrounded.

Desire is desire of the other precisely *as* other, and it characteristically includes the longing for closure. The quest for closure represents the wish to master difference, the very alterity on which desire depends.[39] This, in the end, not the unity of mind and body, nor unity within the subject, is desire's impossible project. Barthes is right, in my view, about desire, but reductive about reading, when he proclaims an antithesis between the text of pleasure, that contents and satisfies the reader, and the text of *jouissance*, which imposes a state of loss, and brings to a

the end of
proue to ? 37

crisis the reader's relationship with language. I also share his perception that, in so far as it offers the reader specific knowledges, certain non-contradictory ways of understanding the world, at the level of content classic realism is politically reactionary. The sexual politics of most romances are hopelessly unreconstructed,[40] and the racial politics of *Gone With the Wind*, for example, are beyond redemption.[41] But I no longer believe that only the avant-garde is capable of precipitating a crisis in the relationship between the subject and language.[42] (Nor, indeed, that adult sexuality is the exclusive property of the left.)

VII

Many of the great love stories, the ones we remember and distinguish now, do not have happy endings. This is not offered as a universal proposition: *Pride and Prejudice* and *Jane Eyre* are eagerly read and reread. But unfulfilled passion and unhappy love exercise a stronger effect on the cultural imagination, leave an impression of greater intensity, than most of the triumphant Hollywood clinches and Harlequin proposals. Tristan and Isolde, Antony and Cleopatra, Anna Karenina and Vronsky do not sit down to breakfast and smilingly decide to get married. Greta Garbo, who played Anna Karenina (and Camille and Queen Christina . . .) was not only the object of cinematic desire, but its embodiment too, with her ethereal bone structure and a flesh rendered transparent in soft-focus close-up. Garbo sustained in her life the myth that her yearning gaze created on film, by disappearing from the screen and from the public world abruptly and simultaneously. Seen only in glimpses thereafter, she remained a mysterious, elusive, solitary figure. And of course she never married.

Like Garbo's greatest films, *Brief Encounter* and *Casablanca* also finally separate their romantic lovers.[43] These productions of the 1940s show desire and morality in conflict, and in both cases morality triumphs, thus proving that the relationship between the protagonists was indeed true love. Both films reaffirm the obligations of marriage, but they take it for granted that marriage is without desire. Desire preserves its precious rarity and its momentariness by virtue of the fact that an eternity of domesticity is not an option.

Desire is predicated on lack, and even its apparent fulfilment is also a moment of loss. Similarly for the reader of romance, the fulfilment of desire in a happy ending is also the unhappy end of the story, since the characters now move on to that transcendent domestic plane where they live happily ever after, immobilized by their own reciprocal happiness. 'Happy love has no history.'[44] No more events are scheduled to happen to the protagonists, and there can therefore be no more story – and in consequence no more delighted, fearful, uncertain, desiring reader-subject. The only way to sustain the reader's desire would be to continue the narrative, and this in turn would be to tear the lovers apart again, to reintroduce the absences which are the necessary condition of desire, or the impediments on which narrative depends.

This is roughly the strategy of soap opera, where the narrative can continue for as long as invention (or attention) lasts. But soap opera is commonly episodic: it expands the narrative possibilities by inter-weaving several related stories, so that by the time one episode comes to an end, others are already under way. The desire of the audience is sustained by dispersing it.

The classic stories of Lancelot and Guinevere, Romeo and Juliet, Abelard and Héloise, do not end happily, but they do end. In *Brief Encounter* and *Casablanca* the plots are to some degree resolved in renunciation, but what is immobilized and thus perpetuated is not domesticity but desire itself, and the central figures are invested with a corresponding heroism, since only unsatisfied love is truly heroic. Love transfigures; it elevates and transforms the lover as well as the beloved, since desire inhabits a secret realm which is paradoxically more real and more luminous than the light of every day. Tragedy immortal-izes the glory of the lovers, lifting them clear of breathing human passion.

In the catalogue of modern love stories, *Gone With the Wind*, whether the novel or the film, holds an extra-special place. The film is commonly regarded as the most successful movie ever made. In 1990 its earnings were estimated at $840 million. It has been shown to a larger audience world-wide than any other film. The novel, published in 1936, sold a million copies in the first six months, and another twenty-five million copies have been sold since then. Some of its most famous lines have become proverbial, and it is the subject of endless pastiche and parody. In the context of twentieth-century romance, *Gone With the Wind* is unique.[45]

What is the secret of this exceptional quality? Perhaps that Margaret Mitchell's story makes no promises it cannot keep. The world it depicts is already lost, gone with the wind that has swept away the 'civilization' of the American South. Extra-textually, we know that this vanished civilization was based on a slavery that is passed off as devotion and patriarchal values that masquerade as chivalry. In its fictional version, however, the Old South is characterized as vain and absurd in venial ways, but it is also depicted as the last home of courtesy, beauty and heroism. Its proffered charm resides at least partly in the fact that it will never return. According to the opening titles of the film, the ante-bellum South is 'no more than a dream remembered,' and the desire of the audience is encouraged to thrive on an idealizing nostalgia. Moreover, the central figure does not so much as glimpse the possibility of a happy ending. Married three times, Scarlett never settles into domestic immobility. The problem she encounters and the text confronts is the lack of harmony between mind and body. What makes Scarlett heroic is not only her determination to survive, but also a doubly unsatisfied desire that she does not understand until it is too late.[46]

Not that understanding the dualist analysis of desire would necessarily solve the problem. Ashley understands all too well, and suffers: 'Love isn't enough to make a successful marriage when two people are as different as we are . . .'[47] And Rhett understands Ashley, as well as Scarlett: 'He can't be faithful to his wife with his mind or unfaithful with his body . . .' (The Hays Code did not encourage the mention of bodies. In the film Rhett speaks of 'Mr Wilkes, who can't be mentally faithful to his wife, and won't be unfaithful to her technically.') But Rhett, though he elicits a sensual response, cannot for most of the story get Ashley out of Scarlett's mind, and her mind is what he wants.[48]

Gone With the Wind stages the Cartesian dualism that other romances offer to dissolve, puts it on display and shows it to be tragic. In consequence, paradoxically, it does not disappoint its audience. The story remains unresolved. Its inconclusiveness is commonly discussed in terms of what happens 'next': does Scarlett get Rhett back, or doesn't she? When Helen Taylor put that question to readers of *Gone With the Wind*, she found that they divided almost equally on the issue.[49] Margaret Mitchell emphatically refused to comment and treated the possibility of a sequel as a joke.[50] (Alexandra Ripley's existing sequel, published in 1991, is no more than a very protracted formula romance.

Its Rhett is a characteristic blend of brutality and sentiment; Scarlett matures into a real woman; and eventually the two get together to form a nuclear family, complete with a new daughter to replace the dead Bonnie.) One of Taylor's readers, however, silently acknowledged the *textuality* of *Gone With the Wind*, when she commented on the implications of the ending for her. While she felt cheated by it, she saw the novel's lack of resolution at the same time as 'part of its haunting resonance. Because the characters are not safely tucked up in bed together they stay with you.'[51] At the 'sneak preview' of the film the audience was polled, and the director, David O. Selznick, noted:

> To my great pleasure, not one preview card mentioned that they wanted to see Rhett and Scarlett together again. I think they hope they will get together, but it leaves them something to discuss, just as the end of the book did.[52]

By withholding closure, by continuing to tease, elude and frustrate, *Gone With the Wind* succeeds in sustaining the desire of its central character and of the audience simultaneously. Narrative strategies and plot converge, not on an immobilized happiness which fails to satisfy, but on end-less indeterminacy, which is also the condition of desire itself.

Desire deconstructs the opposition between mind and body and yet, paradoxically, it is precisely the reaffirmation of the opposition which in this instance has the effect of sustaining desire. Modern Western culture multiplies desire by holding mind and body apart, and then celebrates the desire it reproduces as at once unfulfilled and thrilling, thrilling to the degree that it remains unfulfilled. Meanwhile, the stories that culture acclaims can be read as indicating not only a dissatisfaction with official, institutional values, but also a delight in the power of textuality to defer closure, to postpone the knowledge which would restore to the *Cogito* the solipsistic mastery it so eagerly seeks.

3

Desire in Theory:
Freud, Lacan, Derrida

I

What is the truth of desire? Can it be defined, specified, theorized? Is it possible to pin desire down, to locate it in a system and subject it to the scrutiny of science? Attempts have, of course, been made, most notably by sexology and sociobiology, but perhaps only psychoanalysis addresses the question without divorcing the organic human animal from the signifier that identifies it as human. And yet its psychoanalytic inscription leaves the truth of desire radically in question.

In 1912, Sigmund Freud published an account of true love as the union of two distinct currents in sexual life, the affectionate and the sensual. As an effect of this ideal state of affairs, Freud argues, 'the greatest intensity of sensual passion will bring with it the highest psychical valuation of the object'.[1] Here the new psychoanalytic science perfectly reproduces a dualism already familiar to us from romance and the popular psychology it reaffirms. In Freud's version, mind and body, psyche and sensuality, join to unite man and woman in a healthy sexual relationship.

The essay is 'On the Universal Tendency to Debasement [*Erniedrigung*] in the Sphere of Love', and its ostensible topic is psychical impotence. This condition, Freud the clinician briskly explains, affects men of perfectly normal sexual appetite who find themselves unable to carry out the sexual act, despite a strong psychological or emotional inclination to do so. On investigation, it appears that this disturbance inhibits intercourse only with certain individuals, and that it is commonly accompanied by the sense of an obstacle inside the sufferer: a 'counter-will', which he cannot explain, interferes in specific circumstances with his conscious intention.

Freud goes on to give what appears to be a characteristically lucid account of the psychosexual development of this disorder.

> Two currents whose union is necessary to ensure a completely normal attitude in love have, in the cases we are considering, failed to combine. These two may be distinguished as the *affectionate* and the *sensual* current. (p. 248)

The affectionate current reaches right back into early childhood. In the interests of self-preservation the child develops a close relationship with those who care for it. This primary object-choice carries with it a sexual component, which of course is not able to fulfil its aims. At puberty the affectionate current is joined by a powerful sensual current, which reinvests the child's original objects with an explicitly erotic desire. This time, however, the sexual drive encounters the obstacles that have been set up by the taboo on incest, the result of the Oedipus complex and its resolution. The drive therefore seeks other objects, outside the family, with whom real sexual relations are admissible. These new sexual objects in due course attract the affection that was initially directed to the child's original objects, and in consequence 'affection and sensuality are then united' in the mature adult (p. 250). Unless, that is, something interferes with this normal developmental process. An unconscious inability to surmount the original incestuous attachment to a mother or a sister can isolate the affectionate current from the sensual current. Then the affections seek out objects of desire who recall the family members, and excite a high degree of respect and admiration, while sensuality can find satisfaction only with women of a wholly different kind, who do not recall the original incestuous objects in any way. Love subsists within the sphere of legality and sex outside it.

Some of the decisiveness, the clarity of the scientific explanation Freud gives in this essay, and its consequent persuasiveness, stems from the sustained metaphor which defines the psychosexual process. In Freud's account the psychosexual impulses resemble waterways which flow from different springs. First one current pursues its course and then is diverted; subsequently another current joins it, but runs up against obstacles; the second current then finds a means to bypass the impediments, and in this way it becomes possible for the two streams to unite – or to diverge. We could draw a sketch-map of this developing waterscape, a hydraulic topography charted in words by a master of rhetoric. How transparent the narrative seems, how true, how inevitable.

And the oppositions it identifies are, of course, already familiar: affection and sensuality, mind and body, ideally in harmony, rarely so in practice. The classical distinction between *agape* and *eros*, reformulated at intervals throughout Western culture, is here scientifically accounted for, and an aspect of the history of fine art is shown in consequence to reveal an explicable kind of pathology: 'The whole sphere of love in such people remains divided in the two directions personified in art as sacred and profane (or animal) love' (p. 251). Freud's analysis is triumphantly confirmed by an aphorism that perfectly specifies a tragic duality: 'Where they love they do not desire and where they desire they cannot love' (p. 251).

Meanwhile, the division within masculine sexuality leads in turn to the identification of another antithesis, again already familiar, already 'obvious', between two feminine sexual types, the idealized, chaste wife and the despised but sexy prostitute:

> the man almost always feels his respect for the woman acting as a restriction on his sexual activity, and only develops full potency when he is with a debased sexual object; and this in its turn is partly caused by the entrance of perverse components into his sexual aims, which he does not venture to satisfy with a woman he respects. He is assured of complete sexual pleasure only when he can devote himself unreservedly to obtaining satisfaction, which with his well-brought-up wife, for instance, he does not dare to do. This is the source of his need for a debased sexual object, a woman who is ethically inferior, to whom he need attribute no aesthetic scruples, who does not know him in his other social relations and cannot judge him in them. It is to such a woman that he prefers to devote his sexual potency, even when the whole of his affection belongs to a woman of a higher kind. It is possible, too, that the tendency so often observed in men of the highest classes of society to choose a woman of a lower class as a permanent mistress or even as a wife is nothing but a consequence of their need for a debased sexual object, to whom, psychologically, the possibility of complete satisfaction is linked. (p. 254)

The tendency in question, we are to remember, is a 'disorder', but one which is much more widespread than most people suppose. And in fact, Freud has already confided, to a certain extent this dismal division can be said to characterize the sexual life of civilized man in general (p. 253).

For thus gradually but decisively normalizing a perverse male sexuality, in conjunction with a succession of crude patriarchal female stereotypes of class as well as gender, Freud surely merits all the wrath directed at him by feminists from Kate Millett to Luce Irigaray and beyond. It is as if the reader is invited to share the masculine attribution of ethical and aesthetic inferiority to working-class women, to endorse male promiscuity, and at the same time to recognize as inevitable the fact that men are simply like that, that they can't help it, that there's nothing to be done. Possibly the most brilliant analysis of Freud's misogyny is Sarah Kofman's account of his ad hoc invocation of penis envy in order finally to *guarantee* the debasement of *all* women. The theory of penis envy, she points out, has no place in the logic of Freud's account of psychosexual development, but it does have the virtue of founding women's inferiority in biology. And by depreciating women in general, it solves the problem of the division between wife and whore set up in the essay on Debasement: 'Woman's penis envy is certainly the best solution for Freud, the solution that makes it possible to dispense with the dangerous solution of recourse to prostitutes, those women of humble birth sufficiently debased to exalt man's sex and to banish any association with incest . . .'[2] If all women are naturally and necessarily envious of men, then they are all in that sense debased, and big men can have nothing to fear from even the most admirable of them.

Of course, the antithesis between the chaste but chilling wife and the uninhibited working-class mistress has a distinctively Victorian flavour, even if it goes back at least to Renaissance religious iconography, and although traces of it still survive even now in the preferences and practices of certain prominent politicians and television evangelists. In the nineteenth century in particular, in view of the Victorian idealization of feminine purity, it must have been particularly difficult to solicit participation in eccentric sexual practices from the Angel in the House. No wonder it was necessary to turn to 'uncultivated' prostitutes in whom polymorphous perversity was widely perceived to persist.[3] Today's superwoman, however, a product of the twentieth-century

45

sexual revolution, is expected to take sexual eccentricities in her stride, and indeed to dress up in black leather as required, in between organizing the household and accepting well-deserved promotions at the office. The problem is now surely largely solved. And yet the underlying opposition Freud's text depicts is remarkably close to the dualism identified by the romances: minds and bodies out of line with each other in a slightly different way; two distinct currents converging only coincidentally, if at all; a version of love which strives to reconcile sensuality and affection, while driving them in practice further apart than ever.

The essay on Debasement is divided into three sections and the second of these inaugurates what is apparently a new beginning. The account of psychical impotence, it appears, was merely a prelude, an introduction which now makes way for an approach to Freud's 'proper subject' (p. 252). The problem with the theory as it stands, Freud points out, is that while it explains why some men are psychically impotent, what it leaves out of account is how any succeed in escaping this affliction. And it is at this point that Freud reveals the widespread character of the disorder he is considering: a degree of psychical impotence is the rule rather than the exception.

Something of the same problem affects women too, it now appears. For young women sexuality is so long prohibited, Freud explains, that it is often difficult for them to undo the connection between sensual activity and prohibition. Legitimate sex leaves them frigid, while forbidden sensuality, by contrast, often releases a capacity for pleasure which cannot be found elsewhere. Clandestine love, for example, is a parallel experience for women to the masculine recourse to prostitutes: 'unfaithful to their husband, they are able to keep a second order of faith with their lover' (p. 255). There is thus a certain symmetry between men and women in this respect. Women share, after all, in the 'universal' tendency towards prohibited sexual pleasure.

Freud had already argued in *Three Essays on the Theory of Sexuality* (and would reiterate) that there is only one libido, whether it occurs in men or women, and that if desire is 'masculine' in character, it is so primarily in the sense that 'masculine' means 'active', since a drive is always 'active'.[4] This notorious passage, with its long subsequent footnote, displays a characteristic Freudian pattern of affirmation followed by hesitation when the issue is sexual difference. Here male sexuality is taken as the norm; sexual difference is brought into being with the ending of the phallic phase; female sexuality is thus different – and the same; and in any case, in human beings pure 'masculinity' and pure 'femininity' do not exist. In the Debasement essay men and women share a pleasure in forbidden love. The situations are not identical: women neither overvalue their husbands nor experience a corresponding need to debase their lovers. But both men and women are adversely affected by the long delay, 'which is demanded by education for cultural reasons,' between the moment of sexual maturity and the arrival of the time for legitimate sexual activity (pp. 255–6).

If the affectionate and the sensual impulses commonly fail to coalesce, that is seen at this stage of the argument as a consequence of the cultural practice which separates marriage from the onset of puberty. The victim of psychical impotence in this second section of the essay is no longer a number of unfortunate marriages in which pathology regrettably plays a part, but the institution of marriage in general. And the culprit is not so clearly an inadequate resolution of the Oedipus complex, leading to an unconscious attachment to forbidden, incestuous objects of desire, but rather the chronological gap between the development of a sexual capacity and its legitimate exercise. Freud's 'proper subject', it appears, is not so much a clinical disorder as civilization and its discontents. And in case the reader might draw from this analysis a precipitate inference that earlier marriage would make for happier marriage or, more radically, that marriage itself might not be the happiest location for sexual activity (a case that Freud had already argued vehemently four years earlier[5]), the essay disarmingly draws back from any implied prescription:

> In view of the strenuous efforts being made in the civilized world today to reform sexual life, it will not be superfluous to give a reminder that psychoanalytic research is as remote from tendentiousness as any other kind of research. It has no other end in view than to throw light on things by tracing what is manifest back to what is hidden. It is quite satisfied if reforms make use of its findings to replace what is injurious by something more advantageous; but it cannot predict whether other institutions may not result in other, and perhaps graver, sacrifices. (p. 256)

The final note of warning is chilling. What are these 'graver sacrifices' that the text hints at but does not define? And are they incidental to the argument, or part of the 'proper subject' of the essay? What, indeed, is this 'proper subject'? Have we reached it when the opening of the third section of the essay alludes to 'the curb put upon love by civilization' (p. 256)?

The transparent scientific text has begun to cloud over as Freud takes away with one observation what he gives with another. A disorder becomes a common condition, at least in 'civilization'. But the most obvious remedy will not necessarily produce the cure. The problem is inevitable; there is nothing to be done; and in any case another state of affairs might be worse. Meanwhile, as the discussion develops, or rather doubles back on itself, a new set of oppositions begins to emerge, replacing the text's earlier dualities: no longer mind and body, or man and woman, but sexual pleasure and marriage, sexuality on the one hand and 'civilization' [*Kultur*] on the other. And what is the alternative to this 'civilization', its defining difference? Savagery? Primitivism? Uninhibited working-class sexuality?[6] Or nature itself? And if so, where in human experience might this nature be found? In the pre-Oedipal, instinctual life of the infant, perhaps.

The opening of the third section of the argument, which constitutes something like another new start, simply effaces most of the distinctions the first two sections have set up, by alluding to the title of the essay: the topic is a 'universal' (*allgemeinste*, most widespread) tendency in sexual relations.[7] Since it seems that the question is no longer primarily one concerning differences of culture, class or gender, the essay goes on to clarify its project by attention to the nature of the sexual drive itself. The initial frustration of sexual pleasure [twice over, we must suppose – by the castration complex and again at puberty by 'education'] has the subsequent effect of inhibiting legitimate sexual activity. And yet delay is not after all to blame: '*But at the same time, if sexual freedom is unrestricted from the outset the result is no better*' (my italics, p. 256). As the decline and fall of the ancient civilizations demonstrate, Freud goes on, easy sex is worthless sex. 'An obstacle is required in order to heighten libido; and where natural resistances to satisfaction have not been sufficient men have at all times erected conventional ones so as to be able to enjoy love' (pp. 256–7). Now it appears that nature and convention are not antithetical, but in alliance, producing 'resistances' which enhance desire. Medieval Christian asceticism, for instance, 'created psychical values for love which pagan antiquity was never able to confer on it' (p. 257). Forbidden love is more not less thrilling. Civilization increases the value of the erotic; culture invades sexual life with the effect of intensifying it.

How, the essay goes on to deliberate, can this be? Is it simply an economic question, a matter of supply and demand? Obviously the psychical insistence of an impulse rises in proportion to its frustration. But does its importance also fall when the impulse is easily satisfied? And here Freud invokes the alcoholic, whose desire for wine is not enhanced by scarcity: 'Does one ever hear of a drinker who needs to go to a country where wine is dearer or drinking is prohibited, so that by introducing obstacles he can reinforce the dwindling satisfaction that he obtains? Not at all' (p. 257). It seems, then, that the character of sexuality is in some way special, that there is something in the nature of the sexual drive itself that is 'unfavourable to the realization of complete satisfaction' (even, we must presumably suppose at this stage of the argument, with a debased or prohibited object) (p. 258).

The essay goes on to offer two possible reasons for this new insight. The second of these, the view that genital activity is fundamentally 'animal' and thus incompatible with civilization, apparently reinstates the earlier duality of nature and culture:

> The genitals themselves have not taken part in the development of the human body in the direction of beauty: they have remained animal, and thus love, too, has remained in essence just as animal as it ever was. (p. 259)

This argument carries very little credibility for us now, as products of a culture which, in the wake of D. H. Lawrence, sexology and the sexual revolution of the 1960s, is more likely to idealize sex than to be disgusted by it. Freud seems to be generalizing from his own historical moment, and presenting as universal a problem which has now been solved by sexual liberation.

It is not, however, quite as simple as that. The paragraph as a whole is altogether more puzzling. The second reason why something in the nature of the sexual instinct is unfavourable to complete satisfaction is that sexuality, the sexual drive itself, *develops*:

the sexual instinct is originally divided into a great number of components – or rather it develops out of them – some of which cannot be taken up into the instinct in its later form. (p. 258)

These (animal) components include coprophilia, for example, which is discarded when human beings adopt an upright gait, and which has no proper place in human sexual life. At the same time, however, the fundamental sexual processes 'remain unaltered': 'The excremental is all too intimately and inseparably bound up with the sexual.' Human beings both are and are not 'animal', and the impulses that cannot be incorporated into human sexuality persist and are registered as non-satisfaction (p. 259). Sexual liberation, freeing the erotic from culturally imposed inhibition, is not, after all, quite what is at stake.

The process of development that is identified here is evolutionary, phylogenetic. But a parallel development defines the psychosexual history of the individual human being. The first reason Freud gives in the Debasement essay for the incompatibility between sexuality and satisfaction concerns an originary loss. His account of this process of loss explicitly calls into question yet again the dualities that so much of the essay appears to take for granted. It also tells a story which is implicit in all of psychoanalysis, but which is rarely glimpsed more clearly than it is here. This is the history of a gender-neutral human being, belonging to no particular race or class, which, from its earliest infancy, is already an animal-in-culture, a composite figure in which nature and culture, body and mind are intextricably intertwined, and in which in consequence the great dualism of the Cartesian *Cogito* no longer holds.

According to the text, the first reason why the sexual drive remains unsatisfied is this:

as a result of the diphasic onset of object-choice, and the interposition of the barrier against incest, the final object of the sexual instinct is never any longer the original object but only a surrogate for it. Psychoanalysis has shown us that when the original object of a wishful impulse has been lost as a result of repression, it is frequently represented by an endless series of substitute objects none of which, however, brings full satisfaction. (p. 258)

Every object of adult desire stands in for an original object which is forever lost, and which it represents. Since each substitute, each representation, is always only that and no more, it can never fully be the object of unconscious desire. Loss returns as the impossibility of perfect satisfaction.

surely the Mother ?

But what is this lost object which can never be recovered in adult life? The essay has already told us a good deal about it. The child's primary object-choice is directed towards those who look after it, and is formed 'on the basis of the interests of the self-preservative instinct' (p. 248). It is an effect, in other words, of the child's initial dependency, its need for food and warmth, and its fundamental impulse to survive. This impulse 'carries along with it' sexual components, Freud argues, but these become attached only secondarily to the child's valuation of the attentions originally necessary to the preservation of life. It follows, as Jean Laplanche has argued on the basis of a parallel passage from Freud's *Three Essays on the Theory of Sexuality*, 'that *on the one hand there is from the beginning an object, but that on the other hand sexuality does not have, from the beginning, a real object*'.[8]

Laplanche argues that in psychoanalytic theory human sexuality is not simply and unaccountably given in nature. On the contrary, the sexual drive (*Trieb*: the psychical representative of an instinct[9]) is 'propped on' the impulse to survive. Sexual excitation comes in the first instance from outside, from adults, from the necessary process of caring, which is associated with sexual meanings.[10] But it comes to the child too early to be intelligible. In consequence, the child reaches puberty only after sexuality has already been invested with a whole range of repressed because unintelligible meanings. These meanings are learned from those who bring up the child, from the significances and fantasies which are inseparable for them in turn from love and care. Sexuality, according to Laplanche, is initially supplementary to self-preservation.[11]

Moreover, adult sexuality, it appears, is subsequently 'propped on' the requirements of the ego (which explains, for instance, the narcissistic element in object-choice). In Freud's own words in the essay on Debasement:

> the sexual instincts find their first objects by attaching themselves to the valuations made by the ego-instincts precisely in the way in which the first sexual satisfactions are experienced in attachment to the bodily functions necessary for the preservation of life. The 'affection' shown by

the child's parents and those who look after him, which seldom fails to betray its erotic nature ('the child is an erotic plaything'), does a very great deal to raise the contributions made by erotism to the cathexes of his ego-instincts. (p. 249)

It seems, then, that there is no primordial, original, founding sexual object at all, but only an object subsequently sexually cathected, and invested with sexual meanings initially learned from others, in the course of the necessary process of caring for a human infant whose physical autonomy is so long delayed. The mother, or those who care for the child, by their attentions first *teach* the child how to love.[12] This means, as Laplanche points out, that the object of adult desire

> is not the lost object, but its substitute by displacement; the lost object is the object of self-preservation, of hunger, and the object one seeks to refind in sexuality is an object displaced in relation to that first object. From this, of course, arises the impossibility of ultimately ever rediscovering the object, since the object which has been lost *is not the same* as that which is to be rediscovered.[13]

It also means that sexuality does not exist in a pure state prior to the meanings and fantasies with which it is invested by the caring adults. There is no erotic life outside what is learned, no infantile instinctual sexuality untrammelled by meaning, no body independent of mind, and no lost golden world outside 'civilization' or culture.[14] Human sexuality is inevitably bound up with representation. Civilization is present from the beginning in the world of the little human animal, even before the awareness of castration impels it to submit to the imperatives of the cultural order and renounce incest.

A Third Party thus always attends the sexual relation, and this is culture itself, the location of both sexual meanings and proprieties and prohibitions. Desire, the Debasement essay indicates, commonly repudiates the specific norms subsequently affirmed by 'education', with its delays and deferments, seeking out instead in illicit relationships the pleasure so long forbidden by the cultural order. Far from inhibiting libido, prohibition promotes unconscious desire for an object that can never be found.

There is, in consequence, a resemblance between Freud's analysis of desire and the brilliant account Denis de Rougemont gives of passion as suffering. Tristan and Isolde, de Rougemont points out in *Love in the Western World*, repeatedly seek out impediments to satisfaction. This adulterous love, the ideal type of passion in Western culture, depends on dangers, is enhanced by absences, and has recourse to self-imposed obstacles. At one point in the story Tristan implicitly reaffirms the threat of castration as the penalty for forbidden love by placing his naked sword between the bodies of the lovers as they sleep. Later Tristan perfectly voluntarily marries another woman, another Isolde, but continues nevertheless to long for his first love, refusing to consummate the marriage. The jealous wife finally brings about Tristan's death, and then her own, when she lies to him about the colour of the first Isolde's sails as she comes to cure him. Neither legitimate love nor illicit passion finds perfect fulfilment.

Something in the nature of the sexual drive, Freud has argued, is unfavourable to the realization of complete satisfaction. The Third Party, civilization, the cultural order, which irretrievably differentiates human beings from animals, cannot be fully reconciled with the sexuality which it itself makes possible. What is at stake is not an opposition between an uninhibited nature and a repressive civilization, but a human organism-in-culture impelled by desire for an object that it can neither identify nor find, and motivated by meanings which cannot be entirely recovered.

Freud's essay finally reverts, of course, to the Enlightenment categories with which it began, in order to argue that although the sexual drive is not able to be reconciled with the demands of civilization, although sexual activity does not in the end satisfy human desire, the sublimation of the sexual impulse produces the noblest human achievements. In this way the text furnishes itself with a happy ending. But which of the questions it addresses, we might wonder, is its 'proper subject'? Is it the set of oppositions of race ('civilization' and its unspecified – perhaps primitive – alternative?), class and gender, which cannot be made to stay in place as the text moves on? Is it instead the Enlightenment dualisms of mind and body, culture and nature, which are the only categories apparently available for discussing and analyzing sexuality? Or is it finally a radical reinterpretation of human desire which refuses to conform to any analysis that isolates mind from body, culture from nature, and civilization from what the English translation calls 'instinct' (*Trieb*, drive)?

II

As so often in Freud's work, the scientific clarity of the text is an illusion. The writing doubles back on itself, never reaching the promised goal, but offering another in its place. The process of displacement and substitution mimics, we might argue, the ways of desire, and makes of the text itself an object of desire for the reader. Redactions of Freud, mapping, schematizing, systematizing, and eliminating in the process the seductive duplicities of Freud's texts, too often close on a theology without mysteries and a science which has about as much plausibility as astrology or black magic.

In this sense Freud's best reader has surely been Jacques Lacan, whose dense, difficult, elusive texts make no promises of an illusory transparency. Lacan's writing explicitly foregrounds the processes of enunciation by simulating the modes of speech which are its primary theme. In a direct challenge to the institutional tradition of scientific psychoanalytic writing, his texts are associative, allusive, figurative, digressive. The signified slips and slides under the signifier as the meanings produced by the Lacanian system of differences, 'other' and 'Other', '*objet a*', 'imaginary', 'real', and 'desire' itself, refuse to stay in place. Lacan's 'algebra', the literal symbols, diagrams, graphs imitate – and parody – the 'objectivity' relentlessly pursued by the will to truth.

Meanwhile, the lapses, jokes and narratives, which disrupt and illuminate the texts, mimic the interventions of the unconscious in all human utterance. To schematize Lacan's work, however helpful the process, is in the end to do an injustice to the texts' complexity, and at the same time to diminish their power of seduction. In what follows, a reading of one of Lacan's accounts of desire, I try to reproduce Lacan's own text wherever possible.

Lacan's essay, 'The Signification of the Phallus', was originally delivered as a lecture in 1958. His discussion begins with a 'knot' that fastens together the identity of the human being: 'We know that the unconscious castration complex has the function of a knot.'[15] The castration complex is also a knotty theoretical problem which psychoanalysis sets out to untie, and this second knot at the level of the signifier is formulated in the lecture as a riddle or a mathematical puzzle which confronts both Lacan and his audience: 'what is the link between the murder of the father and the pact of the primordial law, if it is included in that law that castration should be the punishment for incest?' (p. 282). What, in other words, is the connection between the Oedipus complex and the order of language and culture, if castration is the punishment for forbidden love? How does psychoanalysis chart the relationship, which is constitutive for human beings, between prohibition, loss and sexuality? In answer, 'The Signification of the Phallus' recounts the birth of desire, and if it 'solves' the riddle, it also paradoxically defers it by invoking the question of sexual difference.

The essay makes explicit the importance for Lacanian psychoanalysis of the post-Saussurean distinction between the signifier (the acoustic or written image) and the signified (meaning). Although Freud was not in a position to take account of modern linguistic theory, his work, Lacan argues, not only anticipates its findings, but brings out their full implication. This is above all the discovery that language is constitutive of meaning, that signification differentiates, and in consequence,

> that the signifier has an active function in determining certain effects in which the signifiable appears as submitting to its mark, by becoming through that passion the signified. (p. 284)

Lacan offers three terms where Saussure provided two. Signifiers actively transform into meanings an undifferentiated signifiable real, which pre-exists it as unknowable and unintelligible. As a result of the work of the signifier, 'there is born the world of meaning of a particular language in which the world of things will come to be arranged'.[16]

For Lacan the real seems to submit to the signifier, and its transformation is defined as a 'passion': that is to say suffering, something which is endured and, supremely in Western culture, the suffering of Christ on the cross. Lacan's own signifier is not idle. There is a birth here, the birth of the world of meaning, but also a death, since 'the symbol manifests itself first of all as the murder of the thing'.[17] Language erases even as it creates. The signifier *replaces* the object it identifies as a separate entity; the linguistic symbol supplants what it names and differentiates, relegates it to a limbo beyond language, where it becomes inaccessible, lost; and in consequence 'the being of language is the non-being of objects'.[18] The symbolic 'passion' institutes a lack which does not exist in the real.

By its attention to the signifier, and to the primacy of the symbolic in the construction of the world of meaning and difference, Lacan goes on to argue in 'The Signification of the Phallus', psychoanalysis gives a new account of the human condition, 'in that it is not only man who speaks, but that in man and through man *it* speaks (*ça parle*)' (p. 284). 'It' here represents language, the symbolic order, the word as Law, which forms the human subject in its own image;[19] at the same time 'it' signifies language as the material of psychoanalysis itself, the 'talking cure'; and this is so in turn because '*it*' (id) is also the unconscious which is presented, made present for the first time, in signification – as marks on the body, or in verbal slips, jokes told and dreams recounted. There 'resounds', therefore, rings out in the (hollow, perhaps; certainly echoing) human being, what the essay calls 'the relation of speech' (p. 284). No longer an organism in the real, the speaking human being encompasses a void, a lack under the Law.

Speech is a 'relation', the possibility of dialogue, of demand, of community, reciprocity, love. As the condition of subjectivity, permitting a difference between 'I' and 'you', speech is also necessarily the possibility of intersubjectivity, of address and response, question and answer. But this liberation is at the same time a constraint. To the extent that the subject can come to exist in language only under a name (or a pronoun) which is not chosen but allotted from elsewhere, by the Father as representative of the Other, the symbolic itself, that name (*le Nom-du-Père*) supplants what it constitutes. In consequence, 'I identify myself in language, but only by losing myself in it like an object.'[20] Moreover, the place of the ' "intra-said" (*intra-dit*)' within the relation of speech between two subjects is also the place of the '*inter-dit*', the location precisely of interdiction, prohibition and Law (*le Non-du-Père*), and therefore of a split in the subject between what can be acknowledged and what cannot be recognized.[21] The fear of castration and the consequent submission to the (paternal) Law, to the symbolic order, releases the possibility of speech and at the same time divides the subject from itself, instituting and simultaneously outlawing the unconscious. Unconscious desire is thus caught up with what is prohibited.

The unconscious speaks, however, in the symbolic. The repressed returns in the process of speech, putting on display the division, the difference which inhabits and defines the speaking subject:

It speaks in the Other, I say, designating by the Other the very locus evoked by the recourse to speech in any relation in which the Other intervenes. If *it* speaks in the Other, whether or not the subject hears it with his ear, it is because it is there that the subject, by means of a logic anterior to any awakening of the signified, finds its signifying place. The discovery of what it articulates in that place, that is to say in the unconscious, enables us to grasp at the price of what splitting (*Spaltung*) it has thus been constituted.

The phallus reveals its function here. (p. 285)

The phallus, the protagonist in Lacan's narrative of the birth of desire, is defined in the first instance by a series of negations. It is not, we are to understand, a 'phantasy'; it is not an 'object' in the sense in which the term features in object-relations theory; and finally, 'it is even less the organ, penis or clitoris, that it symbolizes' (p. 285). The phallus is not an anatomical feature, whether male or female. On the contrary, 'the phallus is a signifier', Lacan affirms, in a witty repudiation of any dualism that opposes meaning and the body (p. 285), and what it signifies, the essay will later reveal, is desire, 'the desire of the Other' (p. 290). But it signifies, we should remember, only by means of a submission to the symbolic order which Lacan has already figured as a 'passion'. The phallus occupies its privileged position at the price of a loss, and this loss is represented in the Freudian economy as castration. Through the passion of the real, irretrievably separated off from the organism, the phallus (as $-\phi$) comes to stand for the *objet a* which is lost for ever.[22]

How does this loss come about? What are the effects of the advent of signification in the human being? First, the essay proposes, signification causes a 'deviation' of organic needs in the process of transforming them into demands. Subjected to the signifier, these needs return to the speaking subject 'alienated', other than they are, since it is from the Other, the locus of speech which already exists outside the subject, that the subject's message is emitted (p. 286). 'That which is thus alienated in needs constitutes an *Urverdrängung*', disappears from view in an ur-repression, an anterior, prior, primal repression. But this in turn gives rise to something which does appear, namely desire (p. 286). Desire is the effect of the lost needs: loss returns and presents itself as desire. Desire is not *the same as* need: analytic experience certainly demonstrates 'the paradoxical, deviant, erratic, eccentric, even scandalous character' which distinguishes desire from anything that could possibly be *necess-ary* (p. 286). The erotic capabilities of the human animal are way in excess of nature's reproductive imperative. In any case, the needs in question were a matter of survival, not sex. What returns as desire is quite other than the repressed needs that are its cause.

In this morality play of the advent of signification, Lacan presents three allegorical figures, need, desire, and demand. 'Demand . . . bears on something other than the satisfactions it calls for. It is a demand of a presence or of an absence . . .' (p. 286). Demand is ultimately the demand for love, and its mythological founding moment is the story Freud tells in *Beyond the Pleasure Principle* of the child with the cotton reel. At the age of eighteen months, little Ernst, Freud's grandson, took to symbolizing his mother's alternate absence and presence with a cotton reel attached to a piece of string. As he threw it away, the little boy uttered a long-drawn-out sound which approximated to *'fort'* (gone), and when he pulled it back, he greeted the cotton reel with a joyful *'da'* (here).[23] This elementary system of differences, however imperfectly under control, represents the child's entry into the symbolic order, in accordance with which its existence will be structured.[24] But the moment of naming absence is also the instant of the birth of desire, since the signifier, while it *replaces* the mother, does not *fill* her place, makes nothing present. The *fort/da* game represents both command and loss. It is in the mother's absence, in solitude that the child makes itself 'master' of her desertion, by acknowledging the otherness of its mother, and her independent existence (with, indeed, her own separate object of desire).[25] The process of symbolic mastery thus has the paradoxical effect of rendering desire itself indestructible.[26] In addition, Freud suggests that by throwing away the cotton reel the child enacts an emblematic revenge on the mother who has abandoned it.[27] The game is therefore also an act of hostility, a dismissal of the loved object, a figurative destruction. 'Thus the symbol manifests itself first of all as the murder of the thing, and this death constitutes in the subject the eternalization of his desire.'[28]

Murder; the symbolic pact which subjects the human being to the Law; loss; and desire: the strands which make up the knot that con-stitutes the signifying animal, fastens it together, indeed, begin to distinguish themselves at the level of theory (though to untie them in practice would be to precipitate psychosis). At this stage, however, it is

the 'mother' who is the murder victim, since language is first invoked
in the relationship with the 'mother', which is described in the essay as
shown to be 'pregnant with that Other to be situated *within* [*en deça de*:
some way short of[29]] the needs that it can satisfy' (p. 286). Ultimately
the 'father' will stand for the symbolic order in its entirety, the paternal
authority representing Law, which will be invoked in order to impose
limits on the imaginary omnipotence of the now differentiated other,
the arbitrariness of the signifier, and the anxiety of desire.[30]

Or rather the Father. Lacanian psychoanalysis is not much concerned
with narratives of childhood, except in so far as these lay down a
structure which defines the subject. Lacan's theory is not a version of
child-psychology, and is not usefully read as an account of the roles of
mothers and fathers.[31] The stages of psychosexual development have a
mythological status: the 'story' of the child is important only in so far
as it is perpetually recapitulated in the experience of the adult. The
Father is a signifier, and it is the Name-of-the-Father which authorizes
meaning, the paternal-signifying Law which holds in place the ordering
mechanisms of the symbolic.[32] The Mother, too, is crucially a signifier,
not a person, 'the signifier of the primordial object'.[33] With the resolution of the Oedipus complex, which is the entry into the Law, it will
be the symbolic Father who belongs with death:

> How, indeed, could Freud fail to recognize such an affinity, when the
> necessity of his reflexion led him to link the appearance of the signifier
> of the Father, as author of the Law, with death, even to the murder of the
> Father – thus showing that if this murder is the fruitful moment of debt
> through which the subject binds himself for life to the Law, the symbolic
> Father is, in so far as he signifies this Law, the dead Father.[34]

Demand is the possibility of love – and hate. Demand constitutes the
Other as able to satisfy needs, or to withhold satisfaction. 'That which
is thus given to the Other to fill, and which is strictly that which it does
not have, since it, too, lacks being, is what is called love, but it is also
hate and ignorance.'[35] The Other, however, which is not a person but
the locus of speech, is not *full*. Since what the Other can give is not
substantial, demand 'annuls' the specificity of what is given by turning
it into a proof of love. 'It is necessary, then, that the particularity thus
abolished should reappear *beyond* demand' (p. 286). What appears be-

yond demand, 'in the interval that demand hollows within itself',[36] in
the place of the loss brought about by the signifier, is desire.

[handwritten: Desire = Demand — Need]

> Thus desire is neither the appetite for satisfaction, nor the demand for
> love, but the difference that results from the subtraction of the first from
> the second, the phenomenon of their splitting (*Spaltung*). (p. 287)

Neither natural nor cultural, neither a need at the level of the
organism, nor a demand formulated by the *Cogito*, desire is a *difference*.
It is an effect of the alienation in the human animal of the requirement
for gratification as the demand for love. Desire thus deconstructs the
opposition between mind and body. And if the sexual relation 'occupies'
the field of desire, that is because sexuality delivers its appeal at once to
the lost, absent, 'murdered' *real* of the organism and to the Other for the
proof of love. From the gap that necessarily appears within this doubly
barred appeal in antithetical directions, it follows for both the partners
in the sexual relation that 'it is not enough to be the subjects of need,
or objects of love, but that they must stand for the cause of desire'
(p. 287). The cause of desire, Lacan's *objet a*, is the lost object in the
unknowable real. Desire is thus 'a relation of being to lack. This lack is
the lack of being properly speaking. It isn't the lack of this or that, but
the lack of being whereby the being exists.'[37] Desire is a metonym
(a displaced version) of the want-to-be[38] that necessarily characterises
a human life divided between the unmasterable symbolic and the
unreachable, inextricable real. And desire itself is split between the
quest for satisfaction in the real, 'a refusal of the signifier', on the one
hand, and the desire of (for) the Other, the origin of meaning, which
entails 'a lack of being'.[39] This must be so because if the subject longs
to find the real again, it also yearns to find the self which is perpetually
created and destroyed by the signifier.[40] And where else is the signifying
subject to be found but in the Other? Lacan's repeated insistence that
desire is the desire of the Other is his most plural, most elusive formulation. It can be read as meaning variously (at least): desire originates in
the Other (the symbolic); it inhabits the Other (the unconscious); it is
for the Other (the recognition of the other at the level of the unconscious); it is for the Other (the subject-presumed-to-know, the analyst
in the transference); it is for the Other (a guarantee of meaning and
truth in the symbolic, a transcendental signified, 'God').

[handwritten margin notes: Ursula / God / I-God / UCs / beyond language]

How absurd in these circumstances to suppose that desire can be met by 'leaving it to the virtue of the "genital" to resolve it through the maturation of tenderness' (p. 287). Lacan has nothing but contempt for the view that true love leading to happy marriage is the project of desire, since desire precisely exceeds the dualism of sensuality and affection, resides beyond both need and demand. As early as 1948 he invoked La Rochefoucauld's maxim that there are good marriages, but none that are exciting (*délicieux*).[41] Imagining a marriage between Dora and Herr K, Lacan commented that it would be 'as unhappy as any other marriage'.[42] Whatever the nature of desire, genital harmony in conjunction with affection is not its object. Even the most fulfilled relationships involve so many *debasements* (*Erniedrigungen*), Lacan insists, in consequence of the Oedipal drama which conjoins desire with love but also with ('murderous') hate, the dark God 'in the sheep's clothing of the Good Shepherd Eros'.[43] Desire subsists both within and beyond the realm of the pleasure principle; it cannot be contained by the stable, institutional, public *legality* which is marriage. On the contrary, desire, which is absolute, *knows no law*.[44]

For Lacan, as for Freud, then, there are three parties involved in sexual desire, this time the subject, the Law, and the unconscious as outlaw. The subject is an effect of the *Nom-/Non-du-Père*; it inhabits the symbolic order which both produces and prohibits unconscious desire. In consequence, the object of unconscious desire cannot be identified. It is precisely 'the desire for nothing nameable'.[45] This is what it means to say that desire exists beyond demand, beyond the signifier. And yet desire speaks, in the unconscious, in the Other. And its own signifier is the phallus.

Why the phallus, Lacan's essay asks? Partly, of course, the reader must suppose, because this is a reading of Freud, and the argument consequently starts from the infantile phallic stage, which in Freud's account leads up to the castration complex. The phallic stage is the same for boys and girls, and precedes sexual difference (p. 282). In Freud's version sexual difference is produced in relation to the phallus. And perhaps, Lacan adds, the phallus is the privileged signifier of desire because it is the most salient of what can be seized (*le plus saillant de ce qu'on peut attraper*[46]) in the real of sexual copulation, the element which makes visible the sexual incompleteness of both individuals, and which in heterosexual relations promises to join each partner to the real. This is one of the most evasive moments in an essay which is very far from transparent. The phallus is a signifier; it *symbolizes* the penis or the clitoris; but it *is* also the penis – perhaps ('It can be said . . .'). Moreover (perhaps) it represents the copula typographically in the symbolic [as the equals sign (=)?]. And (perhaps) it offers an image of the vital flow transmitted in generation (p. 287).

But then the essay takes back what it might appear to have given: 'All these propositions merely conceal the fact that it can play its role only when veiled, that is to say, as itself a sign of the latency with which any signifiable is struck, when it is raised (*aufgehoben*) to the function of signifier' (p. 288). The phallus is no more, after all, than a signifier, and it can play its role as a signifier only when it appears as such, that is to say when it seems to render 'latent' the real of which it is only the representative, and which it cannot make present. The moment it is 'unveiled', it becomes the bar which 'strikes the signified', which bars the subject's access to the lost (*urverdrängt*, primally repressed) real and the unacknowledged ([secondarily] repressed) meanings which constitute the unconscious (p. 288).

Much of the rest of the essay is concerned with sexual difference. And here it is difficult to avoid the conclusion that Lacan, like Freud, is inclined to take cultural stereotypes for structural effects. Women, it appears, tend to want to *be* the phallus, the object of desire, whereas men want to *have* it. And yet almost at once a (somewhat confusing) allusion to the 'masquerade' of femininity calls this conclusion into question (p. 290). In her essay on 'Womanliness as a Masquerade', first published in 1929, Joan Riviere proposed, with whatever hesitations and reversals, that femininity was *no more than* a mask adopted to deflect male retribution and elicit sexual approval. Riviere's account is psychical, but the hierarchized eroticism that it describes is palpably articulated with the social and cultural, with a sexual identity which is learned.[47] What is 'behind' the mask, what woman might (learn to) be(come) remains to be seen.

Lacan's essay reverts, however, to stereotypes and hierarchy. Women, it argues, wanting to be the phallus, tolerate frigidity, while in men, who want to have it, the dialectic of demand and desire produces a tendency to debasement (*Erniedrigung*) and a consequent 'centrifugal' inclination to infidelity (p. 290). And yet, the essay continues, 'it should not be thought that the sort of infidelity that would appear to be constitutive of the male function is proper to it. For if one looks more closely, the same redoubling is to be found in the woman . . .' (p. 290). True in the end to Freud, Lacan cannot sustain the opposition he seems to want to set up. There is, after all, only one libido, even if it is 'masculine' in character (p. 291).

If this account of sexual difference is finally inconclusive, it is also possible to argue that it is incidental to Lacan's gender-neutral account of desire. But is it? The identification of the phallus as the primary signifier has been critical in the feminist denunciation of Lacan's phallocentrism. 'The Signification of the Phallus' is certainly phallocentric in the most literal sense of the term. And the story Lacan tells there of sexual difference is not one that feminism could easily endorse. Why, then, or how, would any feminist find the essay sympathetic?

The question seems to turn on the meaning of the phallus. As I have already suggested, there is a certain slippage here, or perhaps a certain textual teasing. The phallus is a signifier. No one has it, neither women nor men. It signifies the unnameable object of desire, the desire of the Other, and it re-presents (stands in the place of) the *objet a*, the lost object in the real. And yet it 'can be said' that *this* signifier is chosen because it stands out as what can be seized in the real of the sexual act. It *can* be said. But is it *being* said here? The answer is not obvious,[48] but the evasion is crucial to Lacan's anti-dualist project. In addition, the essay reproduces the Freudian account of the Oedipus complex, to the extent that it portrays the child as longing to be the phallus, which is to say the object of the mother's desire. What the child discovers is that the mother does not have the phallus (p. 289). Does this mean that she does not have a penis, or that she has a desire of her own?[49] The latter, I think, but in reading such an elusive text, a text which so palpably reproduces the elusiveness and the plurality of the signifier, who can be sure? And finally, the essay tells us in its account of the differential relation of men and women to the phallus, the woman 'finds the signifier of her own desire in the body of him to whom she addresses her demand for love' (p. 290). This *is* an organ, even if it is also a signifier (and in the following sentence a fetish). Lacan's essay flaunts the issue of sexual difference by so explicitly, scandalously, privileging the phallus, and then evades the question it has raised by refusing to 'fix' the meaning of its central figure. The text's phallic teasing thus preserves the anonymity, the tantalizing incognito of desire's true object.

The issue of sexual difference is critical for psychoanalysis, and indeed for feminism.[50] Feminism has tended to consider the question by differentiating between anatomy (sex) and gender (culture). Evidently there is an anatomical difference between men and women. Does this imply an essential female sexuality? Or are women not born but made sexually, and made differently in different cultural and historical locations? If we answer 'yes' to the first question, we are in danger of eliminating the differences between women; if we answer 'yes' to the second, do we not risk ignoring the difference between women and men?

Psychoanalysis defers both questions – to the degree that it repudiates the dualist opposition between nature and culture. In psychoanalytic terms it is not a matter of sex *and* gender, still less sex *or* gender, but of a 'knot' which ties together the signifying subject and the lost but inextricable real. This knot is indissoluble, and it is tied 'without regard to the anatomical difference of the sexes' (p. 282).[51] Its consequence is the indestructibility of unconscious desire. The question whether the character of this desire is sexually differentiated is perhaps one that theory is not yet equipped to answer satisfactorily.

III

René Magritte's famous painting of a pipe incorporates its own 'title' within the frame of the picture: 'This is not a pipe.' The painting is then independently named *The Treachery of Images*. Illusionism in painting, logocentrism in philosophy, the metaphysics of presence easily betray us into taking the symbol for the object, or the signifier for its meaning. A picture is not a pipe. *The Treachery of Images* first appeared in 1929.

Subsequently Magritte intensified the joke, and in the process complicated the issue, with *This is a Piece of Cheese*, which shows a framed painting of a slice of brie, perfectly illusionist in its execution. The picture stands on a pedestal under a glass dome. Where now is the 'truth' which images betray? Of course, we could not eat the cheese: the process of symbolization does not make it present. But to name a piece of cheese, to mention it, to write of it, is not to eat it either. On the contrary, the signifier precisely defers, supplants, relegates the imagined presence it sets out to name. But the piece of cheese we eat is always already named, with the consequence that its imagined presence independent of the deflecting, deferring, differing signifier is not an option. There are not, then, two separate orders, the object on the one hand, given in its pristine integrity, and the signifier on the other, a transcription of the object, secondary. On the contrary, there is a condition which is also a process, and it is in order to name this that Jacques Derrida has coined the term 'differance'.

In '*Le Facteur de la vérité*' ('The Factor/Postman of Truth'), first published in 1975, Derrida launches an uncharacteristically vehement attack on Lacanian psychoanalysis in general, including 'The Signification of the Phallus' in particular. Lacan's work, Derrida insists, is phallocentric, logocentric, metaphysical. The insistence that the phallus is not an organ is, he maintains, an evasion. A whole theory of sexual difference is elaborated on the basis of woman's castration:

> the phallus is not the organ, penis or clitoris, that it symbolizes, but it mostly and primarily symbolizes the penis. What follows is obvious: phallogocentrism as androcentrism, along with the entire paradoxical logic and reversals this engenders.[52]

Derrida's main case against Lacan and against psychoanalysis is that they promise to deliver the truth, a truth beyond language, however inscribed in it. Pyschoanalysis, for all its attention to the signifier, in practice sets out to 'decipher' the 'semantic core' of a text or an utterance, the primary content veiled by the signifier. The psychoanalytic process, Derrida argues, is thus an unveiling of truth, and psychoanalytic theory offers itself as the truth of truth.[53] Of course, he concedes, Lacan is not naive enough to suppose that truth is simply a matter of self-expression, or that it is a question of correspondence between a signifier and a referent. On the contrary, Lacan's 'full speech' is full of 'itself, of its presence, its essence';[54] this presence is the (unconscious) truth of the subject's desire; and it is made manifest, unveiled, only in verbal exchange with the analyst, who knows how to read it.[55] 'The values of presence (in person), of proximity, plenitude, and consistency form the system of authenticity in the analytic dialogue.'[56] The psychoanalytic truth is always linked, Derrida goes on, to the power of speech, and its evidence is repetition, which is possible only on the basis of a buttoning down of the sliding signified in a *point de capiton*. Psychoanalysis is thus phonocentric and logocentric, as well as phallocentric: if the phallus is the prime signifier, the truth-full voice is its vehicle:

> Only a speech, with its effects of presence in act and of authentic life can maintain (*garder*) the 'sworn faith' which links it to the desire of the other. If the 'phallus is the privileged signifier of that mark in which the role of the logos is joined with the advent of desire', the privileged site of this privileged signifier, then its letter is the voice: the letter as spokesman, the letter-carrying-speech. The letter alone – as soon as the *point de capiton* of the signified ensures its repeatable identity – carries the necessary ideality or power of idealization that can safeguard (in any event this is what it means) the indivisible, singular, living, non-fragmentable integrity of the phallus, of the privileged signifier to which it gives rise. The *transcendental* position of the phallus (in the chain of signifiers to which it belongs, while simultaneously making it possible) thus would have its proper place – in Lacanian terms, its letter exempt from all partition – in the phonematic structure of language. No protest against metalanguage is opposed to this phallogocentric transcendentalism.[57]

The problem here is not that Derrida is wrong: if psychoanalysis divorces truth from the *Cogito*, the object of knowledge from the knowing subject, it is only in order to reinstate truth elsewhere, in the unconscious (Freud), or in the Other (Lacan), even though we might suppose that this is already a 'Copernican' break with Enlightenment rationalism and empiricism. What is odd here is that Derrida repeats what he denounces in Lacan: he sets out to decipher the semantic core of Lacan's text, treating the signifier as nothing more than a veil.[58] Thus, Derrida re-Freudianizes Lacan's account of desire, ignoring the Lacanian want-to-be in favour of Freudian castration, and he barely acknowledges the implications of the textuality of Lacan's writing: 'Lacan's "style" was constructed so as to check almost permanently any access to an isolatable content, to an unequivocal, determinable meaning beyond writing.'[59] This reads more like an accusation of obscurantism than a recognition of indeterminacy. It quite discounts the effects of Lacan's radical break with the scientific tradition of psychoanalytic writing, and the generic disruption the wilful elusiveness of his writing effects. What disappears from Derrida's version of Lacan is the textual

66

teasing which unfixes the meaning even of the privileged signifier, the *performance* by which the Lacanian text enlists the desire of the reader in a quest for a truth that is withheld even in the moments when it is most apparently on display.

The denunciation of Lacan, in conjunction with the dismissal of Lacan's textuality, is even odder in the light of 'To Speculate – on "Freud"', Derrida's brilliant reading of *Beyond the Pleasure Principle*, which precedes '*Le Facteur de la vérité*' in *The Post Card*. This tour de force is precisely an account of Freud's text as performance (though it is also a critique of Lacan, who took it, Derrida says, for truth). 'To Speculate – on "Freud"' traces the outline of 'Freud's' own desire, the textuality of the desire inscribed in the text, and its hopes, fears, anxieties and repetitions. In a series of oppositions, which turn out in practice not to be oppositions after all, the *fort/da*, absence and presence, the death drive and the pleasure principle, the text both delineates and enacts a struggle for sovereignty which remains unresolved. Freud's sequence of 'speculations', which are not to be confused with 'philosophy', Freud insists, are 'a-thetic': they put forward no thesis and take up no (final) position. This is a text, Derrida demonstrates, 'which advances without advancing, without advancing itself, without ever advancing anything that it does not immediately take back, for the time of a detour, without ever positing anything which remains in its position'.[60] On the contrary, it repeats itself and its speculative differentiations, just as little Ernst repeats the alternation of unpleasure with pleasure in the *fort/da* game. Freud's text repeatedly distances the pleasure principle only in order to bring it back so that it (and Ernst, and his distinguished grandfather) retain their authority, their mastery of the founding moment of psychoanalysis.[61] Like a promise or an oath, the text performs what it defines, Derrida maintains. His infinitely supple and subtle reading identifies in the twists and turns of *Beyond the Pleasure Principle* a kind of performative, which carries out in its writing the process of production (and protection) of psychoanalytic theory. And Derrida's own text, which is more a celebration than a critique, endorses the a-thetic character of Freud's writing which it affirms, and its lack of systematicity, which reveals it as performative of desire.

Lacan's supreme error, then, we may construe, is that he systematizes desire, substituting theory for performance, and in the process laying claim to a single truth which is constitutive for human beings. In

essentialist – ontology

67

Derrida's account, psychoanalysis is thus no more than another, and perhaps the supremely privileged, metaphysics of desire.

Derrida's own text(s) of desire, the 'Envois' which make up the first half of *The Post Card* is (are) anything but systematic. Defying synopsis for this reason, the 'Envois' have perhaps received less attention than is their due. These (love)letters (or postcards), the fragmentary inscription of forbidden love, identify neither their author(s?) nor their addressee(s?) and refuse all the oppositions on which theory is necessarily based. They are intense, passionate, elliptical, elusive, impenetrable. They undermine our confidence in our ability to read by refusing to indicate how they are to be read, when they are coded to avoid a possible censor, when they are ironic, when they allude to 'reality'. They blur the boundaries between fact and fiction. And in all these ways they constitute textual performances (performatives) of desire.

Who is the 'author' of these 'missives' (dispatches, in-voices)? At one moment a figure whose (punning?) signature is *'j'accepte'*;[62] at another a person whose initials are J.D. (pp. 202–3); someone who travels – to Oxford, Yale, Geneva, Brussels . . . and theorizes (or rather, speculates?) about Oxford philosophy, Plato and Socrates, psychoanalysis. But elsewhere it is impossible to be sure. And who is addressed? A woman? Sometimes, but at other times the genders of the correspondents are left in question. And the text is determined not to clarify the situation:

> Who is writing? To whom? And to send, to destine, to dispatch what? To what address? Without any desire to surprise, and thereby to grab attention by means of obscurity, I owe it to whatever remains of my honesty to say finally that I do not know. Above all I would not have had the slightest interest in this correspondence and this cross-section, I mean in their publication, if some certainty on this matter had satisfied me. (p. 5)

It is open to the reader to note that desire defers and destabilizes identity, calls it into question. In love identities are gained and lost. Lovers speak from a range of subject positions. 'I' is ungendered, its sex veiled (pp. 178–9). The addressed, idealized, fantasized other, object of love and hate, is a displacement, a metonym, perhaps a succession of surrogates. It is *open* to the reader to note all this . . .

Meanwhile, what is the genre of this text as a whole? Is it an epistolary novel? Is it, as Derrida's blurb claims, a satire on epistolary fiction? Is it an 'apocryphal' text, doubtfully attributed to a phil-osopher, like Plato's letters, perhaps? Or is it (tempting, tantalizing thought, which must of course immediately be resisted as 'unsophisti-cated') the coded remainder of the real correspondence that it (fic-tionally?) claims to be? (After all, 'real' figures appear in it: Hillis, Jonathan and Cynthia, Neil Hertz, Paul de Man. But the text takes account of that.[63]) And is there a relationship between this generic undecidability and desire? As it fantasizes, imagines, idealizes, over-values, not only at a distance, but as the condition of sexual pleasure, is desire fact or fiction? Or does it precisely exceed those alternatives?

The 'Envois' are full of gaps. 'You might consider them, if you really wish to, as the remainders of a recently destroyed correspondence. Destroyed by fire or by that which figuratively takes its place' (p. 3). You might . . . The later 'Envois' are full of references to a fire, a pro-jected incineration of the correspondence itself, or parts of it, and to publication, with the names withheld, identities confused, ciphers introduced to protect the anonymity of the participants. Fifty-two typographical spaces mark ellipses within the texts. Who can say what is lost here? What is deleted, censored, repressed? What is not said? 'Desire is that which is manifested in the interval that demand hollows within itself, in as much as the subject, in articulating the signifying chain, brings to light the want-to-be, together with the appeal to receive the complement from the Other . . .'[64] To quote Lacan, however, is to suggest that the repudiated psychoanalysis returns in the Derridean performance of desire. But is it repudiated, or is it only the metaphysics of psychoanalysis that is rejected, its systematicity, and its truth-claims based on 'values of presence (in person), of proximity, plenitude'?

The existence of this correspondence assumes an absence, the separ-ation of the lovers. And the ostensible project of the letters, like the many telephone calls which are referred to but not recorded, and even the air mail cassettes the lovers send each other, is to bridge the gap, to fill it with 'truth', with presence. It cannot, of course, be done. The love letter demonstrates the impossibility of communication as the trans-mission of im-mediate, transparent meaning. All signification is at the mercy of 'the Postal Principle as differantial relay' (p. 54): meaning and truth are necessarily differed and deferred, 'differantiated' by the intervals, time differences, delays which interfere with transparency. No letter, the text insists, can be guaranteed to reach its destination. Much of the correspondence concerns a lost letter, which was 'true' and definitive for the relationship. The now 'dead' letter was never delivered and is finally returned to the sender. It remains unopened, and yet continues to haunt the living love affair. *Fort/da*, gone/here: the alternatives do not hold as opposition.

Moreover, the addressee may be 'present', that is to say not at a distance, in the same room: 'I believe that I prefer to write to you (even if you are facing me, or as at this moment at your secretary, just next to me), you push me away less' (p. 174). What then is the actual project? 'Do I write to you in order to bring you near or in order to distance you, to find the best distance – but then with whom?' (p. 78) And what is the difference? 'Absent or present . . . (you are always there, over there, in the course of going back and forth [*en train d'aller-venir*⁶⁵])', like the cotton reel in the *fort/da* game (p. 181). And yet the difference is critical: 'no, it happens that without you I lack nothing, but as soon as you are there I cry over you, I miss you to death, it's easier to bear your departure' (p. 250). *Fort/da:* command and loss. It is in the mother's absence that Ernst renders himself master of her desertion. Differantiated presence, which is always and inevitably differed and deferred, and which in consequence exceeds the alternatives of presence and absence, is the condition of desire.

But presence itself is its object.

> You have always been 'my' metaphysics, the metaphysics of my life, the 'verso' of everything I write (my desire, speech, presence, proximity, law, my heart and soul, everything that I love and that you know before me). (p. 197)

> You are the only one to understand why it was really necessary that I write exactly the opposite, as concerns axiomatics, of what I desire, what I know my desire to be, in other words you: living speech, presence itself, proximity, the proper, the guard, etc. (p. 194)

And it is unattainable – of course, since we desire what we don't have:

> you are now the name, yourself, or the title of everything that I do not understand. That I never will be able to know, the other side of myself,

eternally inaccessible, not unthinkable, at all (*du tout*), but unknowable, unknown – and so lovable. As for you, my love, I can only postulate (for who else, with whom would I have dreamed this?) the immortality of the soul, liberty, the union of virtue and happiness, and that one day you might love me. (p. 147)

The trace of the other in the selfsame exceeds the alternatives of presence and absence, which differance defines – and simultaneously prohibits. Differance gives rise to desire and at the same time prevents its fulfilment:

> differance makes the opposition of presence and absence possible. Without the possibility of differance, the desire of presence as such would not find its breathing-space. That means by the same token that this desire carries in itself the destiny of its non-satisfaction. Differance produces what it forbids, makes possible the very thing that it makes impossible.[66]

It follows that it is not possible to tell the truth of desire, or about desire. Between the lovers truth merely distances, and the desire for truth is 'perverse' (pp. 82–3). The dead letter is in one sense 'true' – and therefore both formative and irrelevant. The truth is always and inevitably the non-truth: Freud knows this (p. 82). Because it refuses the usual oppositions, all the familiar dualities of Western culture, desire cannot be theorized, systematized; the truth of desire can neither be seen nor shown. Desire cannot be put on display.

Unless, perhaps, in its inscription as a succession of postcards, its textual enactment, its non-systematic, untheorized, elliptical, incomplete, uncertain, elusive performance, in a work which mimes desire and mimics fiction, which is inconclusive, apparently inconsequential – a text which is above all and in all kinds of ways *neither here nor there*.

4

Postmodern Love

Can't buy me love.

To the degree that the postmodern condition implies an unbridled consumerism, the cultural logic of late capitalism, pleasure for cash and a product to gratify every possible impulse – if not, indeed, to construct the impulse in the first place – love is a value that remains beyond the market. While sex is a commodity, love becomes the condition of a happiness that cannot be bought, the one remaining object of desire that cannot be sure of purchasing fulfilment. Love thus becomes more precious than before because it is beyond price, and in consequence its metaphysical character is intensified. More than ever, love has come to represent presence, transcendence, immortality, what Derrida calls proximity, living speech, certainty, everything, in short, that the market is unable to provide or fails to guarantee.

To the degree, however, that postmodernity in general, and Derrida's work in particular, also represents a radically sceptical attitude to metaphysics, a fundamental questioning of presence, transcendence, certainty and all absolutes, the postmodern condition brings with it an incredulity towards true love. Where, we might ask, in the light of our experience, the statistics, our philosophy, or any documentary evidence outside popular romance, are *its* guarantees, its continuities, proof of its ability to fulfil its undertakings?

At the same time, no amount of scepticism does away with desire which, if it is the destiny of a signifying organism, is fashioned, but neither produced nor erased, by the specific cultural order which gives rise to our hopes and doubts. Love, as the 'Envois' indicate, thus occupies a paradoxical position in postmodern culture: it is at once infinitely and uniquely desirable on the one hand, and conspicuously naive on the other. Like the writer of Derrida's postcards, we *know* exactly the opposite of what we *desire*, of what we know our desire to be.

When Ferdinand de Saussure drew attention to the problem of translation, he enabled his readers to recognize the inevitability of cultural difference, and the impossibility of legislating for its resolution. Words, Saussure pointed out, do not necessarily have exact equivalents from one language to another. As any practising translator knows, not only nuances but pronouns, genders, tenses, distinctions can be untranslatable.[1] It follows that meanings are not held in place by objects in the world, or by concepts independent of language. Meaning resides in language or, more broadly, in signifying systems (including visual images, for instance) and it is to be found nowhere else. Signification is differential, but the differences are not guaranteed by the world or by ideas. The world may be encountered as resistance, but it cannot be *known* outside the systems of differences which define it. Ideas are an effect of difference, not its cause. They are, moreover, deferred by the signifier which produces them. Differed and deferred, supplanted, relegated by the signifier, the signified has no autonomy, no substance.

There is thus no certainty that our linguistic, signifying, differential cognitive maps are accurate. We cannot think, argue, reason, dispute or know outside the differences that precede our entry into the cultural order, and which, therefore, we have learned from it in the first place. This does not mean that we make everything up, or that whatever we happen to believe is equally plausible, equally valid. If I suppose I can fly, I am likely to encounter the world as resistance . . . Nor does it imply that we cannot learn other languages, inhabit alternative systems of differences. It does mean, however, that we cannot guarantee the positive content of what we know by pointing to some extra-linguistic ground of truth: certainty itself exists only in the language that is invoked to justify it. It does not mean, on the other hand, that nothing changes. On the contrary, knowledges inscribed in language collide and clash, producing alternative forms of understanding; resistances generate new developments; refutations efface old convictions. But the possession of truth is not an option.

The Enlightenment took a judicial stand on cultural difference. It assessed and weighed the meanings and values taken for truth in different cultures and found many of them wanting – primitive, ir-rational or unscientific. But while it repudiated fundamentalisms of all kinds, it participated nevertheless in another kind of metaphysics, by laying claim to a place from which to assess and weigh and judge. That place, which was held to be independent, objective, precisely 'en-lightened', now seems as culturally relative as the judgments them-selves, and from a postmodern perspective this ultimate complacency of the Enlightenment, however well intentioned, has come to look like the last infirmity of noble minds.

Or worse. Because truth is a legislator, and it has imposed its values on all those who have had a more restricted access to it, who have not been entitled to authorize it: the working class, the non-Western world, women. As palpably as any fundamentalism, if less spectacularly, middle-class, white, patriarchal truth has legitimated exclusions, oppressions and violence; it has justified appropriation, damage and destruction.

And true love, too, itself another kind of fundamentalism, has legal-ized prohibitions, coercions, narrow proprieties, expropriations and the transformation of people into property. With the best of intentions, the metaphysical ideal of true love, and the concomitant efforts of the modern Western world to confine and contain desire within the legality of marriage, have produced, we are now in a position to acknowledge, at best a lifetime of surveillance and self-surveillance for the couple in question, and at worst the perfect opportunity for domestic violence and child-abuse, concealed within the privacy of the nuclear family.

II

Love is thus at once endlessly pursued and ceaselessly suspected. Can such a paradoxical value speak or be spoken? Sought after as the ultimate good, feared as constraint, doubted as an illusion, postmodern love is both silent and garrulous. It cannot speak, and yet it seems that it never ceases to speak in late twentieth-century Western culture.

It is silent, first, in recognition of its banality. 'Every other night, on TV', Roland Barthes points out, 'someone says: *I love you*'.[2] How can we, unique and autonomous as we long to be, capture the extraordinary experience of desire by echoing this worn-out commonplace, this blank performative, which lacks nuances and 'suppresses explanations, adjustments, degrees, scruples'?[3] 'I love you' obliterates the distinctiveness of the desire it sets out to capture, and affirms at the same time the difference it sets out to efface, the gap between 'I' and 'you', investing the performance in the process with a certain solitariness. *Desire never*

Love is silent also because it does not know how to speak. If Lacan is *knows* right, desire inhabits the unconscious, and its motive is a lack, an absence at the heart of identity. In consequence, it is speech-less, hollowed within the utterance which is a demand for love. Itself a metonym, a displacement of the want-to-be, desire is unable to name itself: it speaks only in substitutions, in figures, without truly *knowing* what it says.

In *The Differend*, Jean-François Lyotard writes of 'the unstable state and instant of language wherein something which must be able to be put into phrases cannot yet be'.[4] The differend is a case of conflict which cannot be resolved because no single rule of judgment is applicable to both sides. Two discursive genres come into collision, and no meta-language is available to legislate between them. Litigation smothers one side or the other, and in the process the extent of the wrong which has been done simply slips away, though it reappears as a feeling in quest of an idiom. The differend is signalled by silence. His book is about politics, not love, about litigation as an affirmation of power which effaces injustice, but Lyotard acknowledges an analogy with 'the immediate incommunicability of desire'.[5] Paradoxically sought and doubted, and at the same time in excess of the oppositions which structure Enlightenment thinking, beyond the alternatives of mind and body, presence and absence, fact and fiction, love has no satisfactory metalanguage in which to communicate, if communication is understood as full, living, substantial.

Radically heterogeneous, even to itself, desire cannot be presented, made present. The vocabulary of true love, with its vows and contracts, its controls and complacencies, suppresses this heterogeneity, which returns as forbidden desire. Marriage as litigation, or the invocation of family values, offer what now seems only a precarious resolution. In the words of the narrator of Jeanette Winterson's *Written on the Body* (1992), 'Marriage is the flimsiest weapon against desire. You may as well take a pop-gun to a python . . . You'll still lie awake at night twisting your wedding ring round and round.'[6]

Desire is what is not said, what cannot be said. 'What we cannot speak about, we must pass over in silence,' Wittgenstein stated.[7] But paradoxically, twentieth-century Western culture in its entirety constitutes a repudiation of Wittgenstein's laconic and apparently irrefutable conclusion. 'What cannot be said above all must not be silenced, but written,' Derrida replies,[8] and his own writing can be read as a refusal to settle for the silence which attends the limits of formulation. Instead, Derrida's texts invoke every imaginable linguistic and typographical device to go beyond the contradictory point that if we cannot escape the language of metaphysics, we can no longer simply inhabit it either. What is not able to be said is what presses to be given form. Psychoanalysis itself, of course, depends on this assumption: analysis is the process of listening to what cannot be said. And Lyotard's point in *The Differend* is that, since silence aids and abets injustice,

> What is at stake in a literature, in a philosophy, in a politics perhaps, is to bear witness to differends by finding idioms for them.[9]

Desire finds idioms in spite of itself. And even in all its banality it continually attracts an eager audience. '"I love you" is always a quotation,' acknowledges the narrator of *Written on the Body*; nevertheless, 'the most unoriginal thing we can say to one another is still the thing we long to hear'.[10] In the twentieth century, desire is more voluble than ever before – in operas and musicals, poems and pop videos. It produces a proliferation of knowledges: therapies, sexologies, arts of love. The nature of desire is discussed in manuals, counselling sessions, agony columns. It has also extended the field of its operations: desire is now known to be a property of the very young and the very old, as well as all those in between. Sexuality acknowledges no generic limits: desire invades education and advertising; it pervades magazines for men and women. And above all desire tells stories – at the cinema, in the popular press, on television ('every other night, on TV, someone says: *I love you*'). Love stories sell like hot cakes; they also win literary prizes. And all this to disguise the unpresentability of a condition so common, so inevitable, so improbable and yet so precious that we must repeatedly signify it and witness its signification.

III

The postmodern condition might be characterized as the recognition of the implications of differance. Postmodern writing knows that metaphysics is not an option; it takes for granted that the process of representation can never be the reconstitution of presence; it repudiates the modernist nostalgia for the unpresentable, ineffable truth of things; and it variously celebrates or struggles with the opacity of the signifier. Postmodern fiction precisely refuses to be silent in the face of what cannot be said. On the contrary, the impossible generates an extraordinary loquacity, a proliferation of textuality which calls into question the proprieties, complacencies and certainties of the past. If signification is a detour, it is none the less the only track we can confidently claim to follow. The subject is what speaks, writes, reads, signifies, and it is no more than that. Silence is death. Desire lives, then, in its inscription. *we must 'speak' or die.*

Postmodern writing triumphantly affirms its own capacity to escape the limiting oppositions which once promised to deliver the truth. Indeed, the nature of truth itself becomes the elusive stake in the textual games that characterize novels invoking history, fiction representing fact, and presenting it as fiction. D. M. Thomas's *The White Hotel* (1981) scandalously recounts from the point of view of a victim the story of the massacre of Babi Yar, and it does so by 'plagiarizing' Anatoli Kuznetsov's *Babi Yar*, itself a work of fiction, based on the documents recording the event. Where, in what seems an almost infinite regress, *The White Hotel* might be read as asking, are we to find the event itself? The unsettling answer, of course, is that it cannot be found, if to 'find' it is to make it present, full, substantial, living. History is always a narrative, always recounted from a point of view. Timothy Findley's *Famous Last Words* (1981) is an account written by Ezra Pound's creation, Hugh Selwyn Mauberley, on the walls of his war-time prison, of the relationship between Edward VIII and Mrs Simpson in its personal and its political implications. This fictional problematizing of history, of our access to 'the facts' is so common in recent novels that Linda Hutcheon has coined for it the term 'historiographic metafiction', and treated it as the paradigm case of postmodern fiction.[11] Historiographic metafiction calls into question, she argues, the relationship

77

between past and present, event and text, by rendering critical the 'obvious' distinction between fact and fiction.

Is desire a matter of fact or fiction? Fact, self evidently: its effects are visible on the surface of the body; its experience changes lives. Or fiction? The role of fantasy in the construction of desire cannot be overestimated. The same events, the same bodies, differently imagined, differently interpreted, generate different effects. The fascination of the beloved stems to an unknown degree from meanings and values, some personal, some cultural, which invest this body, these actions. People fall in love with film stars, or with voices on the telephone, or with the authors of the books they read. They imagine what is absent. This is only mildly eccentric. 'Isn't desire always the same', Roland Barthes asks, 'whether the object is present or absent? Isn't the object *always* absent?'[12] Is desire real, the only reality, or unreal, precisely romance, fairy tale, a temporary madness, an obsession from which we recover ('what *was* I thinking of?')? The reaffirmation of Law, of everyday obligations and preoccupations, can render desire an absurdity.

Jeanette Winterson's novel *The Passion* (1987) throws into relief the issue of desire's reality. Henri's first love is Napoleon, a man apparently beyond the reach of Law, who set out to conquer the world. Napoleon, Henri explains,

> was in love with himself and France joined in. It was a romance. Perhaps all romance is like that; not a contract between equal parties but an explosion of dreams and desires that can find no outlet in everyday life. Only a drama will do and while the fireworks last the sky is a different colour.[13]

Watching Moscow burn, Henri finally recovers from his passion and love turns to equally obsessional hate and self-disgust.

Here the reader is entitled to suppose that fantasy gives way to truth as Henri sees the real effects of the romance he has subscribed to, and returns in consequence to the realm of Law. But the story of Villanelle, the novel's cross-dressed, bisexual, web-footed heroine, is altogether less conventional. Villanelle falls in love across the roulette wheel with a woman identified only as the Queen of Spades. Throughout Villanelle's narrative, love is figured as gambling, the 'passion' of the title: 'You play, you win, you play, you lose. You play.'[14] Love and gambling are

compulsive, unpredictable, thrilling, dangerous. What is at stake is a
loss: 'We gamble with the hope of winning, but it's the thought of what
we might lose that excites us.'[15] And Villanelle recounts the story of a
man who gambled for his life, and lost. Hers is a desire which is way
beyond the pleasure principle. Villanelle loses her heart to the Queen of
Spades. Henri has to steal into the house and bring it back to her in a
jar. She does not take the same risk again.

Running through Henri's account of Napoleon, his habits, his dis-
likes and preferences, is a refrain addressed to the reader: 'I'm telling
you stories. Trust me.'[16] We don't, of course. Napoleon was real; he
belongs to history; the facts can be checked. On the other hand, Patrick,
the Irish priest with one telescopic eye, tells a story of goblins who
reduced his boots overnight to the size of a thumbnail, and he too adds,
'Trust me, I'm telling you stories.'[17] This time we long to, because
stories are where goblins properly belong. But when Villanelle, cross-
dressed and in love, recounts how she walked on water with her webbed
feet, the repetition of the same refrain implicitly poses a question:

> Could I walk on that water?
> Could I?
> I faltered at the slippery steps leading into the dark. It was November,
> after all. I might die if I fell in. I tried balancing my foot on the surface
> and it dropped beneath into the cold nothingness.
> Could a woman love a woman for more than a night?
> I stepped out and in the morning they say a beggar was running
> round the Rialto talking about a young man who'd walked across the
> canal like it was solid.
> I'm telling you stories. Trust me.[18]

What would it mean to trust her? to distrust her? This is a love story.
Where does love belong?

At the end of the novel Henri finally believes that he has dis-
entangled fact from fiction, reality from invention:

> I am in love with her; not a fantasy or a myth or a creature of my own
> making.
> Her. A person who is not me. I invented Bonaparte as much as he
> invented himself.
> My passion for her, even though she could never return it, showed me

the difference between inventing a lover and falling in love.
    The one is about you, the other about someone else.[19]

This sounds eminently familiar, plausible. The advice columns in
women's magazines would say much the same. This is how you recognize the real thing. But at this moment Henri is mad, alone,
imprisoned on a rock, exactly like Napoleon . . .

IV

Postmodern fiction shamelessly mixes genres. Julian Barnes's *Flaubert's
Parrot* (1984) is a historiographic metafiction which is also literary
criticism and at the same time a love story. Flaubert's narrative *Un Coeur
simple* tells of a lonely old woman who loves a parrot, Loulou, has it
stuffed when it dies, comes to believe that the Holy Ghost must have
been a parrot, and sees a giant parrot welcome her into heaven as she
dies. While he wrote it Flaubert placed on his desk a stuffed parrot,
borrowed from the museum at Rouen. *Flaubert's Parrot* is the story of
Geoffrey Braithwaite's quest for the authentic original Loulou.
    Braithwaite is not naive. He is perfectly clear from the beginning
about the absurdity of the desire for relics of the author, the impossibility of the biographer's task, the incompleteness of diaries and
journals.[20] Nor does he make the elementary error of supposing that if
you can't get it right, it follows that you can't get it wrong. The literary
critic, Dr Enid Starkie, got it wrong by misreading and misrepresent-
ing Flaubert's text, in what Braithwaite describes as an instance of
'magisterial negligence towards a writer who must, one way and
another, have paid a lot of her gas bills'.[21] The novel is not naive either.
Initially there are two candidates for the position of authentic parrot.
Gradually it emerges that three more are still extant out of a possible
original fifty . . .
    Parrots are taught to talk. They reproduce fragments of dialogue.
How, Braithwaite wonders, does the parrot differ from the writer, who
composes texts out of fragments of other texts?[22] And who is Flaubert's
parrot? Zola, perhaps, who learned so much from him? Or Henry
James and the author's other literary descendants? Or alternatively the
professional literary critics, who pay their gas bills by plundering and

reproducing his work? Or is it perhaps Geoffrey Braithwaite himself, who seeks Flaubert's authentic parrot, while insisting that we cannot have access to his authentic life, and discovers that even the parrot cannot be found? Geoffrey Braithwaite, whose wife shared Emma Bovary's initials, and committed adultery and then suicide, even though she did not get into debt, and did not suffer the agony and indignity of death by arsenic-poisoning? Dr Geoffrey Braithwaite, whose life in consequence is restless, unsatisfied, lonely, like Dr Charles Bovary's, or like Flaubert's, perhaps, just possibly, if we only knew . . . ?

'"I love you" is always a quotation.' Isn't desire inevitably allusive, derivative, citational? How else do we learn to speak it, or even to recognize it? Every night on TV someone turns into a parrot. Here is Oliver, from Julian Barnes's *Talking It Over* (1991), debating the implications of his desire for Gillian, wife of his friend Stuart:

> What has to happen is this. Gillian has to realize she loves me. Stuart has to realize she loves me. Stuart has to step down. Oliver has to step up. Nobody must get hurt. Gillian and Oliver must live happily ever after. Stuart must be their best friend. That's what has to happen. How high do you rate my chances? As high as an elephant's eye?[23]

This tissue of clichés and quotations is ironic. Oliver, we are to understand, is arch, literary, flamboyant, knowing and cynical. Even his desire itself reads like a pastiche of René Girard's account of triangular passion in *Desire, Deceit and the Novel*: Oliver wants Gillian because Stuart has her. He also wants her because desire, and talk about desire, 'talking it over', have a long literary pedigree stretching back to the Elizabethan poets and beyond them to the pastoral idylls of Theocritus. Oliver again:

> Would you renounce your love, slip gracefully from the scene, become a goatherd and play mournfully consoling music on your Panpipes all day while your heedless flock chomp the succulent tufts? People don't *do* that. People never did. Listen, if you go off and become a goatherd you never loved her in the first place. Or you loved the melodramatic gesture more. Or the goats. Perhaps pretending to fall in love was merely a smart career move allowing you to diversify into pasturing. But you didn't *love* her.[24]

Oliver's love is intimately involved with power and possession. In a modernist text its citationality might lead us to conclude that it is somehow not *genuine*, not real. This novel does not allow such complacent distinctions to hold. Gillian, who has no style, acknowledges her seduction, her surrender in the simplest terms: 'I feel lost'. But at once she turns the utterance into a quotation: 'Lost and found.'[25] And Stuart, who works in a bank and has no imagination, laments his lost love by quoting Patsy Cline lyrics.

Desire was probably always citational. Certainly the Elizabethan poets knew this when they translated, cited, adapted and reformulated Petrarch, not to mention Theocritus, and Ovid and Catullus. As Shakespeare's plays make clear, Elizabethan lovers conventionally indicate their condition by writing sonnets. This is how we know they are in love. The vocabulary of desire shifts as alternative traditions come into view and new sources are appropriated and adapted. What is specific to postmodern writing is that it foregrounds the citationality of desire, affirms it, puts it on display. And in doing so it both speaks desire and defers it, draws attention to the loquacity, the excess of textuality that constitutes the postmodern recognition of the implications of differance.

V

This explicit citationality roots desire not in nature, not in presence, but in texts, and above all in fiction and the products of the entertainment industry. Stories promise a kind of redemption: they offer coherence, resolution, closure. They appear to reconcile the distinct discursive genres in which love makes itself at once desired and doubted. Lyotard puts forward the same point about the narratives which constitute history:

> Narrative is perhaps the genre of discourse within which the heterogeneity of phrase regimens, and even the heterogeneity of genres of discourse, have the easiest time passing unnoticed. On the one hand, narrative recounts a differend or differends and imposes an end on it or them, a completion which is also its own term. Its finality is to come to an end. (It is like a 'round' in a tournament.) Wherever in diegetic time

82

it stops, its term makes sense and retroactively organizes the recounted events. The narrative function is redeeming in itself.[26]

But postmodern narrative is at best ambivalent about its readiness to inscribe redemption. The promised consolation is not, on the whole, delivered, and not only at the level of plot. Discursive heterogeneity is not effaced but foregrounded by the refusal of first-person narration, by discontinuity of time and place, by quotation, allusion, pastiche and parody. In place of redemption, postmodern love stories pose a question about the strange im-personality of desire. Who is speaking when Oliver invokes Rodgers and Hammerstein or Stuart quotes Patsy Cline?

Lovers, the texts propose, are other than they are, beside themselves, dis-placed. They act uncharacteristically. This is one of the reasons why a romance which is over is so easily forgotten: it was oddly out of character. What is the role of sexual difference here? Do all women share unconscious processes closed to men? Freud and Lacan say they do – and they don't. Do women in love need to quote women, men men? Or is the sexual difference neither here nor there? Can a woman inhabit, appropriate, re-enact, cite the desire represented by Donne, Shakespeare, Yeats, Cole Porter? Stuart identifies with Patsy Cline. Can't a singer of either sex appropriate the same song by switching the pronouns? Is homoerotic desire special, more violent for men, cosier for women? Many homosexuals would say so, but not all. Are hetero-sexual men distanced from the desire represented by Shakespeare, Cole Porter?

Winterson's *Written on the Body* is intense, lyrical, ambitious. And at its heart is the enigma of an unnamed, ungendered, bisexual narrator-protagonist whose identity teases the reader out of thought and into a desire which is precisely desire for nothing nameable. The love the novel records is prohibited, adulterous, threatened by death. It prompts misguided heroics and self-imposed suffering. Love is very explicitly shown to be subject to the dialectic of Law and desire, contentment and passion, boredom and anxiety. The text deconstructs the dualism of mind and body by attributing signification to the flesh: 'Articulacy of the fingers, the language of the deaf and dumb, signing on the body/ longing.' The novel's title itself points to a corporeality shot through with meaning: 'Written on the body is a secret code only visible in certain lights . . .'[27]

The anonymous protagonist recounts a succession of previous relationships – early on with women, and later in the text, though not, I
think, in the story, with men. The text hints now at a male identity,
now at a female one. In the end it is impossible to be sure. The narrative
depends on the discontinuity of the narrator-subject, by turns witty,
reasonable (with the irrational logic of passion), self-accusing, confident, desolate, and always doubling back on what has gone before,
recognizing inconsistency but apparently helpless to prevent it. The
love story is the utterance of a single subject, but this subject does not
offer to speak from a single place. Lovers speak, and yet in doing so
they are spoken by a language that precedes them, that is not at their
disposal, under their control; this language is at the same time dis-
persed among banalities, poetry, the sacred, tragedy. Who speaks?
Who, then, is redeemed here?

VI

A. S. Byatt's *Possession: A Romance* (1990) takes the citationality of desire
a stage further by inventing the texts it cites. These fictitious texts,
however, all instances of pastiche of one kind or another, are themselves
profoundly allusive and citational. The contemporary love story *Possession* tells of Roland and Maud is generated by their joint quest for
the texts of a love between two Victorian poets. Where the desire of
Roland and Maud is predominantly silent, suspicious and sceptical,[28]
the 'Victorian' texts, copious, verbose, speak on their behalf from a
period which believed wholeheartedly in love. Roland and Maud thus
explicitly inhabit a story, while recognizing their own cultural determination. 'He was in a Romance', Roland reflects; 'a Romance was one of
the systems that controlled him, as the expectations of the Romance
control almost everyone in the Western world, for better or worse, at
some point or another.'[29] Meanwhile, however, the Victorian story itself
proves ultimately elusive, evasive, differantial. If *Possession* is critical
of postmodern scepticism, it is by no means nostalgic for Victorian
metaphysics.

The story begins in the present, in the Reading Room of the London
Library, with an epigraph from a nineteenth-century poem, *The Garden
of Proserpina*. 'These things are there,' the 'Victorian' text resoundingly

affirms, 'The garden and the tree/The serpent at its root . . .' If these things are there, the knowing twentieth-century reader recognizes, it is because 'there' has no location but culturally transmitted mythology, intertextually assembled and reconstituted. Already the Garden of Proserpina is visibly composed of fragments of the Garden of Eden in general and *Paradise Lost* in particular. Proserpina, we also know, is identified by Milton as an object of desire, snatched by the god of the underworld to be his bride, 'which cost Ceres all that pain/ To seek her through the world.'[30] Ceres regained her – for the spring and summer. In winter she returns to the underworld. Proserpina is always already lost or about to be lost. The poet's name is Ash.

The modern hero, Roland, is in the Library to look for textual sources of the poem in Ash's annotated copy of Vico. Roland finds what look like some allusions, but they are inconclusive. They are not (of course!) what he really wants. What he does want, however, enough to steal them from the Library, are two unexpected drafts of a letter from the poet to an unknown woman. These texts, of indeterminate status (is either authoritative? was either sent? on what occasion?) inaugurate the romance of the title, romance as quest, romance as love story, and romance as search for the elusive character of desire-as-possession.

It is impossible not to speculate on the models for the fictional Victorian poets. Tennyson? No. Browning, then? But of course if the texts fit at moments, the life does not. And Christabel LaMotte is obviously modelled on Christina Rossetti – except that she barely resembles her in any significant way. Roland and Maud, however, have their literary antecedents too. Roland is the heir to Browning's questing Childe Roland, himself a descendant of the fairy-tale hero who rescues his sister from the Dark Tower of Elfland, but also, perhaps, to the medieval hero who had a *Chanson* written for him. And Maud is Tennyson's Maud, the text makes clear, from whom she inherits a social standing higher than her lover's and 'a cold and clear-cut face . . . Perfectly beautiful'.[31] But does she not also, perhaps, owe something to Christina Rossetti's novel, *Maude*? And even to Yeats's representation of Maud Gonne ('Pallas Athene in that straight back and arrogant head'[32]):

> What could have made her peaceful with a mind
> That nobleness made simple as a fire,
> With beauty like a tightened bow, a kind

That is not natural in an age like this,
Being high and solitary and most stern?[33]

The whole text is a tissue of allusions. The reader of *Possession* needs a good working knowledge of Victorian literature and its antecedents.

The novel is more, however, than a kind of sophisticated literary Trivial Pursuit, and it is so partly because it knows how to elicit the desire of the reader by its silences and by its refusal to fix the character of the desire it delineates. What is silent, despite Christabel's textual prolixity, is the desire of the women. Christabel's letters to Ash conceal as much as they say; they are seductions rather than declarations. The third-person narration of the Victorian love story in Chapter 15 tells more from Ash's point of view than Christabel's. The most revealing moment is the account of Christabel crying in the middle of their first night together for the loss she already anticipates, and her lover's acknowledgement of her 'inaccessible thoughts'.[34] The modern love story is told primarily from Roland's point of view. Though much is finally explained in the course of the narrative, which offers (the illusion of) classic-realist closure, what is left in shadow is Christabel's relationship with Blanche Glover, and her love-and-hatred of Ash after their self-imposed parting, as well as Maud's final relationship with Roland, which remains to be 'worked out', since it has to be reconciled with Maud's 'self-possession'.[35]

The women are Christabel LaMotte and Maud Bailey. Maud as Christabel's descendant resembles her not only physically but in her fierce defence of her autonomy.[36] Motte and bailey: the central mound and the outer wall of a castle. Both Christabel and Maud invoke castles as figures of their passionately defended isolation. Lacan, who is repeatedly quoted in *Possession*, points out that dreams commonly symbolize the formation of the ego in terms of 'a fortress or a stadium – its inner arena and enclosure, surrounded by marshes and rubbish-tips, dividing it into two opposed fields of contest where the subject flounders in quest of the lofty, remote inner castle', which is the unconscious.[37] Conscious identity is precarious, paranoid, threatened with disintegration.[38] The quotation is from Lacan's essay on the Mirror Stage, which defines the inaugural moment of self-consciousness (that is, of course, self-misrecognition) as the jubilant assumption by the infant before the mirror of 'the armour of an alienating identity'.[39] The identity is alienating to the extent that an imaginary *Gestalt* keeps at bay the infant's actual incapacity, the objective turbulence of its 'fragmented' body, but the repudiated turbulence and the fragments return to haunt the ego as aggressivity, the death drive which precedes Eros and which will come to inhabit desire.

The quotation from Lacan is invoked in *Possession* by the appropriately named Fergus Wolff, who threatens to give a paper on Christabel's unconscious. What is absurd in this proposition is that the predatory Fergus thinks he has something to say about the unconscious of a Victorian woman poet, and not the Lacanian reference. *Possession* is a profoundly Lacanian novel, not only in its explicit invocations of Lacan's texts,[40] and not only in its figuration of a desire which is heroic to the degree that it cannot be fulfilled, but above all in its indications of the extent to which desire is inevitable ('necessity', Christabel calls it, twice,[41]) and at the same time dangerous – beyond the pleasure principle, destructive, angry, 'a *wrecker*', as Maud puts it.[42] 'Don't fight me', Ash says, making love to Christabel. '"I *must*," said she, intent . . .'[43] The imperative of male desire is to take possession, though Roland constitutes a postmodern hero in his reluctance to do so.[44] The Lacan invoked here is above all the Hegelian author of 'The Mirror Stage' and 'Aggressivity in Psychoanalysis', but it is certainly arguable that Lacan never abandoned his early insistence on the dark god in the sheep's clothing of the good shepherd Eros, the hate and ignorance which is the price paid for love by the signifying human animal.[45]

In a poem palpably influenced by Randolph Henry Ash, which draws on places she visited with him, Christabel LaMotte writes about desire. The poem tells of powerful, monstrous women: Medusa, Scylla, Hydra, the Sphinx, and the Fairy Melusine, half serpent, half mortal woman, all punished for their presumption. Melusine, LaMotte's protagonist, seduces by her silence mortal men, and gives them to drink of the Fountain of Thirst. At night Melusine flies outside the castle-keep,

> And ever and again a shuddering cry
> Mounts on the wind, a cry of pain and loss,
> And whirls in the wind's screaming and is gone.[46]

LaMotte, who has lost her lover and her child, is not redeemed. Her final letter to Ash, which offers reconciling knowledge, is buried with him unopened. Ash's last message to her is not delivered. Her desire is figured as unquenchable thirst, beyond the alternatives of life and death, salvation and damnation.[47] It subsists in the novel, however, explicitly as textual performance, as writing.

VII

Melusine owes something to Keats's Lamia, part woman, part serpent, the seductive, uncanny figure destroyed by the rational gaze of the Enlightened Apollonius. Elsewhere a lamia is a demonic woman who sucks children's blood. Christabel LaMotte's unearthly, dangerous, desolate outcast resembles in some respects the protagonists of Anne Rice's phenomenally successful *Vampire Chronicles*, which put on display the relentless imperatives of unsatisfied desire. Rice's vampires draw on what is presented as an infinite regress of textuality: novels and films, and before them legends, mythology. But they are also redrawn as postmodern figures, inhabiting a global present which includes extremes of deprivation and poverty on the one hand and a paradise of consumer pleasures on the other. They can fly, but they also travel in aeroplanes and own fast cars. They practise telepathy and watch television. They are accomplished, elegant, sophisticated – and driven.

Bram Stoker's *Dracula* (1897) has become the classic text from which so many subsequent vampire stories are descended. The nineteenth-century account reaffirms, of course, the Enlightenment values its fictional figures call into question. Bram Stoker's story is narrated from the point of view of Dracula's Western, middle-class, heterosexual opponents, and from this perspective vampires are unequivocally evil. They are threatening, we are invited to understand, however seductive they may also be, not least because they evoke an unbridled and voracious eroticism, especially in women, whose feelings ought to be moral, not sexual. Vampires release unconscious desire; they suspend the symbolic Law. Professor Van Helsing, the doctor-lawyer-philosopher, who represents Enlightenment knowledge and values, selflessly saves lives and puts his vast scholarship to work in defence of the weak: the immediate project is above all to rescue the women from themselves. When Dracula moves to London, Van Helsing recognizes that he must be kept at bay, driven out, destroyed. What is at stake now is no less than Western civilization. With the extermination of Dracula the uncanny is finally excluded, but not before its place has been delineated in considerable detail in the text.

Anne Rice's postmodern move is to make the vampire speak, to tell its own story from this uncanny place, without simply reversing the original opposition. In other words, it is not so much that the reader is now invited to endorse the vampire, identify with it, fill it with imagined presence, as that we glimpse what it would be like to occupy a space which cannot exist. In Rice's fiction the vampire remains mysterious, outside, evil, fantastic, grounded only in other texts. (This is especially so in *Interview with the Vampire* (1976) where the human interviewer registers our norms, keeps them before us.) But in the oxymoron of its alien proximity to the reader, the vampire's thirst for blood here constitutes the figure of the desire of the Other, that unconscious, driving imperative, which is beyond the pleasure principle and which has no name.

At the same time, Rice's postmodern vampires are paradoxically ethical, tormented creatures, possessed by a strong sense of their own evil. *Interview with the Vampire* is an account of Louis's reluctance to acknowledge the implications of his own vampire identity. At first he can bear only to kill animals for survival, but gradually he recognizes that the blood he drinks must be human, that he must take human life in order to live:

> 'I knew peace only when I killed, only for that minute; and there was no question in my mind that the killing of anything less than a human being brought nothing but a vague longing, the discontent which had brought me close to humans, to watch their lives through glass. I was no vampire. And in my pain, I asked irrationally, like a child, Could I not return? Could I not be human again? Even as the blood of that girl was warm in me and I felt that physical thrill and strength, I asked that question. The faces of humans passed me like candle flames in the night dancing on dark waves. I was sinking into the darkness. I was weary of longing.'[48]

But learning to kill human beings does not heal the split between a remembered humanity which is irretrievably lost, and an immortal nature which only sharpens the perception of that loss, the awareness that vampires cannot be redeemed. Rice's doomed, divided central figures revere the Law that they are unable to keep. They are in consequence profoundly unwilling to create new vampires. And in *The Queen of the Damned* (1988) their moral mission is to save humanity from wholesale slaughter.

Moreover, vampires love intensely, bisexually and polymorphously: they kiss each other often.[49] But sexual intercourse is not an option: the supreme erotic experience is drinking blood. Vampires also fall in love with mortals, but to drink their blood is to destroy them – or to damn them. It is possible for vampires to exchange blood with each other, but this circulation of the same blood does not nourish: for survival they need mortal victims. They are thus compelled to cause death, and their deadly compulsion is a source of simultaneous rapture and shame, ecstasy and self-disgust. It represents the ultimate debasement, pleasure radically divorced from love. No closure is available to vampires, no possible resolution of the contradictions they represent:

> She stood listening to the blood inside her, and marveling in a crazed, despairing way that it could still refresh her and strengthen her, even now. Sad, grief-stricken, she looked at the lovely stark wilderness encircling the temple, she looked up at the loose and billowing clouds. How the blood gave her courage, how it gave her a momentary belief in the sheer rightness of the universe – fruits of a ghastly, unforgivable act.
>
> If the mind can find no meaning, then the senses give it. Live for this, wretched being that you are.[50]

The frisson the vampire Pandora's experience elicits here is not one of horror.

In Freudian terms, for vampires the imperatives of sex and survival are reunited, by prising apart desire and love. In Lacanian terms, need and demand are explicitly separated, so that Lacan's hollow becomes a chasm. Vampires are compelled to seek a prohibited pleasure outside the Law that they cannot repudiate. Desire is not repressed, but a perpetual, conscious condition, and it is above all the desire to regain a lost (organic) humanity, for all its limitations and contradictions. The vampire Lestat is, he tells us, 'an anguished and hungry being who both loves and detests this invincible immortal shell in which I'm locked'.[51] 'To be human, that's what most of us long for. It is the human which has become myth to us.'[52] But ironically, when in *The Tale of the Body Thief* (1992) Lestat regains a human body, he cannot bear its organic inadequacies. Meanwhile, the human figures in the stories long to be immortal . . . Desire is thus seen to be forever unfulfilled.

A textual fiction, portrayed as beyond the alternatives of life and death, love and hate, good and evil, Anne Rice's vampire is surely the type of the postmodern lover: at once sceptical and idealizing, and therefore restless, unsatisfied, dis-placed and, in the last analysis, solitary.

Meanwhile, 'Love never dies', proclaimed the posters for Francis Ford Coppola's high-camp film version of *Bram Stoker's Dracula* (1992). The title insists on the textuality of the movie's origins. This, it appears to claim, is the real, true, authentic – which is to say textual – Dracula, after so many shams. With characteristic postmodern irony, it then radically rewrites Bram Stoker's story to make Dracula a fallen angel motivated by an immortal passion. Nevertheless, as a love story the film appears closer in spirit to the Victorian period than to our postmodernity. The screen inscribes romance in every other shot, not only in the curiously non-specific sexuality it portrays, but in recurring images of mist and darkness irradiated by the moon, by lightning, or by flames. Though there are moments of macabre comedy, and instances of pastiche, this is apparently a nineteenth-century, thoroughly 'operatic' account of a desire which finds fulfilment in death. The film also comes across as a comment on the sexual inadequacies of British men. Mina Harker gladly risks damnation for her adulterous Transylvanian lover, who willingly dies in consequence, at her hands and in her arms. As the film ends, he is at peace at last, we are to understand, and she is transfigured.

Those were the days! A certain dissatisfaction with the ending perhaps betrays the gap between that world and our own. Love is a Victorian value. The nineteenth century supposed that the problem was repression: desire released was therefore desire fulfilled. At the end of the twentieth century we know better – or worse. The climax of Coppola's film is gloriously metaphysical, and hopelessly anachronistic. But then the film itself is explicitly, self-consciously a costume Gothic, a spectacular fantasy, extravagant melodrama:[53] it never invited us to imagine for an instant that it was telling the truth.

And that, perhaps, is the key to the postmodernity of this text: it insists on its own fictionality. It therefore feeds our longing for ideal love, our hunger for metaphysics, while at the same time taking account of our scepticism, our incredulity towards romance. Simultaneously sophisticated and naive, the film gives us both what we know, and its converse, what we desire, in a single expensive and beautiful package. You *can* have it all, if only at the cinema.

VIII

I should have liked to write about the work of Toni Morrison, about her inscription of the constant dis-placement which is the condition of African-Americans, whether they choose, like Jadine in *Tar Baby* (1981), to gravitate towards white culture, or attempt like Son in the same novel a return to a black culture which no longer permits the realization of their desires. I should have liked to treat her invocation of the unhomely, and *das Unheimliche*, in the stories she tells of what for black Americans constitutes – and fails to constitute – home.[54] I should dearly have liked to consider how *The Bluest Eye* (1979) records the cultural construction of the object of an unattainable but obsessional desire, and to discuss the brilliant account in *Beloved* (1987) of the imbrication of the deadly past of slavery in a present which cannot in consequence realize the possibilities of life.

I should have liked to do all this, but I have a fear of appearing to colonize her work, or at least of seeming to pre-empt the work of African-American critics. The problem is not that Morrison's work 'belongs' to them, or indeed to anyone. But what she writes about includes the white expropriation of black experience and I am afraid to repeat that process. To make her fiction work for me, to get it to define desire on my behalf, might well be one form of such expropriation; to analyze Toni Morrison, who writes about black experience, is to advance into an area constructed in the first instance by those pioneering African-American feminists who have done so much to put black women's writing on the critical agenda.

It is not simply that I don't have the knowledge – of history, of slavery, of slave narratives: I probably don't, but I could learn. And it is not a matter of experience. This book is not about experience: it is about inscriptions, rhetorics, texts. The problem of writing on Morrison is political. When men began to advance their careers by writing about feminism and feminist criticism, or by producing feminist readings, at least some feminists felt that this was a space we had carved out for ourselves, in the face of considerable institutional opposition, and that until the power relations between the sexes had equalized themselves a little, men might perhaps just be good enough to leave it to us. After all, they had the whole of the rest of the field of literature to analyze (and in the good old days of patriarchy that had apparently been quite enough). Again the question was not one of knowledge or experience: it was political. There is no reason why men should not understand feminist politics or read feminist texts. On the contrary, we want them to be attentive to feminism. But we don't want them to colonize it, to take it over.

I have read Toni Morrison's work with the closest attention. But by drawing an analogy with the position of feminism, I conclude that at this stage of history I ought to feel a certain inhibition about setting out to substantiate in a detailed analysis the case I should like to make about Toni Morrison and her subtle, lyrical account of postmodern love.

Perhaps one day . . .

Part II

Desire at other times

5

Adultery in King Arthur's Court: Chrétien, Malory, Tennyson

I

In the beginning romantic love was not a Victorian value. It is commonly agreed that the poetry of the twelfth century in France effected a transformation of desire. Drawing, either directly or indirectly, on Plato's rhapsodic account of love as divine possession, on Ovid's stories of sexual desire as a burning imperative, and probably on the passionate lyricism of Arab love poetry, the troubadours, along with the narrative poets, Marie de France, Chrétien de Troyes and their contemporaries, produced, it seems, a version of love which did not quite resemble any of their models. Romantic love was both idealizing and sensual, a discipline for the sake of delight. Rewriting the Celtic legends of a magical and heroic Arthurian world, the twelfth-century texts defined a passion which involved a constant commitment and the highest degree of intensity, but which was not yet moralized, domesticated, institutional.

It was not necessarily adulterous either. Since the nineteenth century, and in particular since C. S. Lewis showed the Anglican and humanist romance of marriage triumphant over medieval extra-marital passion,[1] scholars have been busy defending their author-heroes against the charge that they endorse adultery. Not much can be done with the troubadours, perhaps, but Marie de France and Chrétien have both been read as proto-Victorian novelists, solemnly proclaiming the redemptive virtue of true love duly located within monogamous marriage.[2] There is, of course, something in it. Love and marriage are certainly not incompatible in these texts. And marriage is commonly the project of love, since it provides unrestricted access to the object of desire: clandestine passion by contrast is necessarily precarious. But the wish to line up authors for or against their readers' favourite institution impels critics to discover censure or celebration in texts where an alternative mode of reading might find exploration, analysis, definition and re-definition of a condition which is seen as enigmatic and in some respects elusive. We might, in other words, ask different questions in the course of interpreting these early inscriptions of romantic love.

The power of love stories is well attested. In the second circle of Dante's Hell, among the sinners who have subjected reason to desire, are two shades that go together despite the whirling storm, and seem light upon the wind that drives them. Paolo and Francesca greet the narrator courteously, and in response to his prompting, Francesca re-counts the birth of their adulterous love. They were reading a story together, and at the point where the heroine was kissed by so great a lover, their own lips met, and that day they read no more. The book was the prose *Lancelot*, a thirteenth-century narrative which incorporated Chrétien's story of the love of Lancelot and Guenevere.[3] Chrétien's poem, *The Knight of the Cart* (*Le Chevalier de la charrete*), relates how the Queen is abducted by Meleagant and taken to the land of Gorre. In the course of rescuing her, Lancelot undergoes many hardships, among them the public humiliation of riding (anonymously) in a cart for common criminals when there is no other way to find her. Wherever he goes, people jeer at the unknown knight of the cart. The wisdom of chivalry, it appears, is foolishness with love, which demands suffering and sacrifice, including the sacrifice of honour if necessary.

Chrétien's narrative puts a succession of puzzles before the member of the audience who enters into the spirit of the adventure and becomes enlisted in Lancelot's quest. Imagine, for example, it implicitly pro-poses, that a knight offers to help you across a river, on condition that he is subsequently entitled to execute you if he sees fit. You refuse, and he insists that you must fight him. Just as you have reduced him to begging for mercy, a damsel appears and asks you to cut off your opponent's wicked, faithless head. Do you (a) let him go, since you have already won the battle? (b) hand the damsel his head? or (c) retreat from an impossible situation? Solution (a) would display a want of generosity or largesse, an attribute due from knights in all circumstances, but especially to damsels. Solution (b) would be lacking in the chivalric virtues of pity and magnanimity to an enemy who accepts defeat. And (c) is unthinkable when your quest is motivated by love. Lancelot does none of these. Instead, he invites the knight to resume the battle, this time with his head as the stake. Lancelot himself will take on the handicap of fighting without moving from his present position. The knight is defeated again, and Lancelot duly gives his severed head to the damsel. But not before his readers have had time to confront the dilemma and ponder the options.

Chrétien's courtly audience would have included his patron, Marie, Countess of Champagne, her small group of ladies-in-waiting, and the much larger number of knights who constituted her husband's retinue. *The Knight of the Cart* repeatedly invites them to consider the appropriate course of action for a chivalric hero who is also a lover. On one occasion a woman offers Lancelot a night's lodging on condition that he sleeps with her. Many knights, the romance confirms, would have been overjoyed at this prospect, but Lancelot, whose heart belongs entirely to the Queen, is very uneasy about the terms of the offer. They are not, however, open to negotiation: he has nowhere else to stay. Knights, the story makes clear, must honour their pledges: but equally, lovers must remain constant. Lancelot therefore shares her bed, but without touching her. Meanwhile, he has already come upon her apparently about to be raped in her own house. Apart from the knight who is holding her half naked, there are six armed men preventing her rescue. What is Lancelot to do? His project, he reasons, is to find the Queen. But on the other hand, a man with such an objective should not have the heart of a hare. Better to die with honour than live with shame . . . (lines 1097–1115).[4] Mercifully, it turns out that the rape is feigned, and in consequence Lancelot lives to continue his primary quest.

The contradictory imperatives of love and honour run all the way through the story. Catching sight of Guenevere watching from a window while he fights Meleagant on her behalf, Lancelot cannot look away. This puts him in the embarrassing position of defending himself behind his back. When the Queen commands him to perform badly in a tournament, he proves his love by enduring humiliation. Similarly, he has to mount the degrading cart if he is to find Guenevere, but in doing so he incurs the contempt of the courtly world she inhabits.

These paradoxes must have held the full attention of Chrétien's knightly audience. Their effect is to define two distinct discursive realms, discrete regimes of meaning and value, which none the less interlock in the twelfth century as romance supplants the *chanson de geste*. The conflict between love and arms also lies at the heart of two of Chrétien's other romances, *Erec and Enide* and *The Knight of the Lion* (*Le Chevalier au lion*). Erec is so much in love with his new wife that he often stays in bed with her until midday and neglects his reputation as a knight. He does not go to tournaments any more and takes no interest in warfare. When Enide reluctantly draws his attention to the extent of his shame, he takes her out on the road, where he subjects her to every kind of brutality, including making her the bait for adventurers so that he can redeem his reputation by rescuing her. She bears all this stoically and resourcefully, without wavering in her love. This process apparently corrects the balance and proves her fidelity, and they then live happily ever after. At the end of *Erec and Enide* the story of Mabonagrain demonstrates all over again the nature of the conflict between love and chivalry. Enclosed by his mistress in a fertile and beautiful garden of love, Mabonagrain can be released only by a superior knight. Love is both a pleasure and an imprisonment, at once a delight in itself and a danger to heroic ideals. The rejoicing which attends Erec's release of the knight indicates the extent of the anxiety these contradictions elicit.

In *The Knight with the Lion*, by contrast, it is love which is threatened by the world of arms. Yvain marries the heiress, Laudine de Landuc. They are in love, we are to understand, but the interventions of the loyal Lunete also make clear that by this means Yvain acquires territory and Laudine gains a knight to defend her magic spring. Gawain persuades Yvain not to give up tournaments now that he is married: it would be all too easy to succumb to the pleasures of his new life, to luxuriate in domestic comfort and become idle. Besides, Gawain argues, a wife rightly despises a man who goes soft. Yvain therefore secures Laudine's permission to set out in search of adventures for a year. Although he leaves his heart behind with his wife, he has such a good time with Gawain that he forgets the date, and fails to return on the appointed date. Yvain has to demonstrate conclusively by prolonged suffering and madness the full depth of his repentance before they can be reconciled.

In these instances love and chivalry are in conflict, but the second case brings them more seriously into contradiction. Yvain's value to Laudine is precisely his military prowess. Women in these stories are

remarkably independent: they travel alone; they maintain castles; it is
Meleagant's sister who tracks down Lancelot and releases him from an
apparently impregnable tower. But women do not fight, and the stories
make clear that this is a warrior society. Laudine explicitly marries
Yvain because she needs a man to defend her magic spring and, thanks
to Lunete again, she finally forgives his absence for the same reason. To
a knightly audience which both idealized military prowess and also
recognized the advantages of marrying an heiress, it must have seemed
that the spheres of love and war were not always so distinct.[5] But their
integration presents a problem. Laudine needs a man who is there to
defend her, but she also requires a knight whose reputation for prowess
is high enough and widespread enough to deter attacks. *The Knight with
the Lion* is remarkably explicit about the issues, even if the difficulties
are finally dissolved in the happy ending.

Lancelot's quest for the stolen Queen leads him to a ford guarded by
an armed knight. Three times the knight calls out to him, but Lancelot,
lost in thought, has already yielded his horse, his shield and his lance
before he becomes aware of the challenger. He is helpless against Love
which disciplines him ('*qui le justise*', line 713) and which so preoccupies
him that he is unaware of his circumstances:

> et ses pansers est de tel guise
> que lui meïsmes en oblie,
> ne set s'il est, ou s'il n'est mie,
> ne ne li manbre de son non,
> ne set s'il est armez ou non,
> ne set ou va, ne set don vient.
>
> (714–19)

(and his thoughts are such that he forgets himself, that he does not know
whether he exists or not, does not remember his name, whether or not he
is armed, where he is going or where he comes from.)

It might appear that Lancelot's abstraction from his surroundings affirms a dualism of mind and body, an absent *Cogito avant la lettre*. But
this is a mind removed *from its own knowledge*, from itself. The self that
Lancelot forgets is not a body but another subject position, knighthood,
and the knowledge that Love temporarily obliterates serves *that*. The
distance between the twelfth-century text and our own values becomes

apparent if we try to imagine the hero of a Victorian novel or a Hollywood western so distracted by love that he cannot function properly. Such a figure would be pathetic or absurd, and not heroic at all. Modern heroism consists precisely in refusing to 'surrender' to love, however deeply it is felt.[6] Chrétien's text gives no indication that we are invited to find Lancelot ridiculous here, though some commentators have read the episode as comedy.[7] The precise register of the account is perhaps difficult to recover at this distance of time, but in the twelfth century, the text seems to me to suggest, such reverie is appropriate to a man in love; it is also perilous, however, to a knight whose quest is to rescue the Queen.

The danger of Guenevere's predicament is made clear to the audience. In those days, the text explains, a knight who found a woman alone would be forever disgraced if her raped her. But if he won her in combat from an escort, she was his to do as he liked with (1302–16). Meleagant has taken the Queen from Kay the seneschal by force. (It is not until much later that Lancelot and the audience learn that the Queen has been protected from rape by King Bademagu, Meleagant's father. Bademagu is as courteous as his son in unscrupulous.) Rescue, it seems, is imperative and urgent. Only a lover fully recognizes the urgency. When Gawain is invited to board the cart he refuses, declaring it folly (389); but Gawain, of course, is not in love. Only the best knight, however, is capable of obeying the imperative. The way is arduous; the battles are demanding; and the pain of crossing the Sword Bridge is intense. Despite the episode of the cart, several people realize that the anonymous Lancelot is special, unmatchable (1265–78, 1953–4, 1978–80). He is resolute, brave, skilful, courteous – and unbeatable. Failure seems a possibility only at those moments in the story when the commands of love contradict the injunctions of knighthood.

Love in Chrétien is thus deeply paradoxical.[8] It motivates heroic adventures; it gives strength and courage (631); but it distracts the hero's attention and thus exposes him to danger. The fact that the Queen is watching makes Lancelot fight better – and worse. Love imposes its own discipline, the 'rules' that Andreas Capellanus codified, with whatever degree of irony, in *De Amore*. It is an askesis. Above all, it is a sweet suffering, a trouble gladly undertaken. Desire entails harsh conditions, the endurance of pain, constant perils. Since he had translated *The Art of Love*, he affirms at the beginning of *Cligés*, Chrétien could well have learnt this from Ovid. 'Night and winter, long journeys, cruel sufferings, all kinds of labour are in this sweet camp . . .'[9] But Ovid's account of love's misfortunes indicates the distance between Latin poetry and French romance. Adversity is the price Ovidian lovers must expect to pay if they are to seduce their mistresses: men parade the trouble they have gone to – and women love it. Ovid is ironic and knowing, abstract and cynical. In Chrétien, by contrast, hardship is not a calculated means to an end. On the contrary, Lancelot's suffering is the practice of love itself, and the narrative recording his endurance, adventure by detailed adventure, constitutes the representation of passion, its inscription as experience.

Romantic love is also euphoric, however. It is lyrical, fervent and reverential, devout and at the same time unequivocally sensual. The text is explicit in its account of love enacted. Her rescue finally ensured, Guenevere summons Lancelot to her window at night. They greet each other tenderly,

> que molt estoient desirrant
> il de li et ele de lui.
> (4588–9)

(for they were filled with desire, he for her and she for him.)

With the Queen's permission, Lancelot removes the bars and climbs in. Guenevere holds out her arms to him, draws him into her bed, kisses and caresses him, until they feel a pleasure so great that the story can only leave it untold. Lancelot treats her with an awe bordering on religious devotion. All night long he has great joy and delight, so strong is their reciprocal love, and when they part, he leaves his heart behind (4651–97).

Here, as elsewhere, twelfth-century romantic narrative takes for granted the force of women's desire and their capacity for passion. And yet when Lancelot greets her immediately after his triumph over Meleagant, the Queen unpredictably turns away as if she is angry. In view of all he has undergone for her sake, Lancelot is bemused and Bademagu astounded, but Guenevere does not relent. Why?

Some twenty years before the completion of Chrétien's poem, Thomas had written a long Anglo-Norman romance of Tristran, of which only fragments remain. His account, which is intensely psychological, rehearses the anguish Tristran feels when he is separated from Isolt. His emotions oscillate wildly. Isolt has surely forgotten him, he imagines: she has her pleasures with King Mark, after all, while he has none. He will therefore make do with another woman: why should he hold on to a love which brings nothing but suffering? And yet, he reasons, surely Isolt cannot have changed? And nor, of course, can he. But if she loved him, he argues, she would surely have found a way to comfort him? And yet it would be better for her to forget him. One can still have pleasure, Tristran reflects, even without love. But how can Isolt do so? How could she forget him? He must not hate her, the long monologue continues; it would be wrong to hate her. But he will marry another woman – another Isolt – in order to see whether it is possible to have pleasure without love, in order to be even with the first Isolt.

> A sa dolur, a sa gravance
> Volt Tristrans dunc quere venjance:
> A sun mal quert tel vengement
> Dunt il doblera sun turment.
>
> (265–8)[10]

(For his grief, for his suffering, Tristran thus wants to seek revenge; for his distress he seeks the kind of vengeance by which he will double his torment.)

Fort/da. Gone . . . but surely not gone? Gone. 'All right, then, go away! I don't need you. I'm sending you away myself,' Freud credits little Ernst with saying to his absent mother, who has betrayed him because she has a desire of her own. By this means the child 'masters' privation, first by naming it and then by provoking it.[11] In Isolt's absence Tristran renders himself 'master' of his own desolation by naming her desertion, by acknowledging that she has an independent object of desire. At the same time he enacts a revenge which has the effect of pushing her further away. He dismisses her, ironically rendering indestructible in the process his longing. This symbolic murder 'constitutes in the subject the eternalization of his own desire'.[12] 'I have seen this happen to many', Thomas wisely observes. 'When they cannot have their desire and what they love most, they do what they can, and take actions out of distress which double their suffering' (397–402).

This, he goes on, is neither love nor hatred, but the invasion of the one into the other, love and anger mixed. To act against desire because of some good that is unattainable is to want what is contrary to desire. This, Thomas maintains, is what Tristran does: he wants what he does not desire (405–14).

This remarkable account gives no indication that any of these processes are unconscious. It is only in a post-Cartesian world, where the *Cogito* is officially in control of its own destiny, that the workings of desire learn to conceal themselves from consciousness. If such an analysis of the contradictions of desire was accessible to Thomas in 1160, it was surely available to Chrétien in the late 1170s. Why does Guenevere turn away from Lancelot, rejecting the knight who has risked his life any number of times to rescue her? Because, she later explains, he hesitated for the space of two steps before climbing onto the humiliating cart. Because, in other words, he has demonstrated that he has an independent object of desire, which is his chivalric reputation. She enacts her revenge by sending him away, hurting herself in the process. She wants what is contrary to her desire. Dismissed, Lancelot goes off to look for Gawain. Soon a rumour reaches the court that Lancelot has been killed. Guenevere is in despair, believing that she has murdered him.

It is absurd, of course: as absurd as the behaviour of a child who punishes the mother he loves for her inevitable absences by throwing away the cotton reel that represents her. Ironically, the Queen has hardly more power over her life than Little Ernst. She is the passive stake in a struggle for power between Meleagant and Arthur. Her husband rashly promises Kay the seneschal a boon, and Kay takes the Queen off to meet Meleagant and fight for her. Predictably, he loses. At Bademagu's court she is well treated, but a prisoner. Lancelot's victory means that she is free to return to Arthur, when she loves Lancelot. Her only power is in the sphere of love, and even there, it seems, her sovereignty is not absolute: Lancelot hesitated for the duration of two steps.

In practice, Chrétien's text has already made clear, this hesitation was the space of a struggle between Reason and Love, in which Love was victorious (365–77). Love prevails each time the conflict occurs, but the Queen has to prove it. At the tournament she sends Lancelot word that he must do his worst. At once he begins to lose. The next day she tests his willingness to undergo public humiliation a second time, again he submits without question, and only then is she sure that they belong entirely to one another (5872–4). It is indeed absurd but, this text makes clear, reason and love keep little company together. Love is excessive, immoderate, irrational. It is not open to conviction by argument or persuasion. Reason knows that love is dangerous and destructive, that the game is not worth the candle, that lovers lose infinitely more than they gain. Love, however, is indifferent to reason's analysis.[13]

When the Queen believes that Lancelot is dead, she determines never to eat or drink again, now that she has lost the man who gave her life its purpose. She bitterly repents her cruelty in turning away at his moment of triumph. If only she had held him in her arms before he died. And yet, she determines, she will not die: it would better fit her crime to live and prolong her torment than die and find peace. Thus love 'reasons' in a parody of rational processes. The false premise throws into relief the irrelevance of the conclusion. Meanwhile, Lancelot hears that the Queen has died. He tries to kill himself and fails. He then reviles Death, who refuses to take him. But it is just after all, he reflects, that he should be punished in this way: he should have killed himself the moment the Queen showed her displeasure. She must have had good cause for it, he insists, but what? In any case, he should have made amends. The symmetry between these monologues draws attention to the way both lovers are tossed back and forth by love's irrational 'reasoning'. Love mimics and mocks the thetic; it simulates ratiocination only in order to display its own distance from logical thought. Desire is absolute: it admits no other law, acknowledges no extraneous ordering process.

Chrétien did not finish the story: his heart, the critical tradition invites us to suppose, was not in it; he wrote *The Knight of the Cart* purely to please his patron, Marie de Champagne. Chrétien imprisoned his hero in Meleagant's tower and left it to Godefroi de Leigni to release him and tidy up the loose ends. And yet Chrétien's alternative to closure is emblematically appropriate, a prelude to the later versions of the story, where Lancelot and Guenevere would part more formally, but just as tragically. Desire, it indicates, paradoxical to the last, is curiously solipsistic: it isolates the lover from his beloved and the world, turning a member of a chivalric company into an anchorite.

What has a passion so paradoxical, so unpredictable, so irrational and so unsociable to do with the stabilizing social institution of marriage? In this text, nothing, of course. But I do not mean to suggest that *The Knight of the Cart* is to be read as a celebration of adultery. On the contrary, the question is simply not raised. Arthur is treated merely as ineffectual and irrelevant. In all the close psychological analysis which constitutes a substantial proportion of Chrétien's text, guilt plays no part whatever. Nor does it feature significantly in the Tristan narratives of Béroul, Thomas or Gottfried von Strassburg. There is no serious suggestion that because they betray marriage the lovers deserve to be punished.[14] It is not so much that love is necessarily adulterous, but rather that love and marriage are not yet indissolubly linked.

The lays of Marie de France were in circulation at the English court in the 1170s, the period when Chrétien was composing his romances for Marie de Champagne. In the lays love is passionate, loyal and constant, and it seeks marriage wherever possible. But these texts show no sympathy with loveless marriages: jealous old husbands who lock up their wives deserve to lose them, and in these circumstances no guilt appears to attach to an adulterous wife. In *Yonec*, for example, the imprisoned wife is visited by a hawk, who magically turns into a handsome knight. When the husband finds out, he puts spikes on her window, fatally wounding the hawk. But not before the wife has become pregnant: her son, Yonec, grows up to strike off the old husband's head. Love is what elicits sympathy in these stories.[15] If marriage is an option, so much the better, but selfless fidelity matters more. The most enigmatic of Marie's lays is *Eliduc*, which tells of a loyal and loving husband who none the less falls in love with another woman. This does cause suffering for all three people concerned, but in the end the problem is solved because each of them behaves with appropriate nobility. The wife goes into a convent, choosing a higher form of love. Eliduc and his new wife then live happily together for many years, before they too follow her into the cloister.

Georges Duby has written persuasively of a struggle in twelfth-century France between Church and society, in which the control of marriage was a central issue. The Church was in the process of sacralizing the institution: marriage, it urged, was to be exogamous, monogamous and pure. The nobles, meanwhile, valued lineage and 'blood', and were inclined to take whatever steps were necessary to ensure the future of the dynasty. Love did not feature prominently in the arguments of either side, and as Duby the scrupulous historian reiterates, of the actuality of desire in the period we can say nothing.[16] It would be several centuries before the struggle Duby depicts was finally resolved, and in the process the understanding of marriage was to change, and the meaning of love with it.

Even if marriage were an option, it is hard to imagine Lancelot and Guenevere settling down companionably together. Indeed, companionship between lovers is not a significant issue in the romances. When in Chrétien's *Cligés* Alexander and Soredamors decide to get married, they have apparently never spoken to each other, though they are in love to the point of distraction. It is the Queen who identifies their condition and brings them together. Exceptionally, *Erec and Enide* stresses the nobility of Enide's character. Indeed, the couple are perfectly matched for courtliness. But it is necessary for the text to make this point clear, since Erec is a prince and Enide's father is a poor vavasour. Whatever the relationship between them, however, it is certainly not companionable. While he puts his wife to the prolonged and quite unnecessary test, Erec repeatedly forbids her to speak to him. Companionship, as *The Knight with the Lion* indicates, exists primarily between men, in the shared adventures of Yvain and Gawain, or between women, in Lunete's unremitting loyalty to Laudine.

The twelfth-century romances show love as passionate, extravagant, agonizing and obsessional. In its romantic mode desire is constant, enduring and transfiguring. It is both sensual and rhapsodic; and it involves the most intense experiences of joy and pain. But it has as yet little to do with social institutions or political stability. Indeed, the integration of passion into the meanings and values of twelfth-century secular culture is treated in the texts as a problem still to be resolved. Though we may find some early indications here of a connection between love and marriage, romantic love does not yet appear as the cement of the family, as moral and rational companionship, emotional sympathy or domestic concord. Love as fitness of mind and disposition was to wait several centuries before it would finally come to be taken for granted.

II

When in the 1460s Sir Thomas Malory rewrites the narrative of adultery in King Arthur's court, he tells another story. Some of the details are still there, though often in reduced or altered form. In Malory's version the cart, for example, is used for carrying wood, and Lancelot has to kill one of the drivers before he is permitted to board it. He badly needs transport because his horse is seriously wounded. The Queen reproaches the lady who mentions the cart's resemblance to a tumbril. But this abridged version of the story takes its place in a greatly expanded account of a chivalric world, compiled on the basis of the prose *Lancelot* and other Arthurian narratives in circulation all over Europe in the thirteenth century and later. The network of relations which constitutes this lost, heroic realm is defined with great specificity throughout the whole length of *Le Morte Darthur*.[17]

Malory's text presents a severely attenuated version of the love scene between Lancelot and Guenevere. The knight and the Queen agree that he should climb into her chamber, pulling out the window bars for the purpose. He cuts his hand, and she urges him to be silent. And then, 'sir Launcelot wente to bedde with the quene and toke no force of hys hurte honde, but toke hys plesaunce and hys lykynge untyll hit was the dawnyng of the day; for wyte you well he slept nat, but wacched.'[18] The Queen takes no part, textually at least, in the proceedings. There are no kisses and caresses here; there is no awe, no devotion; and above all there is no joy so great that it cannot be told. The text does not gesture towards a delight which exceeds the signifier: on the contrary, Malory's knowing narration apparently conceals nothing. Instead, it takes for granted that the reader is already fully aware of what happens on these occasions ('wyte you well'). In this account of pleasure without mystery, there is no indication that anything is left unspoken. What takes place, we are to understand, goes without saying, which means, of course, that a good deal remains precisely unsaid.

Passion in Malory is consistently perfunctory. Early in the story, before Arthur marries Guenevere, he is visited by an earl's daughter called Lyonors. In the course of two sentences he falls in love with her and briskly begets a child who grows up to become a knight of the

Round Table. Lyonors does not reappear. Meanwhile, Malory's Isode plays only a minor part in the long story of her relationship with Tristram. This pattern is established early in the tale. When her father sees that they are in love he offers Isode to Tristram in marriage; Tristram explains that it would shame him greatly to break his promise to King Mark; and her father agrees that Tristram must do what he thinks best. Isode is not consulted; she is not involved in the decision which determines her tragic future. Similarly, Guenevere is by far the most shadowy of the central figures in the story of the Round Table, even though her role in its destruction is critical and her love for Lancelot is at the heart of Malory's narrative.

Does it follow that the fifteenth-century text is less sympathetic to passion than Chrétien's? Early in *Le Morte Darthur* a damsel asks Lancelot why he is not married. There are rumours, she affirms, that he loves the Queen. His reply is categorical:

> 'Fayre damesell,' seyde sir Launcelot, 'I may nat warne peple to speke of me what it pleasyth hem. But for to be a weddyd man, I thynke hit nat, for than I muste couche with hir and leve armys and turnamentis, batellys and adventures. And as for to sey to take my pleasaunce with peramours, that woll I refuse: in princepall for drede of God, for knyghtes that bene adventures sholde nat be avoutrers nothir lecherous, for than they be nat happy nother fortunate unto the werrys; for other they shall be overcom with a sympler knyght than they be hemself, other ellys they shall sle by unhappe and hir cursednesse bettir men than they be hemself. And so who that usyth peramours shall be unhappy, and all thynge unhappy that is aboute them.' (p. 161)

Can this really be Lancelot's view of love? Can it be the text's?

Unlike Chrétien's, Malory's narrative very rarely reveals what the characters think. Opinions are given almost exclusively in the form of dialogue. It is thus difficult to tell quite how much of this austere moralizing is to be read ironically. Lancelot consistently denies that the Queen is false to Arthur, even at the end when no one else is in any doubt of the truth, but here he seems to go a good deal further than is strictly necessary in defence of Guenevere's reputation. Some of his reasoning is already familiar from Chrétien's *Knight of the Lion*: marriage and adventures do not go easily together. It must be acknowledged, however, that many of the knights of the Round Table get married, and most of them seem to go on fighting until they die. Moreover, it is not obvious from the rest of Malory's narrative that knights with paramours are unlucky, unless the implication is that casual sex makes a poor motive for heroism. And even if adulterers are not in general fortunate in war, the text repeatedly stresses that Sir Tristram is the greatest of Arthur's knights after Lancelot himself.

Although much of *Le Morte Darthur* thus fails to substantiate Lancelot's unexpected puritanism, there is, nevertheless, a strand of the text which does seem to affirm an ascetic ideal. *The Tale of the Sankgreal* moves predominantly in a realm of dreams and visions, of mystical encounters and beatific experiences. Only Galahad achieves the Grail quest, and Galahad is a virgin. Percival and Bors come close, as a reward for their chastity. But Lancelot fails because of the mortal sin of lechery. He confesses to a hermit that he has loved the Queen 'unmesurably and oute of mesure longe' (p. 539); he has fought his battles, he acknowledges, for her sake and not God's. When Lancelot goes on to promise to do penance for the past and to relinquish Guenevere's company in the future, Christian otherworldliness triumphs over mortal passion. Perhaps surprisingly, the issue here is not specifically adultery. Virginity, not marriage, is the way of perfection: what comes between human beings and God is earthly desire itself, secular love, a commitment to the things of this world.

Lancelot does his best, but before long it becomes clear that he cannot sustain the ascetic ideal: 'Than, as the booke seyth, sir Launcelot began to resorte unto quene Gwenivere agayne and forgate the promyse and the perfeccion that he made in the queste' (p. 611). The text registers no dismay, no moral outrage. As readers, too, we knew, of course, that it must be so, because the story demands it. *Le Morte Darthur* is not, after all, a treatise on the contempt of the world, but a chivalric romance, and the questions it addresses cannot be solved, though they might be shelved, by invoking the religious idea of perfection. There is no doubt that fifteenth-century Christianity condemns secular passion, and Malory's text acknowledges this. But *Le Morte Darthur* belongs primarily to another genre, a different discursive regime. In the fictional world it depicts, passion is inevitable; the more difficult question of its place in that world is not evaded by recourse to moral denunciation.[19]

And yet there is an evasion in the community delineated by *Le Morte*

Darthur – to the degree that desire is *left out of account*. It is neither denied nor condemned; it is not excluded or repressed; but its very inevitability, its obviousness, means that it is readily *overlooked*. Familiar, already known and to that extent disregarded, desire returns to demand attention from the precarious chivalric society that takes it so easily for granted. Chrétien's paradoxes of knighthood have given way in Malory's text to a structural contradiction which both inhabits and endangers the world of chivalry in its entirety.

Notwithstanding Lancelot's uncharacteristic moralizing, *Le Morte Darthur* more commonly presents a remarkably tolerant attitude to desire in general and adultery in particular. Tristram and Isode are treated with considerable sympathy, not only by the text, but also by Arthur's knights. This is a story of lovers kept apart by a jealous husband. King Mark, increasingly villainous and absurd as the story goes on, is condemned for driving the heroic Tristram away from his court, and when Mark in disguise meets Sir Lamorak, the knight does not hesitate to tell him so. The king of Cornwall, Sir Lamorak assures his unknown Cornish interlocutor, is

> 'the shamfullist knyght of a kynge that is now lyvynge, for he is a grete enemy to all good knyghtes. And [that] prevyth well, for he hath chased oute of that contrey sir Trystram that is the worshypfullyst knyght that now is lyvynge, and all knyghtes spekyth of him worship; and for the jeleousnes of his quene hath he chaced hym oute of his contrey. Hit is pité,' seyde sir Lameroke, 'that ony suche false kynge cowarde as kynge Marke is shulde be macched with suche a fayre lady and a good as Le Beall Isode is, for all the wo[r]lde of hym spekyth shame, and of her grete worshyp as ony quene may have.' (p. 355)

The disguised Mark can think of no reply: it is not his affair, he feebly explains. Moments of pure comedy are rare in *Le Morte Darthur*, but here dramatic irony has the effect of identifying Mark with the stereotype of the cuckold, a figure of fun, at once the butt of Lamorak's scorn and the reader's laughter. Any sympathy his plight deserves is consequently diverted to the lovers.

Lancelot himself evidently shares Sir Lamorak's view: he refers to Mark as 'King Fox' in his letters to Tristram (p. 380). When Mark keeps on putting Tristram in prison in spite of his promise not to, Isode and Tristram escape from Cornwall together and Lancelot lends them his castle of Joyous Garde, instructing his people to love and honour them. King Arthur is also 'passyng glad' to hear that the lovers are together, and he puts on a tournament to celebrate (p. 415). Lancelot only once finds himself seriously at odds with Tristram, and this is when he hears that Tristram has married Isode of the White Hands:

> 'Fye uppon hym, untrew knyght to his lady! That so noble a knyght as sir Trystrames is sholde be founde to his fyrst lady and love untrew, that is the quene of Cornwayle! But sey to hym thus,' seyde sir Launcelot, 'that of all knyghtes in the worlde I have loved him [most and had most joye of hym], and all was for his noble dedys. And lette hym wete that the love betwene hym and me is done for ever, and that I gyff hym warning: from this day forthe I woll be his mortall enemy.' (p. 273)

Tristram is appalled, and writes Lancelot an apologetic letter, explaining that his marriage remains unconsummated. He begs Lancelot to remain his friend and Isode's (p. 288). Evidently here, as in the twelfth-century texts, constancy in love is an absolute value, while a loveless marriage entails only minimal obligations.

The text repeatedly brackets its central adulterous couples together. At one point Isode sends a message to the Queen to say that there are only four lovers in the whole country, and they are Lancelot and Guenevere, Tristram and Isode (p. 267). There is thus a sense in which their stories stand in for one another, so that the accounts of Tristram and Isode invest Lancelot and Guenevere with a corresponding romance, and elicit a corresponding sympathy. But Arthur, of course, is neither villainous nor absurd. In direct contrast to Mark, he ignores his suspicions until they are forced out into the open and substantiated publicly by Agravain and Mordred. And unlike Mark, he is grateful for his friend's loyal and heroic service (p. 674).

But as far as the personal implications of his wife's adultery are concerned, Arthur is much more concerned about Lancelot's treason than Guenevere's infidelity. Though the narrative centres on the King's suffering as his realm collapses into rivalry, vengeance and war, the text makes no mention of sexual jealousy. On the contrary, Guenevere's betrayal of marriage is not, it appears, what distresses him, except in so far as its revelation has had the effect of dividing Lancelot from Arthur, and Lancelot's supporters from Gawain's:

'And therefore,' seyde the kynge, 'wyte you well, my harte was never so hevy as hit ys now. And much more am I soryar for my good knyghtes losse than for the losse of my fayre quene; for quenys I myght have inow, but such felyship of good knyghtes shall never be togydirs in no company.' (p. 685)

What is at stake in the fellowship of the Round Table is a relation-ship between men. It is homosociality that the *Le Morte Darthur* idealizes, treats as precious and depicts as threatened. Loyalty is the supreme imperative: it is masculine comradeship that keeps at bay the murderous rapacity of unchecked aggression and harnesses violence for virtue. The most intense commitment is that of one knight to another; the most tragic deaths are those that destroy friendship. Only Lancelot was kind to Sir Gareth when he first came to Arthur's court, unknown and untested; Lancelot knighted him; and Lancelot accidentally kills him. The event is at least as painful, and as dangerous to the Round Table, as anything in his relationship with Guenevere. When Arthur leads his army against Lancelot at the Battle of Joyous Garde, Sir Bors has a chance to end the war by killing the King. But Lancelot helps Arthur back on to his horse: 'For I woll never se that moste noble kynge that made me knyght nother slayne nor shamed' (p. 691). And in return Arthur weeps for Lancelot's courtesy and the futility of the war.

The story of Arthur's wedding puts on display the relative values of love and chivalry in the world of Malory's text. The barons press the King to marry and Arthur seeks Merlin's advice. Merlin agrees that he should have a wife, and asks him whether there is any woman he loves more than another. Arthur immediately mentions Guenevere, whose father owns a Round Table. Merlin warns him that she and Lancelot will love each other, but Arthur marries her anyway – and secures the Round Table, which pleases him very much. At the wedding Merlin provides an entertainment for the assembled company: three knights are sent off on quests and instructed to report back on their adventures. Sir Gawain strikes off a lady's head by accident and thus disgraces himself; Sir Tor deals firmly with a murderous knight; and Sir Pellinore ignores a cry for help in his impatience to get on with the main task. When they have all returned and been duly praised or blamed, King Arthur produces a chivalric oath, which the knights of the Round Table will reaffirm each year at the feast of Pentecost: they swear to uphold virtue, to be merciful and to give succour to women. 'EXPLICIT', the text concludes, 'THE WEDDYNG OF KYNG ARTHUR' (p. 76).

Of romantic love between the couple, reciprocal passion, marital companionship or domestic happiness the story of Arthur's wedding has nothing to say. Guenevere is even more noticeably absent from her own marriage feast, textually speaking, than she is from her adulterous relationship with Lancelot. Instead, the wedding constitutes a starting point for an examination of the chivalric ideal in the analysis of the quests and the formulation of the oath. Women, who are the only objects of men's desire in Malory's world,[20] do not, of course, participate in the chivalric oath which defines the values of the Round Table, and in so far as they are its objects, they are seen as passive and helpless. While rape is explicitly forbidden, love is not mentioned. The true ideal, the ultimate object of desire, both for Arthur's court and for the text which delineates it, is a world of loyal friendship and masculine self-restraint, the shared values of noble companionship between men and prowess dedicated to virtue. It is a world in which sexuality plays no part.

At the same time, however, *Le Morte Darthur* is not naive: it does not suppose that sexual desire can simply be wished away. The chapter that recounts the inauguration of the Round Table also anticipates its tragic end. Merlin warns Arthur that Guenevere is not 'holsom' for him to marry because she will love Lancelot, but Arthur disregards his words, since 'thereas mannes herte is sette he woll be loth to returne' (p. 59). There *is* desire after all at Arthur's wedding, on the part of both husband and wife, but Arthur overlooks it. In each case this is a desire which is dangerous and destructive, not domestic. Arthur's desire is bad for the health of his kingdom, and Guenevere's, predicted, though as yet unrealized, will come to destroy the Round Table she brings to their marriage.

The desire which is so obvious that it goes without saying is understandable and inevitable, but also disruptive and destabilizing. It creates dissension between Arthur and his greatest knight, as well as between Lancelot and one of his most loyal friends. Even when the King is willing to relent, Gawain remains firmly resolved on revenge for the death of his brothers. But ironically Arthur's final battle is against the parricidal Mordred, not Lancelot. Arthur is alone: Gawain is dead and Lancelot absent because of the quarrel over Guenevere. Arthur kills

Mordred, but not before his son and nephew has wounded him beyond recovery. Mordred is the fruit of Arthur's doubly forbidden desire for his sister, the wife of King Lot.

Malory's text rarely allows the reader to forget the impending destruction of the Round Table. The story of Lancelot and Guenevere is repeatedly invoked from the beginning. In *The Tale of King Arthur* Merlin's prophecies constantly allude to a future which cannot be averted by human endeavour. Mordred's parricide is foretold soon after his conception and defined as a punishment for incest (p. 29). Arthur did not know at the time, however, that the desire which led to Mordred's conception was incestuous, and the event has already taken place before its implications are revealed. History, it seems, is determined by a desire whose significance cannot but be overlooked, since the necessary knowledge comes too late. Desire takes on its full meaning only retroactively, when what is done cannot be undone. Moreover, Lot is unable to forgive Arthur for his adulterous act (p. 48), and in the battle between Lot and Arthur, Sir Pellinore takes the blame for Lot's death. Thereafter, the feud between Lot's sons, Sir Gawain and his brothers, on the one hand, and Sir Pellinore and his descendants, on the other, not only unsettles the Round Table, but also keeps the story of Mordred's conception indirectly alive. In consequence the present of the narrative is curiously provisional, rendered insubstantial by repeated reference to a tragic future that is known in advance. The text identifies a moment which is displaced as it is created, subject to relegation even in the instant that the signifier brings it into being. Desire, which is so inevitable and so familiar that it merits no more than perfunctory analysis, thus casts its shadow over the whole of *Le Morte Darthur* and the world of chivalry that it depicts.

Malory's elegiac text was addressed to a world in crisis,[21] and specifically to a society in which aristocratic values were rapidly becoming outmoded. His readers were predominantly members of the landed gentry and the urban rich in a period of increasing commerce.[22] Chivalry would never return, except as an idealizing fiction at the courts of the Tudor monarchs. And the desire which endangered it would in due course be classified as illicit and outlawed. True love, meanwhile, appropriately moralized, would be brought firmly under the aegis of the sacred institution of marriage.

One of the many minor stories recounted apparently incidentally in

Le Morte Darthur offers a proleptic insight into the distinction that was to emerge in due course between true love and its ungrounded simulacrum, and indicates the character of an ideal marriage in the process. Sir Pelleas has long loved Ettard, who returns the most shameful humiliations and torments for his hopeless devotion. The Lady of the Lake intervenes on his behalf and casts a spell on Ettard so that she at last falls in love with Pelleas. Tortured beyond endurance, however, he now realizes that he no longer loves the woman who has caused him so much suffering. Instead, he marries the kindly Lady of the Lake and they live happily to the end of their days (pp. 100–4). Their marriage is exceptionally restful for Pelleas, since the Lady of the Lake does not allow him to risk his life again (p. 717). Redeemed by the love of a good woman, and confined to domesticity just as Lancelot feared, Pelleas settles down to a life without adventures, without danger and apparently without further event. He is still comfortably alive when the victims of desire are all lost or dead and the chivalric ideal is no more than a memory.

III

In Chrétien, passion is transcendent and transfiguring; for Malory, desire is more quotidian but no less powerful; in both cases, however, love conflicts with chivalry. But both love and chivalry are secular values. Neither Chrétien's text nor Malory's seriously attempts to bring desire under the aegis of a single, overarching moral and spiritual law. On the contrary, love and chivalry each have their own imperatives, their distinct codes of appropriate behaviour. Doubt is caused not so much by the guilt of the protagonists as by the difficulty of sustaining the auto-erotic dyad outside the network of social relations from which the lovers also derive their identities: the court, the world of knightly adventures, the Round Table. If in the Middle Ages forbidden desire incurs the death penalty, as it commonly does, this is not usually administered by the representatives of a higher order, but by self-seeking villains or jealous rivals. Tristan and Isolde are repeatedly challenged by 'felon' barons, while Lancelot and Guenevere are brought to book by the rapacious Meleagant and the parricidal Mordred.

But in its nineteenth-century rendering, the story of adultery in

King Arthur's court sets forbidden love against moral and spiritual duty, desire in opposition to Law. The central figure of Tennyson's *Guinevere* (1859) breaks a contract which is at once divine and human: the Queen's sin is also a crime against a husband and a kingdom. In a long speech, delivered with the remorseful Guinevere prostrate at his feet, the King forgives her 'as Eternal God/Forgives' (lines 541–2),[23] but refuses to take her back, leaving her nothing more than the hope that, duly purified, she may eventually be reunited with him in heaven. Regulated as well as legitimized by the state, and sanctified by the Church, the Victorian institution of marriage is invested with all the ideality of romantic love, together with a moral and political legality guaranteed by a host of religious, social and economic sanctions. This personal relationship now takes precedence over all others, but the 'pollution' of private life by adultery diffuses 'disease' throughout a whole society (552, 515). In betraying Arthur, Guinevere spreads infection all through the order of the Round Table. The text makes Guinevere's shame exceptionally clear; the moral position is never in doubt at any point in *The Idylls of the King*; and yet it is her story, rather than Arthur's, that *Guinevere* recounts, and her anguish more than his which enlists the imagination of the reader.

The nineteenth century was the great age of the family. Queen Victoria, devoted wife and widow, set a noble example. Marriage, Tony Tanner argues in *Adultery in the Novel*, is the central myth of bourgeois society: passion and property harmoniously aligned; love, loyalty and the reproduction of the next generation all in one place.[24] For respectable people, marriage was the only proper location of desire in the Victorian period. The project, therefore, was to reconcile desire with moral choice, to align it with the *Cogito*, to rational-ize it in the interests of domestic concord.

The stabilizing institution of the family was held sacred – even if its integrity, in London at least, was ensured by an unacknowledged army of prostitutes and female servants, who offered men the erotic adventures a sacred institution tends to inhibit. Women, meanwhile, much more closely tied to the marriage bed, were invited to experience passion in a more rarefied mode. Perfect love was understood to be a fusion of the self with another in a transcendental merging of identities, which drew on and diluted a blend of lyric poetry and the Scriptures for its formulation. Here is Jane Eyre's version of the ideal:

I have now been married ten years. I know what it is to live entirely for and with what I love best on earth. I hold myself supremely blest – blest beyond what language can express; because I am my husband's life as fully as he is mine. No woman was ever nearer to her mate than I am: ever more absolutely bone of his bone and flesh of his flesh. I know no weariness of my Edward's society: he knows none of mine, any more than we each do of the pulsation of the heart that beats in our separate bosoms; consequently, we are ever together. To be together is for us to be at once as free as in solitude, as gay as in company. We talk, I believe, all day long: to talk to each other is but a more animated and an audible thinking. All my confidence is bestowed on him, all his confidence is devoted to me; we are precisely suited in character – perfect concord is the result.[25]

Conversely, 'there can be no disparity in marriage like unsuitability of mind and purpose', *David Copperfield* reiterates.[26] Only when his 'sister' Agnes becomes his wife is David truly blessed. *Jane Eyre* was published in 1847, *David Copperfield* in 1849–50. Mid-Victorian fiction commonly culminates in marriage, and marriage stands metonymically for an eternity of happiness and virtue. There were, of course, exceptions. Charlotte Brontë's *Villette* (1853) more than compensates for the sentimental epilogue to *Jane Eyre* by withholding closure altogether. Unsure whether M. Paul returns to claim his bride, the reader is left to ponder whether the conventional romantic conclusion would be worth the inevitable sacrifice of Lucy's hard-won independence. Nearly twenty years later *Middlemarch* provided the expected happy ending, but inconclusively queried the ideal of fused identities:

Many who knew her, thought it a pity that so substantive and rare a creature should have been absorbed into the life of another, and be only known in a certain circle as a wife and mother. But no one exactly stated what else that was in her power she ought rather to have done . . .[27]

In spite of these radical instances, however, most fiction of the period delivers closure by promising its central figure an unproblematic completion of identity in the love of another person. And if this brings women fulfilment, it offers men a moral foundation that enables them to take up their proper place in society as givers of the Law. Supported by the love of a good woman, Will Ladislaw becomes an ardent reformer, devoted to the redress of public wrongs. Marriage means the end of sexual adventures but the beginning of social responsibility.

This is not, of course, a universal proposition. In France, for instance, in the same period, things were known to be quite different. Flaubert's *Madame Bovary* was published in 1857. A Balzac novel significantly forms the base of the house of cards represented in Augustus Egg's triptych, *Past and Present* (1858), which depicts a family destroyed by the wife's adultery. In Thackeray's *The Newcomes* (1853–5) Clara Newcome is found with 'a heap of French novels' on the sofa beside her, shortly before she leaves her husband with Lord Highgate.[28] A French novel about adultery also features in Meredith's *Modern Love* (1862), which records the torments of marital jealousy. Meanwhile, Wagner's *Tristan and Isolde* (1859) intensified for the nineteenth century the forbidden passion of the medieval stories. And in America, Hawthorne's *The Scarlet Letter*, published in 1850, represents a plea for the relaxation of a moral code which creates transgression only to punish it relentlessly. But British fiction of this time tended to treat courtship as the central moment of romantic adventure, and relegated the anxiety of socially disruptive extra-marital sex to the margins of the story, where it invites an uneasy pity (*Bleak House*, 1852) or a horrified fascination (*Dombey and Son*, 1846–8).

One way of ensuring the continuity of perfect concord in a marriage of true minds is the suppression of female desire. If the majority of women are not, as William Acton maintained in 1857, 'very much troubled with sexual feeling of any kind',[29] then the Angel in the House defines and preserves the sanctity of the home, and guarantees the orderly transmission of property and propriety within the family. Sexually passive, dis-embodied, the model wife has a restraining effect on the wayward desires of her husband, and purges the relationship of its nastiness into the bargain. Companionate marriage becomes in effect a renunciation of desire. Ironically, of course, the process drives the husband to seek satisfaction elsewhere, and at the same time reverses patriarchal values by constituting the wife as the privileged agent of the (Paternal) Law.

Acton's extreme position was not in practice representative of Victorian morality.[30] Indeed, 'representative' moral positions are not necessarily an option: cultural history is at its most reductive when it seeks homogeneity. The nature of marriage was subject to heated debate in the period leading up to the Matrimonial Causes Act of 1857. Divorce reform was thought to be long overdue; there was growing dissatisfaction from the 1830s onwards with the existing legal position. In essence this had not changed since the sixteenth century: divorce was available only by means of a petition to the House of Lords, a long and expensive procedure. Meanwhile, the church courts could grant separation from bed and board, but not, of course, the possibility of remarriage. The objectives of the Government were to put the whole issue into the hands of the lawyers by making both divorce and separation matters for a new secular High Court. The project was not to change the law.

In the event, however, form and content could not be kept apart. Public debate in the 1850s revealed a range of attitudes, from pious Christian opposition to divorce in any form to utopian socialist contempt for marriage as a facade for crime, vice and the oppression of women. In between, there was feminist agitation on behalf of wives left penniless, and liberal resistance to the injustice of the double standard inscribed in the proposed legislation. From a conservative point of view, permanent marriage was seen to serve the interests of society, and the aim of the legislation was to shore up the family by reducing unregulated sexual activity. What finally emerged in the Matrimonial Causes Act slightly modified the existing law, but kept the double standard firmly in place: women could be divorced for adultery alone, while men could be divorced only if their adultery was aggravated by incest, bigamy, desertion or cruelty. The clear implication was that male adultery was only to be expected, while an adulterous wife irretrievably destroyed the marital relationship. The antithesis between the sexes had become a metaphysical fact, a truth of nature: female adultery was widely held to be unnatural, while men, naturally promiscuous, needed legal constraints to prevent them from leaving their wives.[31]

Tennyson wrote three lines of *Guinevere* in the summer of 1857, when the divorce legislation was being pushed through Parliament. They were:

> But hither shall I never come again,
> Never lie by thy side; see thee no more —
> Farewell!
>
> (575–7)

King Arthur, as giver of the law, executes his own divorce on grounds of his wife's adultery. The poem was completed in 1858 and published in the first instalment of *The Idylls of the King* in 1859. The volume was all about desiring women. It consisted of four tales of love, *Enid*, *Vivien*, *Elaine* and *Guinevere*. And if the only story among them which does not end in tears is about marriage, and a marriage, moreover, saved by the selfless, uncritical, unquestioning devotion of Enid, Tennyson's fictional women nevertheless feel intensely, speak for themselves, and push at the limits of a culture which apparently offers them no alternative to self-effacing absorption in the life and work, the dreams and aspirations, of a husband. Vivien seduces Merlin in order to secure his knowledge. When Lancelot will not marry Elaine, she offers to follow and serve him anyway. He refuses this on the basis that the world would disapprove, which leaves her nothing to do but die. Her death is a tragic waste. Guinevere's supreme failure is that she did not share Arthur's moral purpose and rejoice in his joy (483–4).

But for all this, it is her point of view that the text of *Guinevere* presents. The poem, set in the convent at Almesbury, recounts in retrospect the Queen's mounting guilt, her fear of the consequences for the realm of her adulterous passion, her pleas to Lancelot to leave the court. Finally, 'passion-pale' (98), the lovers determine to part, each claiming the greater share of shame. In the nunnery Guinevere's mind runs back to the sinless time, when Lancelot came to bring her to marry the King. 'Rapt in sweet talk', they rode together,

> under groves that looked a paradise
> Of blossom, over sheets of hyacinth
> That seemed the heavens upbreaking through the earth.
>
> (386–8)

And she remembers her disappointment at seeing the King she was to marry: she

> thought him cold,
> High, self-contained, and passionless, not like him,
> 'Not like my Lancelot.'
>
> (402–4)

And as she now remembers this moment, Arthur himself appears before her in the convent. Guinevere sinks to the floor and the King stands over her, righteous, judging, condemning, but also tragic, the purpose of his life lost – and his love too: 'my doom is, I love thee still./Let no man dream but that I love thee still' (556–7). Only then does Guinevere recognize that she has misread him all along, that he is not passionless but 'earth' after all (*Lancelot and Elaine*, 133), 'human,' as well as the best, the noblest, the 'highest' (*Guinevere*, 644). Now, and only now when it is too late, at least in this world, she truly loves him, and knows what her marriage could have meant:

> Ah my God,
> What might I not have made of thy fair world,
> Had I but loved thy highest creature here?
> It was my duty to have loved the highest:
> It surely was my profit had I known:
> It would have been my pleasure had I seen.
>
> (649–54)

Duty, profit and pleasure might have met, to fulfil all the aspirations of Victorian marriage, upholding into the bargain the interests of the state that Arthur created, a model couple sharing, promoting and stabilizing his vision of a well regulated society (451–83). All this might have become a reality – if Guinevere had not made an elementary mistake.

Guinevere got it wrong. A realm is laid waste, a noble dream lost to the world, because King Arthur's wife did not understand him. The banality of Tennyson's account would be laughable, were it not for the fact that it throws into relief the gap Victorian culture was so anxious to ignore between knowledge and desire, the *Cogito* and passion. Desire does not recognize what it does not want to see: in Shakespeare's version, 'Love looks not with the eyes, but with the mind/And therefore is winged Cupid painted blind.' Arthur's supposed indifference licenses Guinevere's adultery; she thinks Arthur cold because she is already in love with Lancelot, and her love has nothing to do with duty or profit or the proper regulation of the state. Desire's imperatives, fostered by sweet talk and sheets of hyacinth, may conflict with moral obligation or social improvement as easily as with the codes of chivalry. Its objects have no necessary connection with the shared visions or merged identities on which the ideal of companionate marriage depends.

The Victorians longed to believe otherwise, to imagine true love as compatible with reason and its failures as rationally explicable. Progressive accounts of female adultery in the mid-nineteenth century commonly invest the erring wife with a motive at the level of the *Cogito*. William Morris's 'Defence of Guenevere' (1858) is at first glance more radical than Tennyson's poem. Unlike Tennyson's prostrate and guilty heroine, Morris's Queen stands in court and defends herself with passion and fluency. Guenevere's defence is that the King neglects her emotionally and sexually:

> 'I was bought
> By Arthur's great name and his little love;
> Must I give up for ever then, I thought,
>
> That which I deemed would ever round me move
> Glorifying all things; for a little word,
> Scarce ever meant at all, must I now prove
>
> Stone-cold for ever?'[32]

Since no one now brings Guenevere flowers or cares to know why she sighs, what can Arthur expect? And yet the poem evades the full implications of its own radical stance. Three times the Queen rounds on her accuser:

> 'Nevertheless you, O Sir Gauwaine, lie,
> Whatever may have happened through these years,
> God knows, I speak truth, saying that you lie.'[33]

Where the lie resides is not made clear. It is as if the poem wants to leave open the possibility that the adultery did not take place, or did not take place *often* . . . with the paradoxical effect of reinforcing the enormity of the act itself.

Reviews of Augustus Egg's triptych *Past and Present* complained that the paintings gave no explanation for the wife's infidelity, so that it was not clear who was to blame. The implication is that female adultery has an identifiable cause, that women must have a *reason* for betraying their husbands. Female desire, in other words, must be accountable at the level of consciousness. *The Athenaeum* went so far as to propose that the husband might be a drunken gamester who had beaten his wife to the floor before reading the letter that disclosed her betrayal.[34] 'Bad husbands will make bad wives': the indifferent Sir Barnes Newcome subjects the wife he has purchased to physical and psychological cruelty, and in learning to dissemble her misery, she also learns to deceive.[35] Marital neglect, gambling, drink and violence recurred as the explanations of female adultery in the mid-century.[36] This had at least the paradoxical advantage for patriarchy of returning the domestic initiative to the husband: a man who exerted due control over his family, and exercised proper Victorian values in his own life, was in no danger, it was implied, of betrayal.

The divorce legislation was evidently still fresh in the public memory when Trollope published *The Belton Estate* in 1864–5. In the novel the appropriately named Mrs Winterfield devoutly hopes that her nephew Frederic Aylmer will make it his mission at Westminster 'to annul that godless Act of Parliament and restore the matrimonial bonds of England to their old rigidity'.[37] The story concerns the choice confronting Clara Amedroz between two men, Aylmer and her cousin Will Belton; and the critical difference between them is their attitude to Clara's friend, Mrs Askerton, who lived adulterously with her present husband for three years before her previous husband died. Aylmer and his family find the friendship unsuitable; Will leaves it to Clara's judgment; and much to the reader's relief, Clara stands by her friend and marries Will. Mrs Askerton's first husband was a drunkard and her life with him was wretched: adultery paradoxically rescued her from shame of a different kind.

To this extent Trollope's novel also provides adultery with a rational motive, and thus once again vindicates the ideal of love as the effect of moral choice. But there runs through the text a more profound analysis of what David Skilton calls love's 'perversity'.[38] All three central figures, he points out, love more intensely the more desire is thwarted: passion here is enhanced by rejection, not virtue. Love, in other words, is precisely *ir*rational. Clara only narrowly avoids the misery of a morally inappropriate marriage based on the misrecognition that commonly attends desire.

Tennyson's Guinevere is also irrational: she perversely misrecognizes Arthur's propriety as coldness, longing for something more than the 'pure severity of perfect light' (641). Arthur's uprightness is palpable in the poem: 'the great pillar of the moral order', Gladstone admiringly called him in an unsigned review.[39] The King's mission is to restore order and conscience to the realm, to redress wrongs and foster chastity:

Figure 1 Arthur and Guinevere. From Alfred Tennyson, *Guinevere*, illustrated by Gustave Doré (Edward Moxon, 1867).

> for indeed I knew
> Of no more subtle master under heaven
> Than is the maiden passion for a maid,
> Not only to keep down the base in man,
> But teach high thought, and amiable words
> And courtliness, and the desire of fame,
> And love of truth, and all that makes a man.
>
> (474–80)

He stands, in other words, for Law in the full Lacanian sense of that term: *le Non-du-Père*, the prohibitions and proscriptions of the (Paternal, patriarchal) symbolic order, which precisely outlaw unconscious desire. But if desire is caught up with what is forbidden, the Law is everything that is not sexy, and morality cannot elicit passion. Perhaps, then, Guinevere's misrecognition is not a simple error of judgment. It is motivated, after all, by Arthur's overwhelming austerity:

> I thought I could not breathe in that fine air
> That pure severity of perfect light –
> I yearned for warmth and colour which I found
> In Lancelot.
>
> (640–43)

She experiences marriage as a 'bond' (*Lancelot and Elaine*, 135): a contract, certainly, and binding, but also a restraint, a fetter, confining precisely in its legality.

One way of sustaining the Victorian ideal of marriage was to differentiate between male and female desire: the sexual impulses of a good man would be held in check by the pure love of a good woman, enabling him to become the Law-giver that civilization required him to be. To this end female desire was brought more firmly than ever before under the control of the law and the Law, legislation and morality, where it rested uneasily, cajoled into place by the promise of lifelong happiness, and held there by the threat of social disgrace and the probability of penury. The infidelity of a wife, more devastating to marriage, was also more self-evidently in need of explanation. To fail to explain it was to reopen the gap between desire and moral choice. Is it possible that Tennyson's poem, by allowing that women desire as strongly as men, that there is no qualitative difference, and by treating Guinevere's *mistake* as the effect of Arthur's *legality*, glimpses a problem at the heart of the Victorian effort to naturalize permanent monogamy? Love does not necessarily choose the best. The glimpse is closed off, of course: Guinevere finally realizes the error of her ways. But there is no redemption, the text makes clear, at least on earth. Arthur's rectitude means that he must leave the wife whose falsehood could not but infect his home and his kingdom (509–23). Even now that Guinevere recants, Law and desire still cannot hope to be at peace together.

In 1867–8 the first four *Idylls of the King* were reissued with illustrations by Gustave Doré. The engravings stress all that is most Gothic in Tennyson's texts, with the effect of deepening the intensity of the desire they record. Doré shows Guinevere at Arthur's feet (Figure 1), abject in her guilt, her long hair dishevelled, one small bare foot visible, a penitent Magdalen – and invested with all the sexuality that characterizes that traditional figure. If Doré's image of Guinevere implies shame, it also suggests the desolation of an appeal without hope. Arthur, crowned, stands vertical as the poem requires, and as befits the Law, but he is an old man, and his stance is more poignant than judgmental, as if he too acknowledges an irrecoverable loss.

Meanwhile, the setting is the cloister of the abbey by moonlight. A bush, prolific, still flowering, spills in from the cloister garth: the organic invades the convent, despite the restraining wall. The flowers allude to Doré's earlier illustration of Lancelot and Guinevere riding through 'a paradise/Of blossom' (386–7). Arthur and the Queen, lit by the moon, are dwarfed by the timeless darkness of the cloister vaulting, which evokes a mystery and an aspiration beyond the reach of rational understanding. Though in Tennyson's account Guinevere slips off her seat at Arthur's approach, there is no furniture in Doré's illustration. The drama of their encounter takes place on the bare and ageless stones. In consequence, the emotions of the human figures lose much of their individuality: they are pitiful rather than tragic. Only desire itself, figured as the setting that frames, contains and so far exceeds them, is seen in Doré's illustration as grand. It is also, however, dark, mysterious, beyond the reach of social exchange, accountability or negotiation.

Like Malory, Tennyson also tells the story of Pelleas and Ettarre. He read Malory's account in 1859 'with a view to a new poem', but the text was not written until ten years later.[40] As in Malory's version, Pelleas tells Gawain how Ettarre torments him, and Gawain undertakes to plead his cause. Pelleas subsequently finds Ettarre in bed with Gawain. In Tennyson's story, however, there is no final domestic happiness for Pelleas with the Lady of the Lake, but only bitter disillusionment at the falsehood of both men and women. At last, learning that the Queen too is unfaithful, Pelleas goes berserk. He abandons his name and his identity, declaring war on Arthur and his hypocritical Law.

Pelleas is very young when he first encounters betrayal, and his youthful idealism turns to despair. The little novice who tries to console Guinevere at Almesbury also thinks in simple antitheses of virtue and vice: shut away from the world, she has heard tell 'About the good King and his wicked Queen' (*Guinevere*, 207). These are not, however, the values of *The Idylls* as a whole. On the contrary, Tennyson's text goes beyond its own moral judgments to affirm the difficulty of inscribing social ideals in human institutions.

Chrétien, Malory and Tennyson offer three different accounts of adultery – and thus of passion in its cultural meaning. Three authors; three points of view, perhaps; three audiences, certainly; but also three distinct historical moments, though it is important to stress that the texts are not offered as representative. They are invoked, more modestly, as evidence of what can and cannot be identified, named and linked at specific times. For Chrétien, love is intelligible as a discipline in pursuit of quasi-mystical experience; in Malory, it is dangerous but inevitable; only Tennyson, as a good Victorian, longs to perceive it as a merging of moral consciousnesses – and simultaneously acknowledges the distance that lies between the *Cogito* and the unaccountable imperatives of a desire which necessarily escapes the discipline consciousness seeks to impose.

6

John Donne's Worlds of Desire

I

In Henry James's novel, *The Golden Bowl* (1904), Adam Verver, as yet unfallen, reflects on the instant when he first discovered that he possessed the spirit of the connoisseur:

> He had, like many other persons, in the course of his reading, been struck with Keats's sonnet about stout Cortez in the presence of the Pacific; but few persons, probably, had so devoutly fitted the poet's grand image to a fact of experience. It consorted so with Mr Verver's conscious-ness of the way in which, at a given moment, he had stared at *his* Pacific, that a couple of perusals of the immortal lines had sufficed to stamp them in his memory. His 'peak in Darien' was the sudden hour that had transformed his life, the hour of his perceiving with a mute inward gasp akin to the low moan of apprehensive passion, that a world was left him to conquer and that he might conquer it if he tried.[1]

By a series of intertextual allusions to Keats's poem about reading Chapman's translation of Homer's poems, *The Golden Bowl* here ident-ifies Adam Verver's utopia, the projected American City, filled with art and antique objects from all over the world, as the object of an epic quest, which is also a conquest, and which is at the same time 'akin to . . . passion'.

This is an American conquest of Europe and its treasures. And the European Prince, ironically named Amerigo, is an integral part, indeed, the most precious component of it. The novel charts Adam's fall from innocence as it emerges that the Prince, this new found land, discovered in Rome, in the heart of the old world, the most expensive item in

Adam Verver's collection, identified in the text as a pure and perfect crystal (pp. 120–1), has in the event a flaw, and the flaw is passion. His perfection is illusory. While the Prince himself has no difficulty in detecting the imperfection in the exquisite golden bowl (p. 108), the innocent American cannot see the Prince as he is. The great collector, so eminently incapable of vulgar mistakes (p. 121), has, unlike the eagle-eyed Cortez of Keats's poem, a fatal blind spot: the image of the Prince that he sees is false. The shock is the more unbearable because it is his character as a connoisseur that makes Mr Verver special – like an artist, the text affirms (p. 122). And it is a work of art (Chapman's Homer) which evokes in Mr Verver's consciousness the sudden vision of the Pacific – and the corresponding wild surmise that there is a new world to conquer.

But Amerigo is also a conqueror. By virtue of possessing such a famous eponymous ancestor, the Amerigo who gave his name to the new continent, the Prince appropriates the resources of the Americans, and the mode of *his* conquest is love. As Fanny Assingham recounts it, his name was the 'sign' that at once endeared him to the Ververs.

> The connexion became romantic for Maggie the moment she took it in; she filled out, in a flash, every link that might be vague. 'By that sign', I quite said to myself, 'he'll conquer.' (p. 81)

For Adam Verver, by contrast, the projected conquest of a world of beautiful objects is an *alternative* to passion, another askesis altogether: his wife, indeed, he reflects, would almost certainly have proved an impediment to his single-minded quest:

> Would she have prevented him from ever scaling his vertiginous Peak? – or would she, otherwise, have been able to accompany him to that eminence, where he might have pointed out to her, as Cortez to *his* companions, the revelation vouchsafed? No companion of Cortez had presumably been a real lady: Mr Verver allowed that historic fact to determine his inference. (p. 123)

II

The project of the insistence in *The Golden Bowl* on these European Renaissance conquistadors, Cortez and his companions, is the invocation of a history of the economic and cultural power relations between Europe and America, and the ironic reversal of this history which the novel charts. Meanwhile, however, one of its side-effects, which may be inadvertent (but in reading the culminating work of such a wily story-teller, who can be sure?), is the construction of a link between a series of terms: discovery and desire, conquest and wealth, Renaissance Europe and works of art. To historians of literature this pattern is an uncannily familiar one. In the well wrought urns and pretty rooms of Elizabethan and Jacobean lyric poetry, it is love itself which expands to fill and take over the known world, 'And makes one little roome, an every where' ('The Good-morrow', line 11).[2] 'She'is all States, and all Princes, I,/Nothing else is' ('The Sunne Rising', lines 21–2). In Spenser's version, 'my love doth in her selfe containe/All this worlds riches that may farre be found'.[3] If at this epoch Cortez himself does not appear in the English poems, for obvious national and political reasons, nevertheless, the heroic quest and the commanding gaze of succeeding imperial adventurers appear as at once alternatives to and analogies for passion:

> Let sea-discoverers to new worlds have gone,
> Let Maps to others, worlds on worlds have showne,
> Let us possesse our world, each hath one, and is one.
> ('The Good-morrow', lines 12–14)

The text of 'The Good-morrow' takes it for granted that what is to be done with these new worlds is 'possess' them, take possession of them. The gaze of Renaissance explorers and cartographers produced a knowledge which was the prelude to the exploitation of local resources. In 1569, Mercator's projection offered for the first time a world map that it was possible to navigate by. Europe was, of course, at the centre, the place from which the rest of the world was visible. In 1570, as a result of a suggestion from an Antwerp merchant, Ortelius assembled the first atlas in the modern sense of the term: a collection of maps charting all four of the known continents. He called it *Theatrum Orbis Terrarum* (Theatre of the World). Contracted thus, the world sold well: the venture was an instant commercial success.[4] With the discovery of the West Indies, the mining of Caribbean gold is added to the oriental spice trade, as 'both the'India's of spice and Myne' come within the purview of Europe ('The Sunne Rising', line 17). And the imagery of Meta-physical love poetry leaves no doubt that the wealth of the new world is available for the benefit of the old.

> Oh my America, my new found lande,
> My kingdome, safeliest when with one man man'd.
> My myne of precious stones, my Empiree,
> How blest am I in this discovering thee.
> To enter in these bonds is to be free.
> (Donne, 'To his Mistris Going to Bed', lines 27–31)

The texts are perfectly uninhibited in their formulations of desire: the entirety of the expanding world is rich and beautiful, and like the woman's body, it is there to be discovered, manned and mined.

So far, from the point of view of either the woman or the colonial subject, so bad. It is easy to find in the love poems of John Donne in particular the imperatives of empire characteristic of the energetic and optimistic beginnings of English expansionism. Desire is boundless, unrestrained and urgent, and it is formulated in a series of imperatives that do not invite debate: 'Come, madam, come, all rest my powers defie . . .'; 'Off with that girdle, like heavens zone glistering/But a farre fairer world encompassing'; 'Unlace your selfe . . .'; 'Licence my roving hands . . .' (Elegy 'To his Mistris Going to Bed', lines 1, 5–6, 9, 25). In the Elegy the project is an exploration of the woman's body, an un-covering which reveals a sensual topography of flowery meads and hills (line 14), an earthly paradise (line 21), and such joys (line 33) as explorers commonly found in the landscapes of the new world.[5] But the process of erotic discovery is to precede a new kind of covering that is also and explicitly both a sexual and a social mastery. Among animals, to cover is to inseminate; a feme covert in the period is a married woman who has surrendered her property and her autonomy to her husband. The Elegy 'To his Mistris Going to Bed' concludes its argu-ment with a pun which is in every sense triumphant: 'To teach thee, I am naked first: Why than/What need'st thou have more covering than a man?' (lines 47–8).

What sort of love is it that persistently finds a meaning for itself in images of discovery and mapping, cosmography and conquest? What is the nature of the worlds of desire which appear so frequently in these love poems of the early seventeenth century? What sexual politics is inscribed in the texts? Historically, this is the moment when the intensity of erotic experience is in the process of being regularized and sanctified as the basis of domestic life and family values. The shared, reciprocal desire of the heterosexual couple comes to stand at the heart of society as a source of stability amid the turbulence of politics and the market. What then has love itself to do with territory, property or conquest?

There has been a tendency to identify sexual politics with the cultural analysis of femininity and masculinity, sometimes independently of each other, and to see reading motivated by sexual politics as concerned with the representation of women and (more recently) men. Such a way of reading (and I have no quarrel with it) commonly finds in heterosexual Renaissance love poems by men the characters of a loquacious and predatory man on the one hand, and a wholly silent woman on the other. But in thus placing these figures in opposition to each other, we risk ignoring the relation which, textually at least, binds them together, the very condition, in other words, of their difference within the text. In a love poem this relation consists not only in the differential meanings of man and woman, but also in the desire which assigns the woman who is its object a textual place for the male voice that declares it. Desire in the poems I want to consider is in this sense prior to gender difference, and the condition of its imagined fixing. The sexual politics in question here is the politics of desire itself, and the inscription of a power which includes but also exceeds the difference of gender. Desire, I suggest, has its own political history, and Donne's poems in particular belong on the threshold of its modernity.

Meanwhile, since Foucault, histories of sexuality are increasingly concerned with sexual identities, tracing, for instance, same-sex desire in the documents of other epochs, other cultures, and its exclusion as perversity at a specific moment in the development of the Free West. Heterosexuality, we now know, was produced as a norm, with all a norm's attendant constraints and coercions: it was not so by nature. This project of denaturalizing heterosexuality is indispensable, but as the work becomes ever more precise, more attentive to detail, there is a danger of leaving unproblematized our account of the erotic relation between men and women, and thus inadvertently reaffirming its naturalness by another route.

In so far as they dramatize the impediments to true love, the texts of heterosexual desire are commonly read as throwing light not on the sexual relation itself, but on the inadequacy of this or that individual as a lover. And this inadequacy in turn is identified according to an implied standard of sexual correctness, a model of true love which is essentially problem-free, the real thing, because it conforms to the requirements of nature. Early modern love poetry, less certain as yet than the Victorians about the social value of the heterosexual nuclear couple, may perhaps be read as indicating that true love is not, after all, quite so simple.

In *Poetry and Phantasy*, Antony Easthope identifies 'To his Mistris Going to Bed' as an instance of scopophilic male narcissism. His persuasive account of the Elegy draws attention to the way its sexual object is constantly desexualized by reference to knowledges which have no erotic associations: theology, geography, classical mythology . . . The woman's body is distanced rather than invoked by the utopian allusions to heaven, paradise and the new world. Meanwhile the male body of the speaker, Easthope points out, is repeatedly made visible in the text, 'standing' (line 4), 'upright' (line 24) and finally naked and 'covering' the woman (lines 47–8). His gaze seems primarily to serve the purpose of installing the subject of the text as the cartographer of an imaginary landscape which mirrors his own ideal image.[6]

> The speaker of the 'Elegy' wants above all to look at the object of his desire, to master it visually as a truth he must see 'reveal'd' so he may 'know' it completely. He desires neither the woman nor sexual satisfaction but rather a transcendent object, one whose perfect atemporal image may return to him an equally perfect reflection of himself.[7]

Easthope's reading is a subtle one, and it goes as far as Freud will take it. Freud does not approve of narcissism. Narcissism is loving what you are, or were, or would like to be. It is an instance of incomplete development. Freud the scientist is no more 'disinterested' than F. R. Leavis when maturity is the issue. Narcissism, Freud says, occurs in people 'whose libidinal development has suffered some disturbance, such as perverts and homosexuals'. True object-love is characteristic of men; it is women who are commonly narcissistic, and all the more fascinating for that, rather like children, cats and large beasts of prey.[8]

But a later psychoanalytic generation acknowledges the inevitability of a narcissistic component of desire. For Lacan, it is one of the tragedies of love that while it is precipitated in the symbolic, it seeks satisfaction in the imaginary. Produced by the inability of the subject to be present to itself in its own utterance, desire seeks reaffirmation of subjectivity in the return of its own image and the assurance of its own singularity: 'the first object of desire is to be recognized by the other'.[9] In Julia Kristeva's version of the Lacanian position, however, the emphasis is on the otherness, the difference, of the other person. While the other offers a mirror to the subject, the lover perceives the other precisely as other. Thus, 'the lover is a narcissist with an *object*'.[10] And the condition of otherness, of difference, is not, of course, anatomy but a Third Party, language, the differentiating practice of signification.

If in the light of this more recent psychoanalysis, the narcissism which is undoubtedly there in the Elegy is an inevitable component of desire, and not necessarily to be classified as perversity, we may perhaps return to the text in the light of Easthope's insights to read it as displaying something of the character of desire itself at this moment in the history of Western culture (probably the 1590s). Easthope points out that the projected uncovering is continually postponed, and is still deferred at the end of the poem. Neither the reader nor the speaker achieves the promised discovery, the mapping of the woman's body: she is still, apparently, in her shift. Easthope compares Ovid's *Amores* I.5, where the text exclaims over Corinna's arms, her shoulders, her breasts. Donne's poem, by contrast, offers inventive analogies in place of flesh, witty comparisons, not the thing itself. Moreover, Ovid ends with sexual fulfilment; Donne's speaker is still exercising his rhetorical skills when the Elegy ends.[11]

In other words, 'To his Mistris Going to Bed' departs radically from its Ovidian model precisely in so far as it consists of a series of imperatives and not a narrative of an event. Nothing, in short, *happens*: nothing sexual, that is. Even within the fiction which constitutes the poem, the action is all explicitly at the level of fantasy, and it is this above all that characterizes the Elegy as a text of desire. Desire is by definition unfulfilled: you want what you don't have. Desire is predicated on absence. Ovid's poem is a text of sexual pleasure, which is not the same thing at all. Desire is thrilling, terrifying, euphoric, but it has no necessary connection with pleasure.

Vision in the Elegy imagines itself as knowledge. The woman's clothes, we are to understand, conceal the mystery of her sexual difference, and it is the lover's privilege that justifies his initiation into this essential secret:

> Like pictures, or like bookes gay coverings made
> For laymen, are all women thus arraid;
> Themselves are mystique bookes, which onely wee
> Whom their imputed grace will dignify
> Must see reveal'd. Then since I may knowe,
> As liberally as to a midwife showe
> Thy selfe.
>
> (lines 39–45)

But at the end of the poem the secret is still not delivered, the privileged knowledge not conferred: the speaker continues to plead, instruct, cajole. In his discussion of the gaze and desire, Lacan argues that to conflate vision with knowledge is always to imagine a full relationship between the subject and the world. Moreover, it is characteristic of the *Cogito* to assume that 'my representations belong to me'. To see, or to see and thereby to know, is thus to take possession, to reaffirm 'this *belong to me* aspect of representations, so reminiscent of property'.[12] But the subject is not where it thinks it is.

> In our relation to things, in so far as this relation is constituted by the way of vision, and ordered in the figures of representation, something slips, passes, is transmitted, from stage to stage, and is always to some degree eluded in it – that is what we call the gaze.[13]

It is as if the gaze itself is a kind of blind spot in the process of perception. Donne's Elegy stages the quest for a completeness of vision as possession, and in the process puts on display the elusive, intervening, distancing and differentiating gaze, which is the condition of perception. What is mapped by the text is not a body at all, not the fullness of a presence, but the unrepresented gaze as the symbol of an absence, the lack that precipitates desire.

Meanwhile, however, all this is to ignore the comedy of 'To his Mistris Going to Bed'. As a characteristically Metaphysical text, the Elegy is a tissue of puns, conceits and outrageous analogies. The mode is consistently mock heroic. At first the encounter with the woman in her bedroom is an epic battle, and the absurdity of this is betrayed by the sexual pun: 'The foe oft-times, having the foe in sight,/Is tir'd with standing, though they never fight' (lines 3–4) Subsequent comparisons are religious: the bed is a temple (line 18); the woman brings to it 'A heaven like Mahomets paradise' (line 21); she wears white, like an angel, and though bad angels also wear white, it is easy to tell the difference between the two: 'They set our hairs, but these the flesh upright' (line 24). Despite its transcendental allusions, the text does not for a moment allow us to forget that all the argument is a shift and an erection, and it invites us to savour the comedy of the discrepancy within its mode of address. In this sense, what the Elegy reveals is not a body but wit, a claim to mastery of the possibilities of signifying practice.

In Kristeva's account love is addressed to a Third Party. The auto-erotic mother-child dyad becomes love when it is offered to an Other (capital O), who is not, I think, to be confused with the father. In Freudian terms the Third Party is 'the father of individual prehistory', but as Kristeva explains elsewhere, this figure 'is not grasped as a real person by the infant, but like a sort of symbolic instance; something that is here that cannot be here – the possibility of absence, the possibility of love, the possibility of interdiction but also a gift'. And later, 'some sort of archaic occurrence of the symbolic'.[14] Like the semiotic in Kristeva's earlier *Revolution in Poetic Language*, this Third Party is evidently a kind of pre-signifying signification, the beginnings of a difference *avant la lettre*. Love, it follows, is a triangular relationship between a narcissistic couple and a shadowy Third, and this Third Party is a differential formation, a 'ghost' which Kristeva locates 'beyond the mirror'.[15]

> The loving mother, different from the caring and clinging mother, is someone who has an object of desire; beyond that, she has an Other with relation to whom the child will serve as go-between. She will love her child with respect to that Other, and it is through a discourse aimed at that Third Party that the child will be set up as 'loved' for the mother. 'Isn't he beautiful,' or 'I am proud of you,' and so forth, are statements of maternal love because they involve a Third Party; it is in the eyes of a Third Party that the baby the mother speaks to becomes a *he*, it is with respect to others that 'I am proud of you,' and so forth. Against this

verbal backdrop or in the silence that presupposes it the bodily exchange of maternal fondness may take on the imaginary burden of representing love in its most characteristic form.[16]

The colonial project is addressed to a Third Party: it offers up the indigenous culture to an Idea: civilization . . . salvation . . . God. Its aim is to be able to say to others of the colonial subject, who comes to reflect back the image of the colonizer, 'I am proud of you'. Donne's Elegy is also addressed to a Third Party. 'Isn't she beautiful?', it wants to be able to say, and we are almost convinced that she is, would be, will be, must be. But the text does not prove it. On the contrary, it explicitly withholds the moment of substantiation. It is in this sense that the Elegy is about love and not about the woman who is its object. Meanwhile, beyond the narcissistic mirror, and beyond the vision of the other who is the object of love, desire subsists in what eludes both vision and representation, in what exceeds demand, including the demand for love. It follows that desire is ultimately desire of the Other (the locus of the deployment of speech), to which the subject symbolically belongs, and which is the source of its subjection to desire. The ultimate object of desire is the unmediated, unimagined, unimaginable I Am.

'To his Mistris Going to Bed' is addressed not only to a woman, but also to this capital Other, the place from which one sees and hears, and from which one is seen and heard. This is the significance of the dazzling array of puns and double entendres. This accounts for the brilliant succession of scandalous comparisons and far-fetched arguments. What is affirmed as beautiful is not, in the end, the woman's body, so much as the text itself in its demonstration of mastery of the signifying difference. The Elegy is a display of wit, designed to be heard or read, and offered to a Third Party by a subject who seeks both to placate the Other and to identify with it, to defer to the Other and at the same time to participate in its power to licence the very processes of perception and differentiation.[17] Inscribed in the unsubstantiated affirmation of the woman's beauty, we can hear in the Elegy a bid to be the origin of difference, and not merely its effect.

The poem is not, of course, in the event, an origin at all. Like any signifying practice, it is necessarily intertextually derived, this time quite overtly from Ovid. As an instance of Renaissance imitation, the poem characteristically owes some of its authority to the fact that the

Latin text has already been there first. In *Amores* I.5 it is afternoon;
Corinna appears in the poet's bedroom with the belt of her tunic
undone; he tears her tunic off; she struggles, like one who does not want
to win; he exclaims over the beauty of her body; and finally (in
Marlowe's translation):

> Judge you the rest, being tyrde she bad me kisse.
> Jove send me more such afternoones as this.
> ('Elegia' 5, lines 25–6)[18]

And yet the distance between Ovid's text and Donne's indicates the
audacity of the Renaissance poet's project. Where Ovid's is a seemingly
transparent narrative of sexual pleasure, Donne presents an intricate,
knotty, difficult, dazzling formulation of desire. What fills the gap is
history, not least the cultural history of the subject. The Elegy puts on
display an emerging subjectivity which is not satisfied with imitation.
On the contrary, it insists on its own specificity. The textual density and
the baroque wit of 'To his Mistris Going to Bed' are there in order to
surpass the tradition to which the poem claims to belong. The Elegy
thus dramatizes, whether consciously or not, the desire which constitutes the subject's defiance of its own subjection.

II

'The Sunne Rising' is no less overtly patriarchal, and no less explicitly
imperialist than the Elegy: 'She'is all States, and all Princes, I' (line 21).
But this time the sexual relationship is marginally more reciprocal, to
the extent that the world in question is no longer the world of the
woman's body, but a unit formed jointly by the lovers. The Third Party
to whom their prince displays the 'India's of spice and Myne' (line 17)
is, in the rhetoric of the poem, the sun, and since its obligations are to
warm the world, 'that's done in warming *us*' (my italics, line 28).

'The Sunne Rising' is also an imitation of Ovid (*Amores* I.13), and
once again with a very considerable difference. This time the specificity of the text is partly the consequence of an intervening medieval
European tradition of *aubade* poems, in which the lover conventionally
reproaches the dawn for interrupting the pleasures of the night. But the

irreverent pose of the speaker and the extravagance of the conceits on which the argument depends are quite without precedent. Once again the poem lays claim both to an intertextual authority and at the same time to a singularity which isolates it from everything that has gone before.

Indeed, the transcendence of the subject-speaker is precisely the theme of 'The Sunne Rising'. The sun, source of life, origin of time and history, is commanded to surrender its sovereignty to the newly emerging sovereign subject of the Free West.

> Thy beames, so reverend, and strong
>   Why shouldst thou thinke?
> I could eclipse and cloude them with a winke.
>   (lines 11–13)

The subject, which by closing its eyes can shut out the sun, is itself a little world made cunningly of elements, and there is a sense in which, just as in the Elegy, the subject is the real protagonist of 'The Sunne Rising'. The poem is an affirmation of radical subjectivism, where the speaker is 'all Princes' and 'Nothing else is' (lines 21–2). Moreover, all existing princes are mere players: in an outrageous appropriation of Renaissance Neoplatonism, the text claims that only the lovers represent true reality: 'compar'd to this,/All honor's mimique; All wealth alchimie' (lines 23–4). Inhabiting a timeless realm beyond the quotidian, the speaker magnificently disdains the trivial world of late schoolboys and reluctant apprentices, sleepy court-huntsmen and busy agricultural labourers (lines 6–8).

It is love which promises access to this 'zenith of subjectivity'.[19] Western culture, which at this moment is constructing the sovereign subject, is also in the process of producing as the heart of society a private world of intimacy and personal experience, to be distinguished from the world of work, and to be valued above the public and the political. In the poem love, which ensures the enlisting of the whole subjectivity in personal relationship, subordinates honour, wealth and the sun itself. It excludes and keeps at bay work and politics. The ideal and the erotic are united, if indeed there was ever any separation between them: love transcends time and place ('no season knowes, nor clyme . . .', line 9), but it also takes place in bed. In the utopian proposition of 'The Sunne Rising' the earth is contracted to the nuclear couple. The lovers' bed which, like a map, systematically corresponds to the larger world,[20] is to be the centre of the sun's daily revolution, and this moment of reciprocal passion is to have the astonishing effect of putting an end to history.

The argument is as extravagant as it is romantic. The wit of 'The Sunne Rising' depends precisely on the impossibility of what it proposes: that the sun should stop in its course in order to sustain the perfection of the present. Palpably it won't; indeed, it hasn't. Ovid's version concludes by acknowledging the fact that poetic remonstration has not helped at all. In response to the poet's complaint in *Amores* I.13, Aurora blushes – which only makes things worse. Traditionally, the *aubade* is a lament, and even if the element of comedy is often not far away, these dawn poems commonly recognize the inevitability of parting.[21] 'It is the lark that sings so out of tune,/Straining harsh discords and unpleasing sharps . . . /O now be gone! More light and light it grows'.[22] In Donne's text, by contrast, the mood of defiance is sustained to the end, making the poem more intensely romantic – or more absurd.

But which? The hyperbole generates a similar kind of uncertainty. Her eyes blind the sun; his eyes can eclipse it. Are we to believe that love has the power claimed for it? Apparently not. And yet subjectively, perhaps we do . . . ? Like Wittgenstein's duck-rabbit, which depends on how you look at it, either love in this poem is very exalted, because it is all-powerful, because it transcends the laws of nature, or it is extremely absurd, because it mistakenly supposes that it is all-powerful and can ignore the laws of nature. Or perhaps it is all the more glorious, after all, because it is happy to be absurd and doesn't see that as a problem: love is noble and thrilling exactly in so far as it rejects common sense?

I do not see any way of resolving these uncertainties, nor indeed any very convincing motive for doing so. It is precisely the undecidability of the text, its lack of closure, which sustains the desire of the reader. 'The Sunne Rising' teases and tantalizes the reader to the degree that it is at once utopian about love and explicitly witty at the expense of the utopia it depicts. What is proposed as beautiful in this text is not a woman, but love itself. In so far as love evades any final definition, however, and so remains indeterminate, the text not only brings to light, but also stages, puts on show, perhaps even celebrates, the lack which resides in the process of signification. The poem, it seems to say (though it cannot possibly do so), the poem, like love itself, originates in the Other, in the symbolic, and desires to return there. But the problem about identifying with the Other, about seeking to be the origin of difference, is that in the Other there is *only* difference. The Other as the place from which one is seen and heard, hears and sees, is both an indeterminate location and the location of indeterminacy.

IV

'The Good-morrow' apparently moves very much closer to portraying the kind of sexual relation that the twentieth century perceives as ideal. In this text imperial and sexual politics diverge radically. Mapping and discovering seem to lead inevitably to territorial possession (lines 12–14), but love is an altogether more mysterious and mystical affair, in which lovers own a single world of love between them and at the same time, and constitute a world for each other: 'Let us possesse our worlde, each hath one, and is one (line 14).[23] Either way, these lovers are equal and the relationship is perfectly reciprocal:

> My face in thine eye, thine in mine appeares,
>   And true plaine hearts doe in the faces rest,
> Where can we finde two better hemispheares
>   Without sharpe North, without declining West?
> (lines 15–18)

Each solicits and finds the gaze of the other: their eyes meet and they encounter in the depths of the other's pupil a perfect mirror image of themselves. This jubilant specular recognition entirely elides the gaze itself: what the lovers see escapes the uncertainty inherent in the process of looking. They know the plain truth, because each has introjected the eye of the other: her eye is in his head, his in hers. Like two hemispheres, they merge into a single world, a perfect sphere, known, mapped, complete in itself.

The auto-erotic dyad is still in practice a triangle, of course: the lover, the woman, and the poem. But this time the text draws less attention to itself. The writing is less intricate, less knotty, more transparent, as befits a celebration of the exchange of true plain hearts. Such confidence, we are to understand, has no need of esoteric allusions and inventive analogies, no need, in other words, of rhetoric.

And yet there is a problem of interpretation here more baffling to editors than any of the conceits in the Elegy or 'The Sunne Rising'. Immediately after the metaphor of the hemispheres has offered an image of perfect reciprocity, there follows what Virginia Woolf in a different context calls 'an awkward break', a significant discontinuity in the text, which in this instance suddenly leads in a slightly unexpected direction.[24] Up to this point the logic of the argument is perspicuous: until we met, it proposes, we were like children, or sleeping, perhaps dreaming; now we wake, and watch, but not out of fear; what we see with our eyes open is a whole world, the world of our love. And then suddenly, in the last three lines of the poem,

> Whatever dyes, was not mixt equally;
> If our two loves be one, or, thou and I
> Love so alike, that none doe slacken, none can die.
>
> (lines 19–21)

This is the first mention of dying in a poem where the previous imagery has all been logically linked. The reference is to the belief that if the elements were perfectly mixed in the human body, as they were before the Fall, we should live for ever. Death is the effect of an imbalance of the humours. This is all very well, but what has it to do with anything in the preceding text? And the 'if' of the final assertion is disappointing after the ringing certainty of what has gone before. 'If our two loves be one' seems to call into question the confident image of the hemispheres and the true plain hearts. Helen Gardner examines the textual variants for an improvement, finds none, and decides that the explanation of the alternative readings must be the poet's rewriting of an unsatisfactory line. 'Neither version', she concludes, 'provides a close worthy of the poem's opening. Conditional clauses must always suggest an element of doubt.'

Helen Gardner ignores the additional problem of the word 'slacken'. Her paraphrase reconstructs the syntax so that not slackening is no longer a *consequence* of loving alike, but a *synonym for* it: 'If our two loves are wholly united in one love, or, if they are always alike and *at the same pitch*, neither can perish' (my *emphasis*).[25] It is Theodore Redpath who brings out the difficulty presented by 'slacken'. It makes, in short, for an affirmation of the deepest banality: if our love is perfectly reciprocated (one, alike), so that it does not diminish, it cannot die. This is barely intelligent: *of course* if it doesn't diminish, it can't die. Redpath comments that on this reading 'the mention of slackening would be redundant to the point of absurdity. Donne demands this close kind of reading,' he goes on, 'and his work usually repays it handsomely. In the present case, however, I cannot help feeling that something may have gone wrong, and prevented this otherwise magnificent poem from achieving a truly satisfying ending.' This will clearly not do, and Redpath sets about producing a properly satisfactory conclusion. On his alternative 'none' means no one, neither of us, and the poem asserts that if our love is perfectly reciprocated, so that we do not slacken in our love, *we* cannot die.[26] This is certainly a utopian claim, and lovers are prone empirically to suppose themselves immortal in the intensity of passion. But Redpath's reading would surely reintroduce the kind of indeterminacy which haunts 'The Sunne Rising'. If the speaker of 'The Good-morrow' seriously believes that lovers cannot die, can 'The Good-morrow' possibly be serious about love?

There is, however, another possibility. Every student knows, as presumably did every seventeenth-century reader, that to die is to come. 'The Good-morrow' has already shown itself to be a sexually knowing poem.

> I wonder by my troth, what thou, and I
>   Did, till we lov'd? were we not wean'd till then?
> But suck'd on countrey pleasures, childishly?
>   Or snorted we i'the seaven sleepers den?
> 'Twas so; But this, all pleasures fancies bee.
> If ever any beauty I did see,
> Which I desir'd, and got, 'twas but a dreame of thee.
>
> (lines 1–7)

The final lines of this first stanza, invoking women previously desired and possessed, surely reflect back on the sucking and snorting and country pleasures that precede them.[27] Beauties desired and got, however, are no more than fancies: true love is something else. If we take the final 'die' to invoke the familiar pun, the text might be read as urging that if the desire of the lovers is one, perfectly mixed, and thus undying, perpetual, so that detumescence is impossible, so in consequence is orgasm itself. If none is able to slacken, then none by definition can ever 'die'.

Desire is desire to achieve presence, to attain the imaginary plenitude of perfect recognition, of full possession. This longing seeks to make itself perpetual, to preserve its intensity so that desire does not die. There is a direct conflict here with desire's other and equally urgent physical imperative. Understood as sexual impulse, desire fulfilled (got) would be desire in abeyance (dead). On this third reading of 'The Good-morrow' true, ideal, equal lovers are immobilized, frozen like figures on a Grecian urn, in a state of perfect reciprocal excitement which remains ungratified for ever.

V

In this version of the text the final conceit is after all witty, and it has some connection with the rest of the poem, but it quite punctures the utopian romanticism of the preceding lines, since true love apparently excludes the possibility of sexual satisfaction. The elision of the gaze in reciprocal specular recognition, the merging of two visions into one, then appears in ironic retrospect as precisely imaginary. Desire, after all, is less optimistic: in Lacan's account of the gaze, 'When, in love, I solicit a look, what is profoundly unsatisfying and always missing is that – *You never look at me from the place from which I see you.*'[28]

The final, authoritative meaning of the text is in my view un-decidable. Possibly all three readings, and perhaps others too, were available to Donne's original audience. If so, however, what emerges on the basis of each of the poems I have considered, is the uncertainty of the lover, registered above all in the indeterminacies of the texts. The object of desire is unsure: a woman; a self-image; writing? Its condition is ambiguous: exaltation; absurdity; self-mockery? And its realization in the subject is indefinite, to the degree that the transcendent union lovers seek is incompatible with sexual satisfaction. No wonder the worlds which were gradually opening up to the gaze of Renaissance explorers and cartographers seemed the appropriate emblem of desire.

They were vast, these territories, perhaps limitless, and enticing, rich and beautiful. They were also dangerous, to the degree that they were uncharted both geographically and anthropologically. Desire in Donne's love poetry is a world that remains paradoxically unknown, and that elicits in consequence a corresponding anxiety, which is registered in the texts as undecidability.

We might be tempted to attribute the uncertainty displayed in these poems to an eccentricity, a quirk specific to their author, were it not for the recurrence of similar imagery and a more intense anxiety in the poetry of Andrew Marvell half a century later. In 'The Definition of Love' a whole world turns on two perfect loves, placed as the North and South poles, which cannot 'close':

> Unless the giddy Heaven fall,
> And Earth some new Convulsion tear;
> And, us to joyn, the World should all
> Be cramped into a Planisphere.
>
> (lines 21–4)[29]

This text is, of course, both puzzling and plural. But 'The Definition', read *as* a definition, and not as a narrative, points to a fateful impossibility in the nature of love. If the two poles are to maintain their difference, their otherness, to sustain the structure of the world of love they constitute, they can never collapse into closure. As in my reading of 'The Good-morrow', perfect, parallel loves cannot 'meet' (line 28). Here anxiety gives way to despair.

And yet, paradoxically, this is the historical moment at which desire becomes the basis of a lifetime of concord. The modern nuclear family is increasingly defined in this period as the centre of society, the place where social values are learned and reproduced. Marriage is no longer a question primarily of property, and the transmission of names, titles, entitlements; and the relation between love and marriage is no longer a matter of indifference. On the contrary, the privileged, intimate world of 'The Sunne Rising' and 'The Good-morrow' is in the process of becoming the foundation of conjugal partnership, where love and consent ensure the harmony of the family and the proper inculcation in the next generation of consensual assumptions, beliefs, meanings.

But, these texts suggest, there is an anxiety at the heart of love itself, an uncertainty about the degree to which is it acceptable or possible to be in possession of the worlds desire makes visible. And it is perhaps to allay this anxiety that notions of property and appropriation reappear in the new model of marriage. In Milton's Paradise wedded love is the 'sole propriety' 'of all things common else', and the word 'propriety' points to the degree of possession – of mind and body, behaviour and disposition – inscribed in the new ideal of marriage.[30] 'For love, all love of other sights controules' ('The Good-morrow', line 10). True love is a mode of policing the gaze, excluding errant desires, bringing the subject into line. As property, as possession, the object of desire now promises to fill the hollow at the heart of the subject, making a totality in the place of lack. The territorial imagery of the poems is thus not incidental. The nuclear family precisely makes one little room an every where, takes possession of the space it occupies, in order to create and populate a microcosmic private realm, designed to keep at bay the public world of the economy, politics and history.[31]

VI

The Renaissance is also the historical moment when love stories begin commonly to end in marriage. Henry James marks the beginning of the end of that epoch – at least in English literature. *The Golden Bowl*, first published in 1904, records Maggie Verver's struggle to preserve the conjugal family by mastering the errant desire of the Prince for Charlotte Stant. It is a battle for propriety in every sense, for decorum, for the Prince as property, for the possession of knowledge, for control of the gaze. By a herculean effort Maggie resists surrender to her own desire, and a consequent submission to the will of the Prince which would lead to complaisance.[32] Their conflict of wills and knowledges holds the couple together 'in the steel hoop of an intimacy compared with which artless passion would have been but a beating of the air' (p. 396). In the end, the American Ververs triumph. But what exactly does Maggie gain? The final words of the novel show the degree to which the Prince gives way:

> He tried, too clearly, to please her – to meet her in her own way; but with the result only that, close to her, her face kept before him, his hands

holding her shoulders, his whole act enclosing her, he presently echoed: '"See?" I see nothing but *you.*' And the truth of it had, with this force, after a moment, so strangely lighted his eyes that, as for pity and dread of them, she buried her own in his breast. (p. 547)

The gesture is a long-deferred embrace, but pity and dread are the emotions of tragedy. The syntax ('He tried . . . but . . .') indicates that the Prince fails to please, to meet Maggie in her own way. She desires him, desires his desire. He tries to be what she wants, becomes her image, declares himself her mirror. But the reflection is too evidently imaginary. And 'he' remains uncannily, unsatisfyingly elsewhere, the isolated subject of his own gaze and his enunciation, recognizing in due course the tragic 'truth' of his utterance. In this text the victory of the family is the defeat of desire.

VII

So much for the epoch of true love and the ideal of reciprocity as a basis for partnership. As for John Donne's poetry, in its minute attention to the perplexities of desire, it can be read as identifying problems that proponents (then and now) of family values centred on the conjugal couple generally prefer to forget.

7

Demon Lovers

I

Tempest-tossed by the winds of Aeolus, and pelted with rocks at the hands of the giant Laestrygonians, Odysseus and his crew are relieved to find shelter on the island of Circe. The beautiful goddess, daughter of the Sun and grand-daughter of the Ocean, welcomes into her palace an advance party from the ship, by offering them a dish of poisoned delicacies that turn them instantly into pigs. Mercifully, Odysseus is not among them. Hermes warns Odysseus of Circe's habitual practice, equipping him with an antidote and clear instructions on how to deal with the goddess. In consequence, Odysseus suffers no ill effects from her ministrations, and when Circe orders him off to the pigsty, he rushes upon her with drawn sword. Realizing who he must be, she at once invites him to her bed, and after extracting her promise to do him and his men no further harm, Odysseus accepts her invitation. In due course, the first group are released from their enchantment; a year passes rapidly in feasting and delight; and at the end of it Circe willingly sends the sailors on their way.

In Homer's account Circe is both seductive and dangerous, but the danger she represents is not directly sexual. On the contrary, it is her cooking that turns men into beasts. There is no indication that Odysseus derives anything but pleasure from sharing her bed, or that he experiences any particular difficulty in leaving it. Sexual relations with a woman who has magic powers are not in themselves either transforming or destructive. Subsequently Ovid retells Homer's story without substantial alteration, though in addition it appears that when Circe's passion is involved and her love is rejected, she also turns women into rocks and men into woodpeckers.[1]

In 1590 Edmund Spenser published the first three books of his allegorical epic romance, *The Faerie Queene*, a text which combines the effects of classical Renaissance, Italian humanism and Protestant Reformation. Here Circe's textual descendant, Acrasia, also turns men into beasts in her Bower of Bliss, but this time the process is explicitly erotic. Long wanton joys, which feed Acrasia's lusts, now rob knights of their honour and their humanity, until they are no better than the animals they finally become. Erotic pleasure, rendered obsessional, humiliates and degrades, we are to understand, and its representative in Spenser's allegory is a woman with magic powers. A compulsion so irresistible that it leaves rational creatures other than they are must be more than human, supernatural; and its un-accountable tyranny is readily projected onto the figure who seems to be its cause. Acrasia is one of a succession of insatiable and remorse-less female objects of desire who have achieved a continuing notoriety in Western culture: the Whore of Babylon, Morgan Le Fay, La Belle Dame Sans Merci, the Fairy Melusine and any number of sirens and mermaids, demonic women beyond the reach of compassion or conscience.

Acrasia's garden of love offers every kind of delight to the senses, and Sir Guyon, the knight of Temperance, makes it the mission of his own odyssey to demolish the Bower and imprison its enchanting mistress. And yet he acts with quite extraordinary violence, laying waste the garden in a storm of rage, turning fair into foul, pleasure to dismay.[2] Offered a bowl of wine by the porter at the garden gate, Guyon overturns it with disdain, and breaks the porter's staff into the bargain. When Excess presents a cup of liquor which she has squeezed from the fruit with her own tender hand, Guyon snatches it from her and dashes it to the ground. Finally, he traps Acrasia in a net from which there is no escape, and rases her palace to its foundations. This oddly intemperate conduct has proved deeply disturbing to twentieth-century literary criticism, which has tended to take sides for or against Guyon's (or 'Spenser's') vehemently puritanical rejection of sexual pleasure. No one in this century wants to appear so naive as to come out against sex in general, and in any case the Garden of Adonis in Book III is a palpable endorsement of reproductive love, so the question confronting Guyon's supporters has been what exactly it is that Acrasia represents and he repudiates.

Almost certainly the most convincing of Guyon's apologists is still C. S. Lewis, who identified in *The Allegory of Love* a duality that runs all the way through Spenser's epic between truth and falsehood. The Bower of Bliss, with its vulgar golden ivy and its staged erotic spectacles, is false, Lewis points out; it is artifice as opposed to nature. The Bower represents a sterile and deadly sexuality, while true love is natural, fecund and vital. And true love, of course, means marriage. In the heroic story *The Allegory of Love* so brilliantly recounts, Spenser features as the knight of matrimony, and Books III and IV of *The Faerie Queene* constitute 'the final defeat of courtly love by the romantic conception of marriage'.[3] Spenser's poem thus inaugurates a new set of values, which is 'now' (in 1936) under attack from many quarters, feminism and psychoanalysis among them, and which Lewis's own account by implication sets out to defend:

> In the history of sentiment he is the greatest among the founders of that romantic conception of marriage which is the basis of all our love literature from Shakespeare to Meredith.[4]

Though I do not share Lewis's values, or his commitment to inaugural moments and founding fathers, I find it hard to resist the outlines of the story he tells. *The Faerie Queene*, we might now want to say, is the product of a culture which is in the process of idealizing marriage as the location of true love. But at the same time, it is tempting to identify in Lewis's critical vocabulary, as he describes *The Faerie Queene*, a certain element of transferential repetition. By its imagery of 'attack' and 'defeat', of 'struggle between the romance of marriage and the romance of adultery',[5] *The Allegory of Love* seems to re-enact Guyon's own battle against false love itself. Meanwhile the reader is incited to be 'armed' against the pleasures of the Bower of Bliss, alert to its 'danger signals'.[6] And to this end the critic denounces the delights the poem depicts with a vehemence which, like Guyon's, seems in excess of the delicate structure against which it is directed:

> The Bower of Bliss is . . . a picture, one of the most powerful ever painted, of the whole sexual nature in disease. There is not a kiss or an embrace in the island: only male prurience and female provocation.[7]

By the time we have finished reading Lewis's account, 'when these facts have once been pointed out',[8] there is nothing left of the seduction of the Bower, or its lyrical invitation. The critic snatches the wine from the reader's hand, and lays waste the garden the text so poetically defines.

The most brilliant of C. S. Lewis's opponents, the most eloquent defender of the Bower's 'intense erotic appeal' and its 'continued sensual power', is surely Stephen Greenblatt in *Renaissance Self-Fashioning*.[9] Greenblatt concedes Lewis's reading at one level: he acknowledges the presence in the text of explicit ethical judgment and moral admonition. But his point is that this does not cancel out the reader's response to the pleasures the poem describes: we long, Greenblatt argues, to 'transvalue' the moralizing vocabulary of the text, even as we recognize the threat our seduction represents. And he goes on to find in the enticing dangers of the Bower of Bliss an analogy for the sensual paradise of the New World landscapes and the seductive intricacy of native American art. These the European colonizers were impelled to resist or destroy, officially in the name of civilization, but also in practice because they found themselves longing for the release and the beauty America represented.[10] Greenblatt's account of the text does much to correct what seems unbalanced in the opposite case, and his colonial analogy has shifted the paradigm for a whole generation of critics. But is there not at work here too, as perhaps in all reading, a certain unnamed transferential repetition? Can we not locate in the sympathy with the figures Guyon repudiates, and in the claims for the values of the New World against European imperialism, an assertion also of the New Historicism against the old, and an affirmation of American independence in the face of a formerly oppressive European critical self-righteousness?

In any case, the problem with both these readings is that by aligning themselves for or against Guyon, and by conflating Guyon implicitly or explicitly with Spenser, they ultimately re-enact the fictional struggle depicted within the narrative, and in the process they tend to efface the critical distance. For all their subtlety, for all their close attention to the text, both interpretations have in the end the paradoxical effect of stripping away the poem's artifice in the course of unveiling its 'truth'. How then might we, without having recourse either to Guyon-Spenser's puritanism, or to an authorial identification of 'civility' with power, make a different sense of the Bower of Bliss and the demonic love it so copiously defines?

In the quest for an answer, I invoke another (American) critic. Paul Alpers sees in the golden ivy which adorns the fountain a *trompe-l'oeil*, but one which makes apparent to the attentive spectator and to the reader its own deception.

> And over all, of purest gold was spred,
>   A trayle of yvie in his native hew:
>   For the rich metall was so coloured,
>   That wight, who did not well avis'd it vew,
>   Would surely deeme it to be yvie trew:
>   Low his lascivious armes adown did creepe,
>   That themselves dipping in the silver dew,
>   Their fleecy flowres they tenderly did steepe,
> Which drops of Christall seemd for wantones to weepe.
>
> (II.12.61)

A *trompe-l'oeil* deceives the eye. Viewed from a slightly different angle, the three-dimensional object dissolves into flat lines on a plane surface, proclaims itself a fake. By analogy, the ivy of Spenser's text is explicitly metal and the colour we are offered is gold, not green. 'Any deception that occurs,' Alpers comments, 'is impossible without our active assent and enjoyment.' But the knowledge that it deceives does not preclude the enjoyment of the luxuriant sensuality the following lines depict.[11] We do the text no injustice, therefore, if in our pleasure we momentarily ignore the simulated character of the voluptuous branches, and the feathery flowers, dripping with water that resembles tears. Like the allurements of the garden in general, like the beckoning maidens displaying their bodies in the fountain, and like the soft sighs of Acrasia herself, the erotic availability of the Bower, its capacity to give pleasure, is an illusion at once pleasing and dangerous, which the text both specifies as illusory and invites us to share.

This reading problematizes on the one hand Lewis's assumption that to see through the deception is to defeat its seductive power, and on the other hand Greenblatt's view that the recognition of its deceptive character does not substantially affect the Bower's erotic invitation. But the value of Alpers's account is not its appeal to the spirit of compromise, a 'poise' or balance between two competing interpretations. 'What is it', Lacan asks, 'that attracts and satisfies us in *trompe-l'oeil?*'

When is it that it captures our attention and delights us? At the moment when, by a mere shift of our gaze, we are able to realize that the representation does not move with the gaze and that it is merely a *trompe-l'oeil*. For it appears at that moment as something other than it seemed, or rather it now seems to be that something else . . . This other thing is the *petit a* . . .[12]

Trompe-l'oeil invokes the *objet a*, the cause of desire. Like the duck-rabbit or the reversing cube, the *trompe-l'oeil* is first one thing, then another, now an object, now a picture of an object. It works only if it persuades *as an illusion*, deludes; and it works only if we can see that it is an illusion, that we were deluded. The gap between the two moments, Lacan proposes, is the location of desire.

It is this lack of a single position of mastery which sustains desire in the Bower of Bliss. Spenser's garden offers an erotic spectacle, seduction staged for a spectator. The narrative leads Guyon through a succession of increasingly enticing scenes until, at the heart of the Bower, he discovers Acrasia herself, a perfect centrefold:

> Upon a bed of Roses she was layd,
>   As faint through heat, or dight to pleasant sin,
>   And was arayd, or rather disarayd,
>   All in a vele of silke and silver thin,
>   That hid no whit her alabaster skin,
>   But rather shewd more white, if more might bee:
>   More subtile web *Arachne* cannot spin,
>   Nor the fine nets, which oft we woven see
> Of scorched deaw, do not in th'aire more lightly flee.
>
> Her snowie brest was bare to readie spoyle
>   Of hungry eies, which n'ote therewith be fild,
>   And yet through languour of her late sweet toyle,
>   Few drops, more cleare then Nectar, forth distild,
>   That like pure Orient perles adowne it trild,
>   And her faire eyes sweet smyling in delight,
>   Moystened their fierie beames, with which she thrild

Fraile harts, yet quenched not; like starry light
Which sparckling on the silent waves, does seeme more bright.

(77–8)

Acrasia offers herself as an erotic spectacle to the (here male, hetero-sexual) gaze; her veil does not conceal, but enhances her beauty. Why then does she not 'fill', 'quench', satisfy the desire she elicits? Is it because at this point she offers no more than scopic pleasure? Or is it rather because the text has already set up as inevitable the moment when she will appear as something other than she seems, not this time a monster, like Duessa, but an illusion, a fantasy, insubstantial?

Since it is a text, the poem can have it both ways repeatedly. The narrative has no obligation to resolve its own indeterminacies, but can keep on alternating descriptive passages with affirmations that they depict illusions, thus sustaining the desire of the reader-critic to possess the single truth of the text, its author-ized meaning. But the evocation of this desire, bringing to light at the level of the signifier the reader's own compulsion to know for sure, might itself be part of the project of the allegory.

Parrhasios, Lacan points out, teases Zeuxis by painting a veil so lifelike that Zeuxis wants to know what is behind it.[13] At the entrance to the Bower is an ivory gate on which can be read the history of Medea's 'furious loving' and Jason's 'falsed faith' (44–6). 'Ye might have seene', the text asserts, the billows beneath the Argo,

> That seemd the waves were into yvory,
> Or yvory into the waves were sent.

Here is another *trompe-l'oeil*, now water, now ivory, so convincingly does the one seem to turn into the other and back again. But the acknowledgement of art's power to deceive does not dispel the associations of the tale it depicts, the love story of Medea, Circe's niece, another dangerous woman with magic powers. The explicit deception does not call into question the appropriateness of an allusion at the entrance into the garden of love to the threat involved in demonic passion. On the contrary, the *trompe-l'oeil* affirms the ingenuity of the artist and the complexity of fiction. The text offers what seems like an infinite regress of textuality: a poem which is nothing if not intricate, describing an ivory gate that is a miracle of art, depicting a mythological story that indicates the dangers implicit in desire for a woman who is not merely what she seems. The text itself is not a covering for a truth, whether this truth is conceived as moral or poetic. Like Acrasia's gossamer veil, like the picture painted by Parrhasios, the text does not conceal a hidden reality. But it falls in folds, producing varying degrees of density in different places. And to the extent that any fiction is itself a *trompe-l'oeil*, it is no use hoping to discover what lies behind the veil.[14]

The Bower of Bliss represents the spectacle of desire. At the same time, as a *trompe-l'oeil*, it invites recognition of the uncertainty that promotes desire and the indeterminacy which threatens to withhold satisfaction. No wonder Guyon has to destroy it. The knight of Temperance aspires to rational self-control, government by the univocal consciousness which constitutes his identity: he cannot recognize undecidability; he must not acknowledge the irresistible power of forbidden desire, or succumb to the otherness of an impulse that a later age would classify as unconscious. Instead, therefore, he captures Acrasia in a net from which she cannot escape. In Lacanian terms Guyon represents the Law, which both produces and excludes desire, the *Non* that invokes castration as the penalty for forbidden love. Understood as a figure in an allegory, not a character in a novel, Guyon can only loathe the seductions that throw into relief the difference between seeing and knowing, and the distance between the aspiration to temperance and the human condition that so far exceeds it. Spenser's narrative records an act of aggression directed not so much against pleasure, as against the desire that challenges the sovereignty of rational consciousness, and thus against a humanity that is both more and less than its own ideal humanist image.

In his account of the *trompe-l'oeil* Lacan is concerned specifically with painting itself, though elsewhere in the same seminar he discusses the scopic drive in more general terms. As painting, of course, *trompe-l'oeil* sublimates desire and thus has a 'civilizing' effect.[15] The declared project of Spenser's poem is 'to fashion a gentleman or noble person in vertuous and gentle discipline', by putting before the reader an example in the person of Prince Arthur, since fictions are often more persuasive than precepts.[16] In the course of its civilizing project, *The Faerie Queene* dedicates rich poetic resources to the pleasures Guyon destroys: the text, after all, produces for the reader the delights that it identifies as prohibited. And it prohibits them in the name of an emerging tax-onomy which later generations would refine, the system of differences which justified the romance of marriage and progressively cemented the triumph of true love. Spenser's reader is to become civilized by learning to choose marriage in place of unsatisfied desire.

The Bower of Bliss will palpably not do as the foundation for a lifetime of concord, not primarily because it is false, but because it is precarious, unstable, insubstantial. The bond of marriage depends precisely on certainty, and it builds an enclosure of a wholly different kind, turning people into birds who do not want to fly:

> Sweet be the bands, the which true love doth tye,
>   without constraynt or dread of any ill:
>   the gentle bird feeles no captivity
>   within her cage, but singes and feeds her fill.
> There pride dare not approch, nor discord spill
>   the league twixt them, that loyal love hath bound:
>   but simple truth and mutuall good will,
>   seekes with sweet peace to salve each others wound:
> There fayth doth fearlesse dwell in brasen towre,
>   and spotlesse pleasure builds her sacred bowre.[17]

In *The Faerie Queene* the proper place for sexual pleasure is the repro-ductive Garden of Adonis. Here there is no *trompe-l'oeil*, no seductive spectacle, no spectator-subject, no appearances, indeed, but only sub-stance, the real thing. There is in consequence certainty, steadfast love and stable happiness, but not, as far as I can detect, any trace of desire.

II

At least Guyon had the good sense not to marry Acrasia. More than two centuries later, however, in Keats's *Lamia* (1820), the hero Lycius makes the mistake of marrying the demon-mistress of his dream. Lycius pays for this error with his life, when Apollonius comes to the wedding, penetrates with his knowing, philosophic gaze to the serpent in Lamia, and causes the bride to vanish. Here again the critical temptation is to seek to uncover what lies behind the veil of the text, to reveal the moral, thematic truth of Keats's poem. Is Lamia good or bad? Is philosophy right or wrong? What is the status of dreams? But *Lamia* too evades our question precisely to the degree that the textuality of the poem exceeds its thematic readings.

To some extent Lamia's identity is given in advance of the text. Keats's immediate source was Burton's *Anatomy of Melancholy*, but Burton in turn draws on a figure who can be traced back to the folklore of the Hellenic world, where a lamia was a night-witch, a vampire, and a shape-changer.[18] No repetition is ever exact, however, and Keats's serpent-woman with the 'Circean head',[19] however ethically casual, is not apparently malevolent. She is not, it must be granted, virtuous, and certainly not a feminist: she takes the gift of human form from Hermes in exchange for facilitating a rape. And she is sexually knowing: 'in the lore/Of love deep learnèd to the red heart's core' (I, 189–90); she puts up no resistance to Lycius's mildly perverse, sado-masochistic notion of pleasure (II, 69–81). Moreover, truth is evidently a matter of indifference to her, but then we should hardly expect anything else.

Like Acrasia's, Lamia's seduction is spectacular. Even as a serpent, she is highly coloured, brilliantly visible, 'rainbow-sided' (I, 54). In the nineteenth-century text the spectacle of desire is less direct than in *The Faerie Queene*, displaced from the body onto Lamia's 'purple-lined' palace (II, 31) with its dark-veined porch, its marble columns, silken couches, and fine-textured curtains which 'unveil' the sky beyond (II, 21). It is the palace itself, constructed in order to be seen, which is most elaborately adorned, decked and garlanded, for the wedding feast.

Lamia's supreme expertise is the feminine masquerade. Like Joan Riviere's competent female analysand, she knows how to deflect male anxiety and reprisal:

> Let the mad poets say whate'er they please
> Of the sweets of Fairies, Peris, Goddesses,
> There is not such a treat among them all,
> Haunters of cavern, lake, and waterfall,
> As a real woman, lineal indeed
> From Pyrrha's pebbles or old Adam's seed.
> Thus gentle Lamia judged, and judged aright,
> That Lycius could not love in half a fright,
> So threw the goddess off, and won his heart
> More pleasantly by playing woman's part.
>
> (I, 328–37)

'A real woman': is the suddenly worldly text ironic here? And what, in any case, is 'a real woman'? In her essay on the masquerade, Riviere's radical proposition is that femininity is precisely no more than 'playing woman's part':

> The reader may now ask how I define womanliness or where I draw the line between genuine womanliness and the 'masquerade'. My suggestion is not, however, that there is any such difference; whether radical or superficial, they are the same thing.[20]

Apollonius, the philosopher, thinks he knows what is real. He subjects Lamia to his piercing gaze, looks behind the veil of her appearance, and finally, triumphantly names her: 'A serpent!' (II, 305). But he is wrong – to the degree that she exceeds the taxonomy available to any analysis which seeks the singular truth of her identity. For she is precisely a lamia, a shape-changer, once a woman, then a serpent with a sad-eyed woman's face, and now 'a lady bright' (I, 171). Moreover, as a lamia, she belongs to the world of dreams, the place where she first encountered Lycius and fell in love with him (I, 215–19). This is a world that is invisible to Apollonius: all he can see is a serpent. 'Philosophy', the poem famously asserts, 'will clip an Angel's wings,/Conquer all mysteries . . . Unweave a rainbow' (II, 234–7). Apollonius is paradoxically blind to the Dionysian spectacle Lamia creates for Lycius, and his blindness has the effect of annihilating the dream he cannot perceive.

What is a dream? It is, Lacan points out, a place of intense visibility, where the world *shows*, highly coloured, brightly lit.[21] Like Acrasia's Bower or Lamia's gorgeous palace, the dream is *spectacular*. But what also *shows* in the dream, however obliquely, however figuratively, is unconscious desire [*ça montre*[22]], and this is so because in the dream the *Cogito* as *self*-consciousness is suspended. It is possible in a dream to reflect, Lacan maintains, but it is not possible to reflect on oneself reflecting, to apprehend the self as thought.[23] The dream is thus a spectacle of desire which escapes the self-conscious, censorious restraints and prohibitions of consciousness.

Desire, meanwhile, is inevitably specular, scopic: it includes the pleasure of looking. And this is true not only for men, as contemporary Western culture often urges, and pictorial pornography commonly implies. In other epochs, the Elizabethan among them, masculinity as spectacle has been taken for granted, and indeed in the animal kingdom display as a mode of seduction is predominantly, though not invariably, male. In the course of this display, during the visual rituals of courtship, which include preening and parading, paint or adornment, a spectacular appearance is adopted and a masquerade performed. 'It is no doubt through the mediation of masks that the masculine and the feminine meet in the most acute, most intense way.'[24] The process, motivated by unconscious desire, renders both sexes other than they are – which is not, of course, to say that what they *are* is either singular or accessible. On the contrary, as desiring subjects, what we are is crucially duplicitous.

In the ordinary course of things, too, human beings look, but they are also looked at, and it is this that in the scopic field turns them into subjects. We make of ourselves a picture for others; we become what they want to see, what they are able to see. But the process entails a loss, a splitting, because it separates off the unconscious, which others precisely cannot see, and so obscures our difference from ourselves; the waking subject is thus confined to what is perceptible. Choang-tsu dreams that he is a butterfly. 'In the dream, he is a butterfly for nobody. It is when he is awake that he is Choang-tsu for others, and is caught in their butterfly net.'[25] By its capture of unconscious desire in a net, the *Cogito* both constrains and reduces what we are. Naming Bishop Berkeley as the philosopher who took the Cartesian tradition to its limits, by holding that nothing exists but what is perceptible, Lacan claims that the philosophic gaze appropriates the power of annihilation.[26]

Lycius determines to marry Lamia in order to put her on show, that is, to make of her masquerade, which is designed for him, a spectacle for others:

> What mortal hath a prize, that other men
> May be confounded and abashed withal,
> But lets it sometimes pace abroad majestical,
> And triumph, as in thee I should rejoice
> Amid the hoarse alarm of Corinth's voice.
>
> (II, 57–61)

As a motive for marriage this is probably not all that eccentric. Lamia, however, immediately grasps the implications of his plan, and weeps;

she beseeches him to change his mind; but he revels in her suffering and refuses to relent. His explicit aim is to capture her in a net, 'to entangle, trammel up and snare/Your soul in mine, and labyrinth you there' (II, 52–3). No sooner, however, has Lycius unveiled his bride, shown his dream to the fixed and fixing gaze of the philosopher, than Apollonius annihilates his object of desire and the desiring subject with her. The dream is dispelled by the waking world of the reductive *Cogito*, which seeks the closure of a single truth.

The question arises, however, whether by interpreting Keats's text as an allegory of Lacanian psychoanalysis, or by invoking Lacan as the key to the 'true' meaning of Keats's text, I do not simply repeat the Apollonian, annihilating gesture of thematic reading. Not quite, I think, to the degree that the reading does not exhaust the poem. For Keats's text is also a *trompe-l'oeil*, in that it moves suddenly and surely between distinct modes. To the degree that it comments, evaluates, explains and, indeed, denounces, the text inhabits the waking world we know. But at other moments it incarnates, as even the Lacanian text does not, the world of dreams, in which nothing is impossible, nothing forbidden. The setting of Lamia's metamorphosis precedes the advent of Law: it exists,

> Upon a time, before the fairy broods
> Drove Nymph and Satyr from the prosperous woods,
> Before king Oberon's bright diadem,
> Sceptre, and mantle clasped with dewy gem,
> Frighted away the Dryads and the Fauns.
>
> (I, 1–5)

This realm, older even than folklore, prior to the coming of those fairy lands that Keats would elsewhere recognize as now 'forlorn',[27] is one of total omnipotence, without monarch or sceptre, without rule. In such a setting rape is miraculously not rape, but love (I, 134–45), since after all dreams know no prohibition. And truth is not an issue because reflection acknowledges no possibility of exclusion:

> The way in which dreams treat the category of contraries and contradictories is highly remarkable. It is simply disregarded. 'No' seems not to exist so far as dreams are concerned. They show a particular

preference for combining contraries into a unity or for representing them as one and the same thing.[28]

Thus in Keats's version, when Lamia makes visible to Hermes the nymph he loves, what she enables him to see is both a dream and its opposite, both non-truth and truth, since these contraries are also synonymous:

> It was no dream; or say a dream it was,
> Real are the dreams of Gods, and smoothly pass
> Their pleasures in a long immortal dream.
>
> (I, 126–8)

Where the negative does not exist, reality cannot exclude the dream, nor the dream reality.

What is most remarkable in *Lamia* is that by a mere shift of register the text easily returns the reader to the arena of knowing wit and worldly wisdom, so that the dreamworld suddenly appears as something other than it seemed. Meanwhile, within the philosopher's regime of truth, Lamia is plausibly enough a lie, and the insistent '*No!*' of Apollonius justified (II, 304), though that regime is characterized above all by loss. Philosophy is the quest for closure in the name of truth.[29] From the point of view of the reader, Apollonius's scopic mastery of Lamia's illusion is now vindicated, now itself illusory, but in either case the source of a deprivation that readily stands for the cause of desire. Meanwhile the poem, refusing to deliver a unified position of certainty for the reader, sustains but does not gratify the desire it constructs for knowledge of its own truth, for closure at the level of the signified.[30]

Within Keats's narrative, of course, Apollonius secures a victory, even if a Pyrrhic one, for truth. How, after all, prior to the psychoanalytic account of the unconscious, could the world of dreams seem other than an escapist invention? More recently Derrida, drawing on Nietzsche's account of the feminine masquerade, has invoked 'woman', as an analogy for writing, to challenge the *Cogito*, the truth-seeking missile of the philosophical tradition. The veiled figure of 'woman', Derrida urges, exceeds the alternatives of truth and falsehood. As with writing, the veil is not there to conceal, but to make visible. In consequence, both 'woman' and writing have the power to reveal the blindness of philosophy, by refusing the distinctions and exclusions, the identities and essences, on which the possession of truth depends. Derrida's interest here is in the capacity of 'woman', as the non-truth of truth, to hurl the questing knight of reason from his [blinkered] horse.[31]

But this triumphant Derridean reversal of the Apollonian victory would return us to the present, and first there is something more to be said about the past.

III

The nineteenth century, as the work of Mario Praz long ago established, was the great age of demon lovers.[32] Romantic agony, the recognition of an intimate relationship between pleasure and pain, desire and horror, love and hate, constituted a form of literary resistance to the clear and distinct ideas that the Enlightenment required in philosophy, as well as to the intense Victorian regulation and moralization of private and public life. It was in the nineteenth century that demonic women, sexually knowing, powerful and dangerous, became widespread enough in fiction to constitute a recognizable stereotype. Tennyson's Vivien and Swinburne's Mary Stuart in the writing of the period, Rossetti's *Proserpine* and *Astarte Syriaca* in painting, all seem to promise the seductive fatality of forbidden love. Meanwhile, as the examples of Coleridge's Geraldine and Le Fanu's Carmilla indicate, demonic women sometimes ignore heterosexual orthodoxy, which in a predominantly homophobic culture renders them at once more threatening and more thrilling.

In other instances, demon lovers also exceed the alternatives of life and death, thus stretching to the limits the distinctions and exclusions on which culture depends. As Edgar Allan Poe's 'Ligeia' (1838) reaches its uncanny conclusion, the narrator's lost love returns to animate the body of his second wife. When the corpse of the fair-haired, blue-eyed Lady Rowena rises from her bed of death, she throws off the grave clothes in which she is shrouded to reveal the lustrous dark hair and the unfathomable black eyes of the long-dead Ligeia.

Like Acrasia and Lamia, Ligeia is not only beautiful but also sexually knowing: she shows a 'more than womanly abandonment' to love.[33] And this time the indeterminacy which also characterizes these predecessors is made explicit in the account of Ligeia from the beginning as 'strangeness'. His first wife's beauty, the unnamed narrator tells us, was pervaded by a 'strangeness' (the word is insistently repeated) that he could neither identify nor explain. It belonged supremely to her eyes, and yet it was not to be found in their physical form, though they were larger than normal. It was, on the contrary, a *depth*, perhaps a forbidden knowledge (p. 114):

What was it — that something more profound than the well of Democritus — which lay far within the pupils of my beloved? What *was* it? (p. 112)

The question is not answered. Many times, the narrator tells us, he has felt as if he is close to grasping its meaning, and each time the explanation finally eludes him (p. 113). The text, indeed, begins with what the narrator does *not* know about Ligeia: 'I cannot, for my soul, remember how, when, or even precisely where, I first became acquainted with the lady Ligeia' (p. 110). Such details are incidental, perhaps, when what is at stake is passion, but the narrator's ignorance about her turns out to include her family, and even, though she subsequently became his wife, her surname. Ligeia is thus from the beginning explicitly mysterious, unknown, inexplicable, uncanny.

Many people, Freud notes, experience a sense of the uncanny especially strongly in relation to death, dead bodies, revenants, ghosts.[34] In Freud's account the uncanny depends on indeterminacy. The essay begins with a kind of linguistic *trompe-l'oeil*. The German *heimlich* means familiar (homely), recognizable, safe, Freud affirms, but a shift of attention brings out another and precisely opposite meaning: the *heimlich* is also hidden, unknown, dangerous.[35] Conversely, therefore, *unheimlich* can also be invested with two antithetical meanings: known and unknown. The uncanny, Freud maintains, is the familiar that ought to have remained hidden, something dangerous which demands recognition, the return, in other words, of the repressed. A frisson marks the moment when two incommensurable knowledges, conscious and unconscious, are brought into play simultaneously. The sense of the uncanny is generated either on the one hand by the repetition at the level of consciousness of repressed material, or on the other by an encounter with ancient cultural beliefs or superstitions which have not been adequately surmounted. It is for this reason, Freud argues, that revenants are especially uncanny. In the first place, the unconscious, as the terrain of desire, knows nothing of death: there is thus a sense in which we all unconsciously subscribe to a 'belief' in life after death; at the same time, modern science has so little to say about death that an archaic fear of ghosts is not far from the surface of our culture. In consequence, the border between life and death is on two counts both clear and unclear, simultaneously fixed and permeable. The revenant thus constitutes the repetition of a knowledge that the unconscious already possesses and the Enlightened *Cogito* forbids.

Ligeia's return is both possible and impossible, and once again the text refuses to resolve the indeterminacies it sets up. Is the animated corpse real or an illusion? Is it indeed Ligeia, or something quite different? If it *is* Ligeia, what *was* she, and are we closer to solving the mystery of her strange and unaccountable gaze? Is the resurrection of the narrator's lost love a welcome reunion or a visitation from hell? Is the figure 'really' alive or dead, and what, in any case, do those terms mean, what is their difference? The text does not say.

All these are in one sense questions of genre. Are we to read Poe's tale, in other words, as a ghost story, presupposing the existence of the supernatural? Or is it, conversely, a realist narrative about a deluded narrator, the subject of an opium dream?[36] The text stresses the power of his addiction to produce vivid hallucinations. During Rowena's unexplained illness, the narrator at her bedside sees, or thinks he sees, 'a faint, indefinite shadow of angelic aspect'. 'But I was wild', he goes on, 'with the excitement of an immoderate dose of opium . . .' (p. 122). Did he really see a brilliant, ruby-coloured fluid dropped into Rowena's medicine, or was it an effect of his morbid, drugged imagination? As he sits beside Rowena's corpse, 'Wild visions, opium-engendered, flitted, shadow-like, before me' (p. 122). How, in that case, are we to assess his final affirmation?

> 'Here, then, at least,' I shrieked aloud, 'can I never – can I never be mistaken – these are the full, and the black, and the wild eyes – of my lost love – of the lady – of the LADY LIGEIA.' (p. 126)

The unconscious does not acknowledge death. But whose unconscious is at stake in this story, the narrator's, or the reader's? Whose wish is gratified (and simultaneously appalled) by this uncanny resurrection? Once again, the question is one of genre. Freud, in quest of the experience of the uncanny, looks above all to fiction, and also confronts in the process the issue of genre. Fairy tales, after all, he points out, depend on an archaic, animistic system of beliefs, but they are not necessarily in consequence uncanny. On the contrary, we simply agree to share for the purpose of reading them the imagined supernatural world they presuppose. Similarly, Dante's souls or Shakespeare's ghosts, however seriously we take them, do not evoke the particular frisson which bears witness to the uncanny, since this depends on a 'conflict' between belief and incredulity. But the position changes when the text appears to represent the everyday world we seem to know. Then the intrusion of the supernatural has a quite different effect. The most powerful instances of uncanny writing, Freud argues, are those which keep us guessing about the presuppositions of the world defined in the fiction, especially if they 'cunningly and ingeniously avoid any definite information on the point to the last'.[37]

'Ligeia' holds out in this respect to the end, and thus provides the promised frisson for the reader. But there is a further evasion in this text, which places its uncanny effect squarely in the realm of textuality itself. 'Ligeia' is intensely allusive. Introducing the question of the protagonist's mysterious attraction, the tale quotes Bacon's *Essays*:

> 'There is no exquisite beauty,' says Bacon, Lord Verulam, speaking truly of all the forms and *genera* of beauty, 'without some *strangeness* in the proportion.' (p. 111)

Ligeia's luxuriant hair evokes 'the Homeric epithet, "hyacinthine"' (p. 111).[38] Her name comes from Milton, who got it from Virgil: in the *Georgics* it belongs to a nymph with shining tresses floating over her white neck (IV, 336–7), while in *Comus* Milton turns his Ligea into something closely resembling a mermaid, and thus yet another kind of demon lover, 'Sleeking her soft alluring locks' (lines 879–81). Poe's heroine reminds the narrator of Hebrew medallions and Greek art. Moreover, the epigraph from Joseph Glanvill, cited three times in the course of the story, invites us to adopt it as an 'explanation' of Ligeia's improbable return:

And the will therein lieth, which dieth not. Who knoweth the mysteries of the will, with its vigor? For God is but a great will pervading all things by the nature of its intentness. Man doth not yield himself to the angels, nor unto death utterly, save only through the weakness of his feeble will.

Ligeia, who did not want to die, was an exceptionally strong-willed woman . . .

The effect of all these allusions is paradoxical. On the one hand, they *authorize* the extraordinary story, invest it with the authority of serious writing, classic texts. 'Lord Verulam' is oddly more dignified than simple Bacon; Glanvill was a Cambridge Platonist. The citations ground the disturbing events of the story in references which are familiar, or are made to seem so. They thus have the effect of reversing the procedures of the uncanny, which disturbs what we (think we) already know. At the same time, however, the ground the allusions provide is precisely textuality, other texts, not an extra-textual truth. And in the case of Milton's mermaid, the reference is overtly mythological. Curiously enough, the Glanvill quotation has not been traced. Is it possible that this is an invention? And is there not something in itself uncanny about an apocryphal quotation, attributed to a philosopher, which 'explains' the uncanny events of a tale about a demon lover?

Possibly the oddest allusion of all is to Ashtophet. The narrator wants to explain why he has forgotten Ligeia's origins. Is it, perhaps, a romantic oversight? 'And indeed', he continues,

> if ever that spirit which is entitled *Romance* – if ever she, the wan and misty-winged *Ashtophet* of idolatrous Egypt, presided, as they tell me, over marriages ill-omened, then most surely she presided over mine. (pp. 110–11)

Ashtophet, the editor explains, is also an invention. The word suggests both Ashtoreth, the fertility goddess, and Tophet, a version of hell associated with the worship of Moloch, to whom children were sacrificed (pp. 527–8). Divine female sexuality on the one hand, death and hell on the other: the exotic name produced to account for the loss of Ligeia's, the name which takes the place of hers, and thus of the protagonist's lost origins, 'Ashtophet' surely reproduces at the level of the signifier, which is to say repeats, the unresolved duality of both the demon lover herself and the text that tells her story.

IV

The presence that rose thus so strangely beside the waters, is expressive of what in the ways of a thousand years men had come to desire. Hers is the head upon which all 'the ends of the world are come', and the eyelids are a little weary. It is a beauty wrought out from within upon the flesh, the deposit, little cell by cell, of strange thoughts and fantastic reveries and exquisite passions. Set it for a moment beside one of those white Greek goddesses or beautiful women of antiquity, and how would they be troubled by this beauty, into which the soul with all its maladies has passed! All the thoughts and experience of the world have etched and moulded there, in that which they have of power to refine and make expressive the outward form, the animalism of Greece, the lust of Rome, the mysticism of the middle age with its spiritual ambition and im- aginative loves, the return of the Pagan world, the sins of the Borgias. She is older than the rocks among which she sits; like the vampire, she has been dead many times, and learned the secrets of the grave; and has been a diver in deep seas, and keeps their fallen day about her; and trafficked for strange webs with Eastern merchants: and, as Leda, was the mother of Helen of Troy, and, as Saint Anne, the mother of Mary; and all this has been to her but as the sound of lyres and flutes, and lives only in the delicacy with which it has moulded the changing lineaments, and tinged the eyelids and the hands.[39]

Walter Pater's prose account, first published in 1873, and later in part relineated by Yeats as a poem,[40] of Leonardo's painting of *Mona Lisa* (or *La Gioconda*), surely recapitulates all the strangeness, all the exotic sexuality, all the citationality of the preceding demonic women. As the cause of desire, Pater's Mona Lisa exceeds rational explanation: she evokes a realm beyond the alternatives of good and evil, life and death and, we might add, truth and fiction. This uncanny revenant, whose troubling beauty seems to indicate a mysterious knowledge, promises both pleasure and danger, divinity and evil. And yet, paradoxically, she conceals nothing. Her occult lore, with its disregard of contraries, is engraved in the flesh itself, and is thus fully legible to the spectator. The 'origin', however, of Pater's account is no more than another text, a

Figure 2 *Mona Lisa*. Leonardo da Vinci, *La Joconde (Mona Lisa)*, Musee du Louvre. © Photo R.M.N., Paris.

picture of a woman about whom we know very little (Figure 2).

Pater's reading of the Renaissance painting would not now qualify as art history. There is no doubt that he looks at the picture, but most of what he sees is not there, is not *in* – that is to say – Leonardo's text. There are in the work of art on show in the Louvre no Borgias or vampires, no lyres and flutes. And yet the most casual visitor to the Louvre, without any knowledge of art history, might be able to recognize a 'troubling' quality that helps to vindicate Pater's reading, or at least invests it with a certain plausibility. Is it an effect of the unfathomable eyes, whose gaze so narrowly fails to meet our own, with the result that, like Ligeia's, they seem to possess a mysterious depth, an unspecified knowledge? Or is it a consequence, perhaps, of the disjunction between the expression of the eyes and the famous smile, now serene, now sinister, according to the position of the spectator?

Leonardo's painting belongs to the threshold of the modern world. It shakes off the ascetic theocentrism of medieval art, and proclaims the beauty and the richness of human flesh. A triangular composition suggests harmony, completeness: the woman is portrayed as unified and self-possessed. Perspective and oil paint permit a new mimetic quality in the finished work: the figure is apparently three-dimensional, the textures of skin and clothing palpable.

But where is this figure located? How does Mona Lisa relate to the remote, rocky setting, the bare cliffs, the water out of which, as Pater points out, she seems to materialize 'so strangely'? She sits in front of a stone parapet, and beyond it the mysterious, mythic background seems to contradict the mimetic effects of the technique, making it hard to recognize this painting as the portrait of an individual in a specific social context. The nature which defines the human being by its difference is as different as it could be: uninhabited, largely undomesticated, gothic. What are the distances involved? Where is the foreground of this wild setting against which the human figure appears suddenly improbable, precarious, cut off from nature by the demarcation line a third of the way up the picture, and yet rising out of it to gaze into an equally mysterious distance beyond the spectator? As the eye of the viewer slips between background and foreground, the woman is now enigmatic, possessed, unearthly; now familiar, self-possessed, supremely human.

On this reading, the painting proclaims the human subject as the location of an otherness which returns to haunt it as the condition of its being. Mona Lisa is not only an object of desire, but also a desiring subject, and thus necessarily other than she is. Pater invests her desire with the specific knowledges and fatalities developed in the nineteenth-century texts: Acrasia, by contrast, is not uncanny, though she is dangerous. But the indeterminacy Pater identifies in Leonardo's painting is surely a condition which defines and constitutes the human subjects of modernity who, by surmounting supernatural belief, have taken conscious and Enlightened control of their own destiny – or think they have.

V

Pater's Mona Lisa is what 'men had come to desire'. All the demon lovers I have discussed so far have been women, exactly as we should expect in a patriarchal culture. The object that comes to stand for the cause of desire, mysterious, enigmatic and elusive, endangers mastery, and mastery is predominantly the property of men. Control is threatened by the figure who throws into relief both the uncertainty of what we can know and the otherness that inhabits the subject, revealing in the process the limitations of the *Cogito*. And historically control is supremely a masculine preoccupation. In Western, Enlightened culture, truth legitimates government: decisions are made and executed in its name; undecidability does not produce legislation. How appropriate, then, and how predictable that the indeterminacy which promotes desire should be projected onto the figure who provokes it, and that this figure should be classified as supernatural, relegated as evil, and named as woman.

And yet there are, perhaps surprisingly, male demon lovers. Milton's Comus is the son of Circe, and though rhetoric is his primary mode of seduction, Comus is as attractive and as dangerous as Acrasia. In Milton's masque of 1634 Comus turns his victims into beasts. Milton's later figure of Satan is, of course, an arch-seducer, and if his approach to Eve is not so directly and overtly sexual, the transformation he effects is a great deal more terrible and more destructive. Like Comus, Satan is also deeply duplicitous: he inhabits other identities, appearing in the character of a mist, a toad, a serpent indiscriminately. Among his nineteenth-century textual descendants, Dracula is variously a bat, a wolf or a cloud of dancing particles. And in this respect, they both emulate the pagan Zeus, whose seductive masks include a bull, a ram and a dolphin, as well as Diana and a shower of gold, in a textual history which descends at least from Ovid's *Metamorphoses* to Yeats's 'Leda and the Swan'.

As king of the gods, Zeus rarely suffers any ill-effects from his erotic adventures, apart from Hera's reproaches and counter-plots. But Satan's malignity is represented as itself deeply tragic, the consequence of his own unfulfilled and unnameable desire to be other than he is. Satan bequeaths some of this anguish to his descendants, including Melmoth the Wanderer, Maturin's protagonist of 1820, who in order to avoid his hellish fate, is compelled to seek a mortal willing to change destinies with him. Melmoth comes closest to success, and indeed to redemption, with the woman who loves him enough to marry him, but even she is not prepared, in the end, to lose her own soul. And if Melmoth, whose eyes have a preternatural lustre, represents the desperation of the desire of the Other, Bram Stoker's Dracula in the novel of 1897 is surely its most stricken, most desolate incarnation.

Like their female counterparts, male demon lovers are represented as eliciting a response so intense that it seems to demand supernatural explanation. Moreover, they are remorseless in the execution of their desires, and in the process they reveal their victims to be helplessly other than they are. Dracula invades the dreams of the innocent Lucy Westenra, so that in sleep she is subject to a strange compulsion which she cannot account for by day. As the vampire effects his mysterious nightly transformation, Lucy sleepwalks to meet the object of her desire, and unknowingly opens windows to admit him to her bedroom. While she sleeps, she inadvertently reveals the sharpening of the canine teeth that disappears by day. In dreams she speaks in an uncharacteristically soft, voluptuous voice.

The male figures resemble demonic women, too, in the degree to which they baffle the oppositions on which the rational recognition of truth depends. They commonly have no single identity. The Great Silkie of the Scottish ballad tradition is a man on land and a seal in the water. He begets a human child, but returns and claims him from his mother in order to 'teach him for to swim the faem'.[41] Milton's Satan is simultaneously both angel and devil, heroic even in his destructive villainy. A familiar passage of *Paradise Lost* compares Satan, his dazzling brightness 'darkened' by his fall, to the sun in eclipse, diffusing an ominous twilight which 'perplexes monarchs' (I, 597–9). And Dracula, neither alive nor dead, neither wholly substantial nor totally immaterial, challenges the oppositions so carefully held in place by Enlightenment science.

Vampires, indeed, which can be male or female, of course, seem to take on a new and unholy vitality at exactly the moment when Enlightenment scientificity proclaims the supremacy of the *Cogito* and the objectivity of truth. Though they have ancient roots, vampires come to prominence in Western culture towards the end of the seventeenth century, at the moment of the Enlightenment.[42] Associated primarily with Eastern Europe, that strange territory familiar from travellers' tales, but seen as just beyond the reach of the new knowledges being produced in the West,[43] vampires initially hover uncertainly between the realms of fact and fiction. These mysterious, alien figures haunt a culture which is busy ridding itself internally of superstition and irrationality. Vampires emerge from the East to fascinate the Enlightened West.

To the degree that they blur the oppositions on which clear rational thinking and empiricist observation depend, vampires come in due course to represent everything that the Enlightenment cannot recognize. Life is the opposite of death: medical science depends on the ability to define the distinction. But vampires are the un-dead; they do not belong with the living; they spend their days in their coffins and inhabit the night; they have no *proper* place. Vampires have a material existence and they bring about material effects, but at the same time they cast no shadow and are not reflected in mirrors: they exceed the alternatives of presence and absence. Blood drinking is explicitly erotic. Love and hate are conventionally antithetical, but vampire love is simultaneously malevolent: it takes possession of the object of desire and in consequence destroys it. According to Thomas Laqueur, anatomy defines men and women as *opposite* sexes for the first time in the eighteenth century.[44] Vampire sexuality immediately deconstructs this newly established opposition: both male and female vampires penetrate their victims, but only after they have been penetrated by another vampire; meanwhile, it is the passive victim who provides the vital fluid.[45] Moreover, the beloved in due course becomes the child, blurring familial difference.

In Britain interest in vampires intensified in the late seventeenth century, just as the witch craze began to subside. An outbreak of East European vampirism was extensively reported in the Western press in the 1720s and 30s; the last British statute against witchcraft was repealed in 1736. This concurrence may be more than coincidental. Witchcraft was held to be real, a possible practice in a world dominated by the supernatural. By contrast, the earliest appearances of the vampire, in travellers' tales and newspaper accounts, tend to be explictly textual, a matter of report or record, not belief or empirical reality. In 1679 the vampire is 'a *pretended* demon, *said to* delight in sucking human blood . . .' (my italics).[46] An account of the *Travels of 3 English Gentlemen* in 1734 locates vampires in Serbia, and while making due concessions to English scepticism, attributes belief in them to a succession of foreign authorities:

> These Vampyres are supposed to be the bodies of deceased persons, animated by evil spirits, which come out of the graves, in the night time, suck the blood of many of the living, and thereby destroy them. Such a notion will, probably, be looked upon as fabulous and exploded, by many people in England; however, it is not only countenanced by Baron Valvasor, and many Carnioleze noblemen, gentlemen, etc., as we were informed, but likewise actually embraced by some writers of good authority. M. Jo. Henr. Zopfius, director of the Gymnasium of Essen, a person of great erudition, has published a dissertation upon them, which is extremely learned and curious, from which we shall beg leave to transcribe the following paragraph . . .
>
> These spectres are reported to have infested several districts of Serbia . . . In 1732, we had a relation of some of the feats in the neighborhood of Cassovia; and the publick prints took notice of the tragedies they acted in the bannat of Temeswaer, in the year 1738.[47]

Textual indeterminacy thus invests these early vampires. They are not likely to be credible to English readers; on the other hand they are more than peasant superstition, since they are vouched for by gentlemen and scholars. But they are identified at one remove, a matter of other people's beliefs, a phenomenon that the travellers are informed about by others, that they read about in works of erudition, or newspapers, where vampires are said to play a part in tragedies. The *Travels* was not published until 1810. By 1819, when Polidori published his introduction to *The Vampyre: A Tale*, vampires are an Eastern 'superstition' which has given rise to 'many wonderful stories', but a case of vampirism in Hungary, he adds, was credibly reported in the *London Journal* of 1732.[48] Neither fully plausible as fact, nor easily dismissed as fiction, vampires are consistently citational: they exist in quotation marks, in stories, in passages transcribed from other texts.

During the course of the nineteenth century, however, vampires are progressively relegated to fiction. Vampires, positivism assures us, do not exist; they are nonsense, non-sense. But they remain fascinating to a culture that confines sense to antithesis, reduces difference to opposition. The symbolic Law, insisting on what is logical, clear, separate, at the same time produces a conception of the invasion of the other into the self-same. Un-dead, in-human, dis-placed: these prefixes bear witness to the unpresentable. Language in its own structure generates phantasms which exceed the alternatives it offers. The more enthusiastically reason offers to police it, the more the symbolic order gives rise to the uncanny. Vampires have survived from a vanished past; they represent everything that the scientific, rational knowledges of the Enlightenment repress. And yet they are disturbingly familiar, recognizable as a linguistic possibility, glimpsed in the interval that the symbolic order hollows within itself.

As the indeterminate and thus disturbing other of Enlightened taxonomy, Bram Stoker's Dracula must, of course, be exterminated, and by men, under the leadership of the doctor-lawyer-philosopher, Van Helsing. This representative of all that is best in the Enlightenment tradition – its generosity and open-mindedness, as well as its knowledge and its relentless logic – recognizes Dracula for what he is, and though Van Helsing himself is not indifferent to the hypnotic fascination of the Count's female companions,[49] he is resolute in his defence of civilized values. The vampire is an embodiment of an archaic indifference, a failure to distinguish adequately, which the Enlightenment must surmount in order to ensure the supremacy of the *Cogito*.

But Dracula also stands, of course, for unmastered desire, and he represents in consequence a danger to the purity of womanhood, on which domestic happiness and harmony in marriage depends. He enlists Lucy's unconscious desire before she is able to marry Arthur Holmwood (home-would?), and he threatens to lure Mina away from the husband she loves, Jonathan Harker. Indeed, the extraordinary scene in which Dracula compels Mina to take blood from his breast occurs in her bed, while Jonathan sleeps beside her. 'Strangely enough', she reflects afterwards, while Dracula held her she did not want to hinder him (p. 370). Mina wears a white nightdress; and Dracula's words make clear the degree to which the episode parodies and imperils Victorian marriage:

> 'And you, their best beloved one, are now to me, flesh of my flesh; blood of my blood; kin of my kin; my bountiful wine-press for a while; and shall be later on my companion and my helper.' (p. 370)

The project is a merging of identities that will transform Mina in Dracula's image, degraded, carnal, cannibal, flesh feeding on human blood, in a repudiation of all the prohibitions on which true love and marital concord depend.

VI

Is there, then, no theoretical difference between male and female demon lovers, no distinction, apart from the obvious anatomical one, to be made between the demonic objects of unconscious desire imagined for men and women? In both cases the unaccountable, irrational, destabilizing character of desire is projected onto the figure who stands for its cause, and each time this figure is represented as dangerous, non-human, demonic. In both cases the demon lover brings about a relaxation of conscious control, and transforms the subject into a being it cannot consciously recognize or acknowledge. The determinations of the symbolic order give way, and prohibition disappears, in a world where impossibilities are possible.

It might be paradoxically reassuring from a conventional feminist point of view, in so far, at least, as the familiar reassures, to find that, while the female figures are objects of desire, only the males are desiring subjects. Certainly male demons are not, on the whole, spectacular, not objects of the gaze. But in practice the females are subjects of their own desire. Lamia is in love and she actively pursues Lycius. Meanwhile, if she is not a hallucination, Ligeia returns, we are invited to suppose, by pure force of will. Alternatively, it would conform to expectation if the male figures were more violent, more invasive, more prone to exercise force when seduction fails. And certainly Comus is ready to rape the Lady, while Satan penetrates the defences of the Garden of Eden like a predator. But conversely, Dracula can enter only where he is at least initially invited, whereas Ligeia commits murder in order to take possession of another woman's body. The conventional gender-differences do not seem to hold. As for power, all demon lovers, whether male or female, possess it in abundance.

But there is, nevertheless, one detectable difference which obtains in the instances I have considered. This distinction is generic rather than thematic: the stories of male demon lovers finally deliver resolution, closure, truth; the generic indeterminacies which characterize the stories of demonic women are not found when the protagonist is male. We never know *for certain* whether Ligeia's resurrection is the effect of an opium dream; it is hard to settle for a univocal identification of Lamia; the meaning of the *Mona Lisa* shifts with the attention of the gaze. But we have no difficulty in classifying Zeus, despite his many different incarnations, or Comus, however persuasive his arguments. Behind their deceptions the stories reveal the single truth of their protagonists' identities. Moreover, there is no indication that they are in any sense illusory within the fictional realm they inhabit. Even the Silkie belongs to a world where 'finns', as they are known, can alternate as human beings or seals. The indeterminacy of these figures is thus thematic but not generic. Satan may have been idolized by the Romantics, but whether he is the hero or the villain of the poem, he is unequivocally real within the cosmos the text depicts. In the same way, though vampires begin as textual indeterminates, located uneasily between fact and fiction, named in quotation marks, when they are once relegated to fiction, the stories they inhabit are generically determinate. As readers we simply agree, for the purpose of reading it, to enter into the supernatural world the narrative presupposes. *Dracula* does not keep us guessing about whether vampires exist: on the contrary, for the duration of the novel, we know that they do. Dracula himself, in consequence, thematically indeterminate, as I have suggested, becomes a textual essence. Within vampire fiction, vampires themselves are a species: they can be unmasked, unveiled to reveal the truth that lies behind the deceptions they practise.

Of course, Bram Stoker's text teases the reader with mimetic promises. The story begins in the everyday world we recognize, and the narrative simulates the strategies of realist fiction by presenting a succession of documents offered as evidence of the truth it tells. There is no single narrative voice: the story is related entirely by eye-witnesses in letters, diaries, extracts from newspapers, and correspondence with estate agents and removal firms. But the specificity of the documents and the convergence of their accounts only serves in the end to validate the 'extraordinary' events they record. From the moment, about half way through the novel, that the stake has been driven through Lucy's heart, there is no more room for doubt about the existence of vampires, and what follows is an adventure story, a struggle between our heroes and a 'terrible and mysterious enemy' (p. 303), who happens to be supernatural. It is also a chivalric romance: Arthur, Quincey Morris and John Seward are all in love with Lucy; after her death each develops a close and courtly relationship with the married Mina Harker, and the novel goes on to recount 'how some men so loved her, that they did dare much for her sake' (p. 486).

Since its publication in 1897, Bram Stoker's story has never quite disappeared from popular consciousness, its hero, at least, kept alive by Hollywood films and narrative fiction. Part of its compelling power surely depends on its generic familiarity, its repetition in another key of the Christian story of human beings as the stake in a cosmic power struggle between good and evil, God and the Devil. Indeed, this is made clear in the story itself. The religious references become more specific as the story goes on. Dracula promises Renfield immortality if he will fall down and worship him (p. 360); the vampire's project, Van Helsing indicates, is to father a new order of beings, 'whose road must lead through Death, not life' (p. 389). Meanwhile, after her encounter with Dracula, Mina bears the mark of Cain on her forehead; only God, Van Helsing tells her, can remove it, and 'Till then we bear our Cross, as His Son did in obedience to His will' (p. 382). At the same time, Christian allusions are interwoven with folk remedies. Van Helsing fights evil with crucifixes and the eucharistic Host, wild roses and garlic indiscriminately. As a doctor, he also draws on modern scientific knowledges.

By this means the supernatural is brought under the aegis of the *Cogito*, where in practice, of course, it had quietly remained throughout the modern period. An ominiscient supernatural being was indispens-

179

able to some versions of Enlightenment philosophy, if a matter of indifference to others. And any universe that does not exclude the possibility of God might perfectly well contain vampires too. The strange compulsion vampires exert in *Dracula*, so that it proves seductive to the purest of women, to the innocent Jonathan Harker and even to Van Helsing, who is intellectually fortified against it, now becomes intelligible, readily recognizable as another version of original sin. We *know* this story. Freud maintained that the most powerful instances of uncanny writing are those which keep us guessing about the presuppositions on which the story is based, the genre, in other words, of the text. If Freud is right, *Dracula* is not ultimately uncanny, since we recognize its genre. And neither, for similar reasons, is *Comus* or *Paradise Lost*, *Melmoth the Wanderer* or 'Leda and the Swan'.

What, then, might we make of a difference, widespread enough, perhaps, to be significant, between female demon lovers on the one hand, who so commonly elude our grasp, and escape the confines of the *Cogito* by exceeding the available semantic and generic taxonomies, and male demon lovers on the other, who, however ambiguous, however disturbing, are finally brought within the sphere of the known, the intelligible, the familiar? One group of stories reaffirms what the text has already taught us to know; the other challenges it; one group resolves textual uncertainties to proclaim a truth within the fiction; the other leaves the idea of truth radically in question.

A criticism which seeks to explain the text by invoking the author could readily resolve the issue. All these texts are produced by men. From the point of view of the author, the female demon lover constitutes an object of desire, and thus retains all the ambiguity, all the mystery with which unconscious desire invests its objects. Male demon lovers, meanwhile, are rivals who must be recognized and defeated. The problem with this straightforward, 'obvious' (and heterosexist) explanation is that it entirely ignores the role of the reader. We should not in practice be reading or discussing any of these texts now, they would not be readily available to us, if they had not already been widely read, had not made sense to generations of readers of both sexes. It seems probable, therefore, that they both draw on and reproduce meanings already in circulation in the culture at large. Some of these meanings are historically specific in the narrow sense: *Melmoth*, for instance, recreates the Byronic figure of the outcast that was widely popular in the aftermath of the French Revolution. But others have a broader currency.

Perhaps, then, the difference between male and female demon lovers belongs with the differential meanings of 'man' and 'woman' in Western culture? Joan Riviere might have agreed: womanliness as masquerade, femininity as veil, calls into question the essences that guarantee truth. Derrida might also agree, though in *Spurs* 'Derrida' himself (as author, as essence) is at least as elusive as Lamia, veiled (but not concealed) as he is by the Nietzschean texts he invokes: 'There is no such thing as woman', this 'Derrida' affirms, 'as a truth in itself of woman in itself. That much, at least, Nietzsche has said.'[50]

> Woman (truth) will not let herself be taken. In truth woman, truth will not let itself be taken (prisoner).
>
> That which will not let itself be taken (prisoner) by truth is – *feminine*, which should not hastily be translated into femininity, the femininity of woman, female sexuality and the other essentializing fetishes, which are exactly what people believe they take when they retain the simple-mindedness of the dogmatic philosopher, the impotent artist or the inexperienced seducer.[51]

'Woman' exceeds what can be taken. Guyon takes Acrasia prisoner in a net, but only in order to avoid taking her, since what she represents so evidently exceeds all that can inhabit the birdcage of true love. Lycius mistakenly imagines that he can trammel up the soul of Lamia; Apollonius wrongly supposes he has captured the truth of her identity. The 'feminine' is in excess of what can be seen. The real secret of the *Mona Lisa* might never be known; equally, there might, in the event, be no secret whatever. It is possible, though by no means certain, that in the depths of Ligeia's lustrous eyes there is a forbidden knowledge; alternatively, there might be nothing at all. The 'feminine' as object of the desiring gaze suspends the opposition between true and false, while the masculine reinstates essence, identity, closure.

The female body makes apparent that, while what there is to see might be either more or less than there is, what you get is, all the same, what you see.[52] *Spurs* accounts for the sexual difference it points to by explaining that 'woman' does not believe in castration: on the contrary, she knows that castration does not take place.[53] This is quite different, of course, from Freud's account of woman as already castrated, which has the effect of premature closure. Knowing that castration does not happen, without fear of the penalty for forbidden love, 'woman' thus escapes the constraints, the exclusions and the oppositions of the symbolic Law on which truth depends.[54] This does not mean that she does not recognize the *Cogito*, but she is not at the mercy of its *Non*. The 'feminine' is sceptical: it mocks naive masculine credulity, and the anxiety which ultimately motivates the need to look behind the veil.

The 'feminine', *Spurs* proposes, therefore offers an alternative view of textuality, liberates it from a metaphysics of reading that stalks the final signified with a net:

> The hermeneutic project which postulates a true sense of the text is disqualified under this regime. Reading is freed from the horizon of meaning or truth of being.[55]

Interpretation seeks what eludes capture, which means, of course, not that any decoding will do as well as another, but on the contrary, since textuality is inexhaustible, that reading 'must be carried to the furthest lengths possible'.[56] The desire, we might add, that motivates the reading process, is not easily gratified.

And women — actual women, in all our range and diversity, in our historical and cultural specificity? Where do we feature in Derrida's account? Who knows? If some of us choose to recognize ourselves there, that possibility is an effect of the place allotted to us by a patriarchal Western culture, which affirms and reaffirms an elusive, enigmatic femininity. What, then, are we to do with this meaning produced for us, this space which we are invited to take up? We could, of course, reject it in favour of our own truth, our essence, submission to our Law, with due penalties for error. We could, that is to say, reproduce in another register the oppositions and exclusions, the restraints and prohibitions of the existing order. Or, alternatively, we could remain elusive, exploit our scepticism and continue to introduce moments of opacity into a patriarchal knowledge dependent on the gaze.[57]

VII

There are in the reading process, I have wanted to suggest, two desires in play: on the one hand the desire of the fictional figure within the text, and on the other the desire of the reader. What the stories of demon lovers suggest is that the desire defined in the fiction cannot be met by a mortal lover, because in the end desire is not of the other, but of the Other, and its gratification is both forbidden and impossible. The desire of the reader, however, is permitted. Metaphysical reading promises the gratification of truth unveiled, the meaning of the text, closure. But the regime of truth is characterized by loss: finite meaning, I suggested in chapter 2, is often a disappointment, and it dispels the fictional world we have inhabited, leaving us desolate, forlorn. The alternative is to seek out the pleasures of the *trompe-l'oeil*, which permits us to shift between incommensurable knowledges without finality, or fear of retaliation. This mode of reading postpones closure. Instead, it acknowledges all that is elusive and enigmatic in the work, and sustains desire by privileging whatever is critically unmastered, textually demonic.

8

━━━◄ ►━━━

Futures: Desire and Utopia

I

Desire exists on Whileaway, but it is understood to be a sickness, a temporary invasion of the person by a parasite which will eventually be expelled. The condition, compulsive, hectic, obsessional, is definable only in a sequence of post-Petrarchan paradoxes: 'pleasant pain, balmy poison, preserving gall, choking sweet'.[1] Janet, who comes from the utopian fantasy world of Joanna Russ's *The Female Man* (1975), recounts with a degree of irony how she first fell in love on Whileaway:

> Love – to work like a slave, to work like a dog. The same exalted, feverish attention fixed on everything. I didn't make a sign to her because she didn't make a sign to me; I only tried to control myself and to keep people away from me. That awful diffidence. I was *at her* too, all the time, in a nervous parody of friendship.[2]

In Janet's account desire manifests itself as at once banal and lyrical; its effects are excessive, irrational, disordering; the condition is barely nameable, but it is citational, turning people into figures from folktale and fantasy; in addition it is impersonal, and also curiously depersonalizing:

> We reached the trees . . . The ground between them was carpeted in needles, speckled with moonlight. We dissolved fantastically into that extraordinary medium, like mermaids, like living stories; I couldn't see anything. There was the musky odor of dead needles, although the

pollen itself is scentless. If I had told her, 'Vittoria, I'm very fond of you,' or 'Vittoria, I love you,' she might answer, 'You're O.K. too, friend,' or 'Yes, sure, let's make it,' which would misrepresent something or other, though I don't know just what, quite intolerably and I would have to kill myself – I was very odd about death in those strange days. So I did not speak or make a sign but only strolled on, deeper and deeper into that fantastic forest, that enchanted allegory, and finally we came across a fallen log and sat on it.

'You'll miss——' said Vitti.

I said, 'Vitti, I want——'

She stared straight ahead, as if displeased. Sex does not matter in these things, nor age, nor time, nor sense, we all know that. In the daytime you can see that the trees have been planted in straight rows, but the moonlight was confusing all that.

A long pause here.

'I don't know you.' I said at last. The truth was we had been friends for a long time, good friends.[3]

Whileaway, as its name indicates, is a place of escape from the society mimetically defined in the novel and recognizable as twentieth-century Western culture. Whileaway represents a world of dreams, where wishes are fulfilled. Desire, by definition unsatisfied, is thus ultimately incompatible with this illusory location, though it is, nevertheless, the condition of its existence. Whileaway is itself an object of desire, the imagined alternative to an insistent and intolerable present. At the same time, however, Whileaway is seen by the reader to be an object of desire to the degree that it includes, contains and satisfies the desires of its imagined inhabitants.

Utopian writing necessarily struggles with this paradox. In the dream-worlds, fantastic islands and speculative futures which, in the Western tradition since Plato, have had the effect of throwing into relief the inadequacy of the reader's own society, desire is at once a tentative presence and a necessary absence, no sooner glimpsed than either met or repudiated. Alternatively, it remains as a problem, a disruption in the smooth economy of an otherwise perfect order. Janet and Vittoria wrestle with each other, sob together and then make love. Afterwards they walk back separately, 'each frightened to death of the weeks and weeks yet to go before we'd be over it'. Subsequently, Janet now adds laconically,

Vitti and I have stayed together in a more commonplace way ever since. In fact, we got married. It comes and goes, that abyss opening on nothing. I run away, usually.[4]

The continued existence of utopian writing in Western culture is evidence of a dissatisfaction with the arrangements successive social orders have made to satisfy the needs and wishes of their citizens. Whether as monastic rules, proposals for ideal commonwealths, nostalgic accounts of a lost golden age, or novels depicting a distant or future society, utopias constitute evidence of a hope, however faint, that the future might be other than the present; they demonstrate, that is to say, a desire for change. The utopian impulse acquires a special intensity in the early modern period, when the secularizing influence of humanism emphasizes the imperative to construct heaven on earth, to seek perfection here, even if not now, not quite yet.[5] But while utopias represent objects of desire, as accounts of improved societies they also tend to indicate a place for passion within an alternative social order, and in utopian writing of the modern period it is possible to trace a deepening critique of the increasing domestication of desire as true love, and its confinement within the nuclear family.

II

The arrangements for accommodating desire in utopia vary widely, both historically and according to the political project of the text. Most utopias have taken some account of the erotic but, perhaps predictably, it is not until the nineteenth and twentieth centuries that sexual desire plays a major part in the imagined ideal world. Reproduction tends to be the issue in earlier texts. Plato's *Republic*, for example, allots sex a fairly minor role. Eroticism is seen as a natural impulse, but among the Guardians it is to be carefully regulated in the interests of the state. To this end, periodic 'marriage' festivals are to be arranged, at which the rulers will bring couples temporarily together, ostensibly by lot but in practice according to eugenic principles, to breed, and in the process to gratify their natural instincts. There is no suggestion that they might resist this or wish to make their own choices, nor that they might seek more sexual activity than the regime permits, but then their education will already have instilled in these people a strong commitment to the common good, which is what qualifies them to be Guardians.

Since women are capable of everything men do, though in general they will do it less well, there is no reason why women should not be Guardians, and be educated with boys to rule the other two classes, the Auxiliaries (the executive) and the third class, which is responsible for production. But despite this modest concession to sexual equality among the elite, the Republic is described exclusively from the perspective of men. Friendship occurs between men; it is women and children who are held in common. Sex is evidently pleasurable: young men will be rewarded for special prowess by being allocated more frequent opportunities to sleep with women. But even from the point of view of men, about desire as longing for the unattainable, 'that abyss opening on nothing', *The Republic* has nothing to say. There is no indication here of the transcendent and transfiguring passion defined in the *Phaedrus* and the *Symposium*, but then the erotic activity specified in *The Republic* is exclusively heterosexual.

Sir Thomas More's *Utopia* (1516) was strongly influenced by Plato, though More differs from Plato at certain critical points, not least on the question of marriage, which in *Utopia* is for life. But once again marriage simply contains and confines a natural and inevitable sexual impulse. In More's account sex is just as functional as in Plato's, and perhaps even more mundane. Sexual intercourse is one of the bodily delights, comparable in degree of pleasure to excretion or the relief of an itch by scratching.[6] The only indication that it might be marginally more compulsive than either of these is the observation that pre-marital sex is heavily punished in Utopia, on the grounds that if fornication were permitted, no one would ever bother to get married.[7] There are no fantastic forests and enchanted allegories here, no moonlight or mermaids, and no inability to formulate words that would do justice to the character of passion.

But if More's account of Utopian sex is perfunctory, in Charlotte Perkins Gilman's all-female, parthenogenetic Herland, created in 1915, desire itself is totally unintelligible, except in the form of a longing to be a mother. This critical cultural difference gives rise to certain difficulties in the relationships the novel depicts between the visiting American heroes and the brides they marry in Herland. The male narrator's hope of eliciting in Ellador a richness of sexual passion corresponding to his own is repeatedly and comically frustrated:

> Then I did my earnest best to picture to her the sweet intense joy of married lovers, and the result in higher stimulus to all creative work.
>
> 'Do you mean,' she asked quite calmly, as if I was not holding her cool firm hands in my hot and rather quivering ones, 'that with you, when people marry, they go right on doing this in season and out of season, with no thought of children at all?'
>
> 'They do,' I said, with some bitterness. 'They are not mere parents. They are men and women, and they love each other.'
>
> 'How long?' asked Ellador, rather unexpectedly.
>
> 'How long?' I repeated, a little dashed. 'Why, as long as they live.'
>
> 'There is something very beautiful in the idea,' she admitted, still as if she were discussing life on Mars. 'This climactic expression, which, in all the other life-forms, has but the one purpose, has with you become specialized to higher, purer, nobler uses. It has – I judge from what you tell me – the most ennobling effect on character. People marry, not only for parentage, but for this exquisite interchange – and, as a result, you have a world full of continuous lovers, ardent, happy, mutually devoted, always living on that high tide of supreme emotion which we had supposed to belong only to one season and one use. And you say it has other results, stimulating all high creative work. That must mean floods, oceans of such work, blossoming from this intense happiness of every married pair! It is a beautiful idea!'[8]

Beautiful indeed – and a long way from the world we know. Which, a reader might be prompted to wonder, is the more utopian vision, Gilman's *Herland*, or the story of true love our culture recounts to itself?

But if some modern representations of ideal worlds simply eliminate desire as incompatible with the fulfilment it is their project to depict, others leave it in place as a problem to be resolved – and conclude that, though there are palliatives, there is in the end no cure. In William Morris's *News from Nowhere* (1890), for instance, love alone causes trouble in an otherwise calm and contented world. Dick and Clara lived together for two years and had two children; then Clara fell in love with someone else and they parted; now they are beginning to re-establish their relationship. The pain this has caused, old Hammond tells the narrator, cannot be avoided. But at the same time, he is careful to point out, in a world without contracts and without property, at least the unhappiness is not compounded by legal struggles over financial support, possessions or the care of the children. Desire is separated from institutional regulation on the one hand and moralistic compulsion on the other. There is no divorce in Nowhere, since there is no marriage:

'At least, if we suffer from the tyranny and fickleness of nature or our own want of experience, we neither grimace about it, nor lie. If there must be sundering betwixt those who meant never to sunder, so it must be: but there need be no pretext and unity when the reality of it is gone: nor do we drive those who well know that they are incapable of it to profess an undying sentiment which they cannot really feel.'[9]

Desire is not always reciprocated; there is no guarantee that it will not alter; but change is not attended by legal and economic penalties or social reproach.

Rivalry in love cannot necessarily be avoided. Later in *News from Nowhere* it emerges that in a struggle between two men for the same woman, one has been killed. And now, in consequence, both the killer and the woman are so full of grief and remorse that they are in danger of self-destruction. '"And all this we could no more help than the earthquake of the year before last."'[10] Again there are no penalties: it falls to the community to heal the survivors. In the same way, in Marge Piercy's *Woman on the Edge of Time* (1976), when Bolivar and Luciente compete for the sexual attention of Jackrabbit, the community steps in with a form of collective counselling which helps the rivals to engage with the problem. But there is no full reconciliation and no solution: in the end Jackrabbit is killed, leaving both Bolivar and Luciente to mourn his death.

Plato and More deal with sexuality by regulating it. In *Utopia* marriage is for life, except in cases of intolerable waywardness or adultery, and in these instances the offender is not allowed to remarry. Adultery is severely punished, the first time by slavery, the common punishment for all crime, and the second time by death. Conversely, Morris and Piercy minimize the degree of regulation, leaving moral issues to the community. In Piercy's Mattapoisett, which is very much a product of the novel's period in the mid-1970s, the sexual impulse is set free from restraint, bisexuality is the norm and lifelong monogamy is unknown, though very intense sexual relationships may develop at intervals.

Modern liberal culture stresses the value of choice – but it also acknowledges the power of inertia. In Fay Weldon's *Darcy's Utopia* (1990) the future promises freedom to change, to experiment, at least discreetly. At the same time, however, this novel, the product of a more sceptical moment, repudiates the idea that unregulated sex will mean a radical liberation of erotic activity:

> 'It will not be like that. The inhabitants of Darcy's Utopia will have as much or as little difficulty getting together as anyone else. Fear of rejection will inhibit many, others will cringe before fear of compli-cations, responsibility, hurting others, failing to perform adequately, or having to reveal physical imperfections. Cellulite of the thighs keeps many a woman chaste: a potbelly keeps a man on the straight and narrow like nothing else. Most will stick to a partner chosen in the madness and self-confidence of youth, as they do outside Darcy's Utopia.'[11]

True love is not a common feature of utopias. In the earliest examples the term would have no meaning, and after the Renaissance true love is either not an option or not an object of desire. There are exceptions, of course: Ursula Le Guin's *The Dispossessed* (1974) depicts 'the bond' which exists for life between Shevek and his partner,[12] but the main concerns of this novel are elsewhere. Two centuries earlier, Sarah Scott's feminist *Millenium Hall* (1762) portrays an ideal community of chari-table women, who include among their responsibilities the education of poor children and the training of orphans to earn a living. They do not discourage the marriages of their former charges, and indeed they help to set up young couples so that they become productive members of society. But their commitment to marriage has little to do with the pleasures of true love, and the account they give of their motives for supporting the institution is notably unenthusiastic:

> 'We consider matrimony as absolutely necessary to the good of society; it is a general duty; but as, according to all ancient tenures, those obliged to perform knight's service, might, if they chose to enjoy their own firesides, be excused by sending deputies to supply their places; so we, using the same privilege substitute many others, and certainly much more promote wedlock than we could do by entering into it ourselves. This may wear the appearance of some devout persons of a certain religion who, equally indolent and timorous, when they do not choose to

say so many prayers as they think their duty, pay others for supplying their deficiencies.[13]

There are love stories in *Millenium Hall*, but they all have unhappy endings. The founders of the Hall, like the women who undertake the retirement prescribed by Mary Astell in *A Serious Proposal to the Ladies* (1694), are in retreat from the vicissitudes of the life available to middle-class women in the period. Amid the accidents and disfiguring diseases which befall them, the secret profligacy of their ancestors, and the sudden deaths of their partners, women, the novel indicates, are commonly left destitute or worse, the prey of seducers or tyrannical husbands. Love exists, but it is rarely without impediment, and the ideal of conjugal happiness is seen as itself utopian when marriage settlements are the primary concern of the families involved. The novel's projected alternative is a community of celibate women dedicated to virtue, 'epicures in rural pleasures', who pool their resources to construct a 'female Arcadia'.[14]

Both Astell and Scott imagine, in opposition to the world they know, a secularized version of the monastic ideal, which was also, of course, initially conceived as a utopian alternative to a fallen world, a community secure from the turbulence of medieval warrior society, dedicated to good works and the love of God. The religious vows of poverty and chastity represent one possible response to the Western anxiety about the lure of property on the one hand and passion on the other. Marriage is another way of dealing with these two dangers. Ideally, marriage works to contain both: it licenses private property and sex, brings them, indeed, into conjunction, but it keeps them within bounds by legitimating each in due measure.

Marriage yokes the transmission of worldly goods to the reproductive process, and cements the alliance between them in the perpetuation of the family name. Most utopias, on the other hand, do away with private property, and where marriage survives in utopian fiction, it is commonly separated from economic inheritance, the passing on of names and the idea of the spouse as property. Even in More's patriarchal version, where women minister to their husbands and are chastised by them, and where life-long fidelity to a single sexual partner is strongly preferred,[15] the family is not in any obvious sense dynastic: there is no patrimony to be passed on to the children; no names of individuals or families are mentioned.[16] Herlanders have only one name each, though a title may be allocated later by the community, according to their roles or functions. There are no family names. The women are horrified when the Americans ask them to change their names on marriage. In the anarchist society defined in *The Dispossessed*, single names are allocated to children at birth by a computer. Mattapoisett names children at birth, but allows them to choose new names when they reach puberty, and any number of times thereafter. There are no surnames. While-awayans inherit their mother's first names, with the additional suffix 'son', though the children are all girls. Janet Evason's mother was Eva; her child is Yuriko Janetson.

Where it exists at all, monogamous partnership in utopian writing is thus little more than residual, and in the feminist versions the conventional conjugal couple we recognize is often derided by the utopians themselves as possessive or tyrannical:

> 'Unstable dyads, fierce and greedy, trying to body the original mother-child bonding. It looks tragic and blind.'[17]

> Iron plunged into ice is cold but colder still is the lot of the young girl who has given herself in marriage. The young girl in the house of her mother is like seed in fertile ground. The woman under the roof of her husband is like a chained dog. The slave, rarely, tastes the delights of love, the woman never.[18]

To the degree that the family survives in these alternative societies it is often radically reinterpreted. At first glance, More's Utopian family structures are deeply conservative. Women move to the husband's house on marriage; male children remain there; and the entire household is governed by the oldest father. But genetic parentage is not sacred. If the household becomes too big, children over fourteen are moved into other households which are smaller than the accepted norm of between ten and sixteen adults. Women nurse their own children (a progressive proposition for the rich in 1516), but they do this in well-appointed communal nurseries; women also organize the meals, but food is taken in common in what look remarkably like Oxbridge dining halls. There is thus only a minimal association between the family and domesticity. As far as supplies are concerned, there is, of course, no competition between households, since there is no property. On the contrary, one city happily provides what another lacks. In consequence, 'the whole ylande is as it were one familie, or housholde'.[19]

Eating is also communal in *News from Nowhere, Millenium Hall, Herland, The Dispossessed, Woman on the Edge of Time* and *Darcy's Utopia*. Evidently home cooking looks more like drudgery from the perspective of an ideal society. Herland miraculously provides all domestic comforts for everyone, apparently without exploitative labour, and every individual has her own apartment. Matapoisett also offers separate accommodation for all its inhabitants. Whileawayans, by contrast, join families of thirty or forty people on the basis of choice, not heredity. The families take responsibility for food, shelter and cleanliness, but mothers of children under five are released from this burden in order to concentrate on the young and enjoy a period of leisure. In Mattapoisett, where babies are delivered in the brooder, three parents of either sex volunteer to mother them without reference to genetic inheritance. As in Utopia, 'the family' is ultimately the community itself.

Predictably, therefore, childcare is commonly a matter for the whole society, not confined to individuals, and strenuous efforts are made to avoid parental possessiveness and control. *The Republic* has children taken away at birth from their genetic parents and brought up communally, without the adults knowing which are which. By this means, Socrates explains, anyone will come to be seen as a potential relation, and the appropriate loyalties will be redirected to the group. There will thus be fewer motives for quarrels and litigation. In the feminist utopias of the 1970s children commonly stay with their parents (however this term is understood) only briefly. Thereafter, they go to school, where they often spend the nights as well as the days. At puberty the young are frequently invited to demonstrate their capacity to look after themselves by some kind of ordeal or ritual, and thereafter they are regarded as independent, though of course the community offers support in a crisis, as it does to all adults.

III

It is clear from these accounts taken together that the nuclear family is not conceptually inevitable. There are, it becomes apparent, imaginable alternatives to the story told by the political right, reproduced by popular romance, and diligently lived out by a great many people in the Free West in theory, if not in practice. This is the conventional tale of desire framed by true love, contained by marriage, and generating the nuclear family, which is understood to be the primary source of domestic comfort and emotional support for all normal members of a civilized society, as well as the only possible setting in which to bring up happy and adjusted children. Throughout its history, though more intensely at certain epochs of dissatisfaction or unrest, and in a continuous tradition since the early modern period first idealized the nuclear family as the basis of social stability, Western culture has generated dreams, fantasies and speculative fictions which propose alternatives to the values this same culture has so strenuously promoted. The world of social and sexual relations, the utopian tradition consistently implies, could be other – which is to say better – than it is.

But would we really welcome the versions of change depicted in any of these texts? Even if specific details are appealing, the alternative arrangements defined in utopian writing are offered as elements in a totality which often seems complacent rather than challenging, simply substituting social coercion for institutional constraint. Understood as blueprints for the future, many of these fictions are no longer especially inviting. The unremitting courtesy of the ideal society, for example, can come to strike the reader as very slightly dull, however worthy. Would we seriously like to emulate More's Utopians, as they solemnly go off to early morning lectures in their undyed linen garments? Even if the food in Nowhere is always excellent, it is the women who serve it. Everyone there wears Pre-Raphaelite costume, and the high point of the social calendar seems to be a haymaking dinner in a disused church. Some of the 1970s accounts have also dated badly: they would hardly do as models for a more sophisticated and certainly more sceptical generation.

But perhaps models are not quite what is at stake. Most utopian writing offers a juxtaposition of the present society with its imagined alternative. A visitor from the existing world (Hythloday, Guest, Connie Ramos) is introduced to the customs and practices of the utopian culture. Moreover, the visitor or an interlocutor, More, for instance, like Glaucon in *The Republic*, comments, judges, resists or is persuaded. The reader's reactions are thus to some degree taken into account, already inscribed in the text, and subjected to examination, counter-argument or counter-example. In consequence, the reader is enlisted in a dialogue, whether explicitly or implicitly, and in the process what is familiar and obvious, the social organization we have taken for granted, gradually comes to appear as one option among others, and thus no longer inevitable. Indeed, the utopian society might not be an ideal at all. As Northrop Frye points out, More's Utopia is not a Christian state, although *Utopia* is certainly a Christian book, admired by the foremost Christian reformers of its period. The alternative society is not necessarily a goal, but a hypothesis, a possibility, which clarifies the present by denaturalizing its practices.[20]

This clarification is an effect of the defamiliarization brought about by an imagined encounter with an alternative culture. Most utopian writing explicitly invokes cultural difference. For instance, Socrates explains that if women are to become Guardians alongside the men, they had better do exercises with them in the gymnasium as part of their education. Glaucon finds the idea of naked women highly comic, but Socrates points out that the Greeks once thought naked men looked very silly, whereas now the practice of exercising naked is taken for granted. Glaucon's values, initially seen as natural, are shown to be culturally relative. The issue is not only which practice is better – more rational, more useful, more coherent – but the distance imposed by examining common-sense assumptions from a different perspective, from elsewhere, subjecting them to 'cognitive estrangement'.[21]

Many of the fictional visitors to the alternative culture experience problems of adjustment. Guest mystifies the inhabitants of Nowhere by offering them money in exchange for services and goods. Connie is appalled to see a man breast-feeding in Mattapoisett. The episode is not necessarily prescriptive: instead, it can be read as denaturalizing the conventional meaning of sexual difference, and addressing a question to the reader in the process. Our own ethnocentrism is similarly denaturalized: to the Utopians 'we' are the ultraequinoctials, and they know very little about us. Patriarchy, too, is correspondingly deflated by distance. When Janet first time-travels to the present from the all-female Whileaway, she happens to land on an office desk. Behind it sits an odd-looking human figure:

a strange woman; thick and thin, dried up, hefty in the back, with a grandmotherly moustache, a little one. How withered away one can be from a life of unremitting toil.

Aha! A man.

Shall I say my flesh crawled? Bad for vanity, but it did. This must be a man. I got off its desk.[22]

The reader is invited to see, at least momentarily, that it is not inevitable that we should take male bodies as the human norm. Monique Wittig's *Les Guérillères* (1969) parodies the patriarchal pleasure in phallic symbols by finding vulval emblems everywhere.

Cultural difference is inscribed in language. The implication of Saussurean linguistics that, since translation is not a matter of simple correspondences between one language and another, it follows that ideas are not universal extra-linguistic concepts, an insight so radical that it has transformed our understanding of our place in culture, has long been obvious to utopian writers who could never have heard of Saussure. More's rulers are called syphogrants and tranibors, and this distinguishes them from Tudor magistrates, who are differently selected to carry out quite different functions. The Herlanders cannot grasp what 'wife' means, and have no concept of 'man' as representative human being. Later, on Le Guin's anarchist Anarres personal pronouns have more or less disappeared, and there are no proprietary idioms for the sexual act:

> In Pravic it made no sense for a man to say that he had 'had' a woman; the word which came closest in meaning to 'fuck', and had a similar secondary usage as a curse, was specific: it meant rape. The usual verb, taking only a plural subject, can be translated only by a neutral word like copulate. It meant something two people did, not something one person did, or had. This frame of words could not contain the totality of experience any more than any other, and Shevek was aware of the area left out, though he wasn't quite sure what it was.[23]

The society of Marge Piercy's Mattapoisett has replaced masculine and feminine pronouns by 'person', and their possessive forms by 'per'. Meanwhile, the women of *Les Guérillères* see existing language in its entirety as subject to revision:

They say that there is no reality before it has been given shape by words rules regulations. They say that in what concerns them everything has to be remade starting from basic principles. They say that in the first place the vocabulary of every language is to be examined, modified, turned upside down, that every word must be screened.[24]

IV

The juxtaposition of cultures, values and meanings has the effect of relativizing current arrangements. Our existing social order is differed and distanced, its inadequacies thrown into relief. Utopian writing does not necessarily prescribe, but by presenting options for debate, it sets out to motivate discontent. In addition, it also implies, however tentatively in some instances, that there is a choice, that things need not be as they are, as we 'know' them.

But utopian writing is precisely speculative. Has it any purchase on the world we know? Is there, in other words, a choice in practice? Self-evidently, the gap between a fantasy and its realization is vast. To plan an alternative future is not necessarily to suppose that the plan could ever be implemented. The most carefully thought-out monastic rules and projected pantisocracies did not in the event succeed in deflecting corruption or preventing human failure. Most recently, speculative futures have tended to be explicitly fictional, utopian novels, not even put forward as realizable practical proposals. In our own present society there are clear and obvious material constraints, ranging from the international capital invested in the current social order, to sexually transmitted diseases, and existing suburbs full of three-bedroom houses and five-seater cars. What use are utopian dreams of alternatives to the nuclear family in a world of Mothercare, AIDS and housing shortages? We derive from the past, moreover, traditions, habits of thought and fiercely held proprieties, as well as inheritance laws and tax incentives, which take for granted the inevitability of monogamy. Since More, the term which identifies all these imagined alternatives etymologically conflates at the acoustic level two incompatible Greek meanings: *eu*topia (good place) and *ou*topia (nowhere). Is not utopian speculation precisely utopian?

Meanwhile, the recognition within utopian writing itself of the role of language in the construction of meanings and values raises the question of the limits culture itself imposes on the range of options available at any specific historical moment. Even if there were no material constraints, and no institutions reinforcing the present regime, does not the analysis of culture that follows from Saussure's insight imply that political choice and deliberate intervention in history are no more than liberal illusions, themselves the effect of a culture which fetishizes 'freedom'? How does post-Saussurean theory, which dethrones the sovereign subject, the autonomous individual as the source of a personal destiny, allow nevertheless a place for deliberate action, and in particular political action? Does poststructuralism permit a theoretical account of choice, without reducing the notion of choosing to a process which is in practice arbitrary for the individual, since it is motivated elsewhere? If, in other words, poststructuralism attributes agency primarily to the letter, and defines the subject as an effect of meanings, how can such an 'effect' make decisions?

Men and women act, but subject to determinate conditions which are not of their making. And if poststructuralism has tended to stress the determinate conditions, that need not lead us to a grim determinism which implies that there is nothing to be done. There was never any danger that twentieth-century culture, to the degree, at least, that it is dominated by the interests of the Free West, would succumb to a world view that eliminated choice. It is worth noting, as an example of the tenacity of individualism, that in practice the prevalence of theory in the academy has by no means eliminated from most literary criticism the notion of the autonomous Author as the origin and guarantee of the meaning of the text. Poststructuralism emphasizes the cultural, linguistic construction of the individual because that is what we are most likely to forget.

It does not follow, however, that we are all confined to reproducing the meanings and values we learn as 'native' speakers, imprisoned in our separate groups within one mother-tongue or another. In the Lacanian analysis of language, signifiers are mostly not 'buttoned down': the meanings we learn are not held in place, but slide beneath the signifier, with the effect that language is necessarily polysemic. Otherness invades meaning, and consequently defines the subject who is its effect. The subject itself, already redoubled and split in its imagined, imaged, speculary wholeness, and divided again in its own utterances between the 'I' who speaks and the 'I' who is put on show there, longs for an 'other' (person, way of life, mode of being) which would make it truly whole and unified.

The fulfilment of this desire is always imaginary. While it finds a series of locations, the object of desire, the other, is always only a stand-in. The ultimate, unconscious object of Lacanian desire is the unattainable Other. This, at least in modern Western culture, is often something very close to the desire for agency, deliberate action in accordance with the determinations of an unrestricted *Cogito*. The desire of the Other is (or includes) the longing to be the undifferentiated origin of difference, to occupy the place of the deployment of speech, to *be* or to *control* the condition of the possibility of subjectivity – and in consequence of desire itself.

When the subject speaks there are on stage in the miniature but recurrent drama of enunciation two figures. The first is the subject which appears (or is able to appear) in the utterance, the imaginary 'I' that is spoken of there. 'To say "I" is to enter the imaginary', Roland Barthes points out.[25] This 'I' is hungry, or thirsty, a feminist, or a revolutionary, it affirms, and it is no more, at that instant, than the imaginary unity it lays claim to. But if to say 'I' is to enter the imaginary, it is not thereby to abandon the symbolic. The second figure in the drama is the subject that speaks, that makes the utterance, inhabiting the symbolic order of language and culture. This second, symbolizing figure exceeds the first in its access to a range of possible utterances, and opts at this moment for this one.

The first figure is the effect of the utterance itself, constituted in and by it. The second figure, the subject of the enunciation, is no less an effect than the first, constituted as it is by the range of meanings in circulation in advance of its entry on to the stage. But the subject of the enunciation has at its disposal the knowledges in which it participates, the understandings inscribed in its culture. And like the utopian text, it is able to move between them, bringing one to bear on another as alternative or critique, and to constitute in the process new knowledges, new understandings, thus modifying for other subjects the range of what it is possible to know, to think, or to say. In this sense the subject deliberates, and chooses.

The choice is not 'free', to the degree that there are limits on what it is possible to say at a specific historical moment or in a specific cultural location, as well as limits on what it is politic to say within the norms of cultural acceptability. It is not 'free', to the extent that the subject does not control the entire range of possible meanings attributable to its utterance, the unconscious motivations in play, or the full set of possible effects of its intervention. Choice is not 'free', if to be free is to stand outside all existing knowledges and occupy a stable position from which it is possible to lever up the world. But conversely, in the drama of enunciation the subject is not a mere puppet. Within the existing constraints it is able to improvise, to reproduce or to contest the existing norms, to reaffirm or to resist the dominant meanings.

The postmodern subject, the subject of poststructuralist theory, is thus capable of choice, and is consequently accountable for its actions. There are no guarantees that its choices are founded in fact or are politically correct. But then there never were. We can, however, read as attentively as ever those utopian narratives which indicate that it is possible at least to imagine a world in which things are arranged other-wise.

Utopian fiction does not spring purely from the head of its creator. On the contrary, it is always intertextually derived – by bringing into conjunction fragments of existing knowledges, as well as by negating what is known of the present. More draws most obviously on Plato and Renaissance humanism, William Morris on socialism and Victorian medievalism, and Charlotte Perkins Gilman and Marge Piercy on different representations of the American dream. This intertextual character guarantees a degree of familiarity for the fiction, and in consequence ensures that it offers the reader an effect of choice – between *this* society and *that*, between the known (empirically) and the intelligible (intertextually). And what, after all, is finally the difference between these two modes of knowing, so often posed as antithetical? If our sense of our own culture is lived (in the economy, in institutions, and in the experience of desire) it is also learned (from the language in which it is inscribed, and from the myths and legends where the culture defines its ideal self and the appropriate objects of desire).

The choice that the utopian vision presents is thus not absolutely free. (But is not absolute freedom itself a utopian illusion, the dream of the Other?) It is subject to certain constraints, constituted as it is by the meanings already in circulation, and it may be motivated by desires which escape recognition. But the subject has at its disposal the knowledges in which it participates, and it is able to move between them, bringing one to bear on another as alternative, improvement or critique.

We can in consequence make choices. Even without the sovereign subject, we can act as agents on behalf of one way of life or another, though we do so subject to the limits of what it is possible to know, and within determinate conditions which we do not control. The material constraints cannot be wished away: the ability to imagine an alternative social order does not guarantee that it can be brought into being. And in any case we cannot expect to define in advance, from within this culture, the social relations that would work in another. But some tentative speculation on what might constitute a better society is probably a necessary though not a sufficient condition of deliberate political intervention in the course of history.

V

Utopias are not blueprints for the future, but they are more than simple critique of the present. As wish-fulfilments devised to supply the deficiences of the current order, they have the status of dreams, and like dreams they may be read as trivial or significant, just as the reader chooses. That indeterminacy, prompting a doubt about how seriously we are invited to take the proposed alternative society, is frequently inscribed in utopian writing itself. Generic uncertainties lure the reader along false trails and into unexpected stances. Lack of closure withholds the security of a clear position of intelligibility and thus of judgment. Precisely by evading straightforward prescription, utopian writing often teases the reader into taking sides on the propositions it puts forward.

More's *Utopia*, for example, is extravagantly equipped with the details that constitute *vraisemblance*. At first glance, this elaboration of verisimilitude seems more like literary high spirits than politics. There is a sketch map of the island, as well as a sample of the Utopian language, contributed by Peter Giles, who supplied a copy of the alphabet and a quatrain written in the vernacular. This is helpfully translated into Latin. Moreover, the text includes a letter from the author to Peter Giles, explaining that there is some uncertainty about the width of the River Anyder at Amaurote. John Clements thinks that the river is only three hundred paces wide, but More believes he remembers Hythloday saying that the bridge was five hundred paces wide. Peter Giles is urged to check this important detail with Hythloday, since the author is extremely anxious not to misrepresent the true state of affairs. What is more, Giles is asked to enquire of Hythloday where exactly Utopia is to be found on the map, since this crucial point was omitted from his account. In his letter to Busleyden, also printed with the text, Peter Giles solemnly explains that in fact Hythloday did say where the island was, but unfortunately More was distracted by a servant at the time, and Giles himself did not catch what was said, because one of the auditors coughed loudly at that moment, having caught cold, no doubt, on shipboard. He is not sure whether Hythloday is still alive.

Even now, in the light of centuries of discussion of *Utopia*, it is momentarily tempting to take all this verisimilitude literally. In 1516, in the context of a tradition of travellers' tales of strange cultures and outlandish customs, Utopia must at times have seemed perfectly plausible. Meanwhile, however, the etymology of the names consistently underlines the fictionality of the island. Hythloday means nonsense-talker, romancer; Amaurote means faint-seen, mirage; and the River Anyder, of course, is waterless. Mimesis is invoked, only to be dismissed. Meanwhile, 'More' repeatedly intervenes to contest Hythloday's evaluation of Utopian practices, and the text ends with an allusion to the author's remaining reservations, saved for discussion at a future date.

This textual teasing pulls against the solemnity of Hythloday's exposition of Utopian customs. There is still a critical debate about whether *Utopia* is no more than a *jeu d'esprit*, and not an account of an ideal commonwealth at all, a brilliant piece of scholarly wit, rather than a serious proposal to sixteenth-century Christendom. Surely, it hardly matters at this distance of time, we might suppose – except in so far as to take sides on that question is also, of course, though sometimes inadvertently, to take a stand for or against the abolition of private property, hierarchy and conspicuous consumption. ('Could anyone as wise as More really have subscribed to Hythloday's values . . . ?') The generic indeterminacies of the text thus have the continuing effect of enlisting the reader in debate, and despite the best efforts of the literary tradition, discussion cannot easily be confined to the question of the author's intentions.

One of the most Brechtian of utopian fictions is surely Marge Piercy's *Woman on the Edge of Time*, where the generic question is foregrounded from the beginning. Even Connie herself is not sure whether she is 'really' in contact with a society a century and a half into the future, or whether she imagines the whole thing. The novel opens with that uncertainty: 'Connie got up from her kitchen table and walked slowly to the door. Either I saw him or I didn't and I'm crazy for real this time, she thought.'[26] For most of the story Connie is a patient in a psychiatric hospital, diagnosed as paranoid-schizophrenic. Is this science fiction or a psychological novel? Is it really a utopia, or instead a critique of the psychiatric institution, like *One Flew Over the Cuckoo's Nest?*

Is Connie simply hallucinating? The community in Mattapoisett 'solves' all the problems Connie as a middle-aged, unemployed Mexican-American encounters in her own society. Moreover, the figures she meets in Mattapoisett are free, healthy and productive parallels for her oppressed friends and relations in the present: Dawn replaces Connie's lost daughter, Angelina, and Bee her dead lover, Claud. Diana is a happy version of Sybil, and Jackrabbit a creative Skip. When Skip kills himself, Mattapoisett holds a wake for Jackrabbit. On a bad trip Connie mistakenly makes contact with another future, where Gildina, bred, reconstructed and drugged to be a sex object, constitutes a projection of Connie's anxiety about her prostitute-niece, Dolly. Connie initially supposes that Luciente's presence is a hallucination. No one else sees her. But on the other hand, Dolly notices that the chair Luciente sat in is still warm . . .

The novel ends with the psychiatric reports on Connie. Is she 'crazy'? The uncertainty lures the reader into consideration of the more important question whether Mattapoisett itself and the values it represents is crazy. In this light it is possible to see that each of the customs described as normal in Mattapoisett is offered for debate in the reader's present, perhaps in the feminist consciousness-raising groups which were so widespread at the time of the novel's publication. Would relegating birth to machines really liberate us, or would it instead deprive us of an intensely important experience which is exclusive to women? Would children be better brought up by people who were not their genetic parents? Given that it is technologically possible, would we want men to breastfeed?

Like *Utopia*, *Woman on the Edge of Time* evades closure. Mattapoisett is constantly compelled to defend itself against the powerful remnants of the old culture: it is a society at war. Connie is also at war, both for herself and on behalf of the new order she envisages. When the psychiatric profession try to commandeer by physical means what remains of her subjectivity, when her attempted escape has failed, and when further resistance seems hopeless, Connie poisons her doctors with weedkiller. What should she have done? What else could she have done? Is murder ever justified? Can a new order founded on violence hope to match the ideals of feminism?

Joanna Russ's *The Female Man* juxtaposes four distinct positions, four voices. The first-person narrator, Joanna, is dissatisfied with the present, intellectual, sardonic, witty. Janet, from Whileaway, is unruly: she cannot make sense of twentieth-century America and behaves gratifyingly badly on social occasions. Jeannine, who appears in the third person, likes being a girl and hates Whileaway, and yet she feels there is something missing from her life. Jael, meanwhile, comes from a much more imminent future and finds all three while looking for her 'other selves'.[27] Jael inhabits Manland, where she survives by ingenuity and violence. Who are these women? Are they all aspects of the same woman, distinct but available subject positions? Do they represent a range of attitudes to feminism? What is the reader to think when Joanna reproaches Janet? Who is speaking in *The Female Man*?

In *Les Guérillères*, which recounts the story of the feminist revolution, the most scandalous propositions are consistently prefaced by 'The women say . . .' The voice of the text itself is thus always deferred. Moreover, vituperation alternates with lyricism, riddles, or lists of women's first names printed in capital letters. There are poems at the beginning and the end. What is the genre of this text? And what exactly does it propose?

Less radically, perhaps, but still problematically, Fay Weldon's *Darcy's Utopia* attributes its utopian vision to the academic, Julian Darcy, currently in prison for attempting to destroy the British economy. But as the novel goes on, it becomes clear that its real author is his non-academic wife, Eleanor, who makes it up as she goes along. Her views are presented in fragments, in taped interviews with two different journalists. Eleanor Darcy, formerly Ellen, before that Apricot, and perhaps soon to be Alison, is inconsistent, inventive, anarchic, brilliant or possibly mad, as the reader determines.

All these texts withhold the luxury of a single position of intelligibility from which the reader can legitimately simply endorse or dismiss an identifiable and coherent set of propositions. By this means each of them invites debate, sets out to enlist the reader in the process of making decisions. The options are not neutrally defined, of course, but nor are they presented in terms of a crude set of oppositions between good and evil, or progressive and reactionary values. The process of choice, since the assumption is that we do participate in the choice between futures, begins with the act of reading itself.

VI

Utopias have the status of dreams: they represent a desire (Hythloday's, Connie's, if not ours) fulfilled. And this at the level of content is the paradox, I have suggested, of utopian writing. In a true utopia the desire of the inhabitants is either met or kept at bay. As a result, the imagined daily 'reality' of utopian life tends to strike the reader as bland, complacent or boring. But in so far as a utopia is an object of desire, the desire inscribed in the text is not necessarily for the way of life of the alternative culture. Utopia is a dream, and the dream, Lacan points out, 'is made for the recognition . . . of desire'.[28] In the dream *it* (the unconscious) *shows*, though not necessarily at the level of manifest content. Dreams, psychoanalysis indicates, have to be interpreted. Some utopian writing may point to a desire which is not found quite where its explicit propositions might be taken to indicate.

Michèle le Doeuff reads More's *Utopia* as a daydream (*rêverie*) in the service of a desire that is not in the end political at all, a longing for a solitary and ultimately narcissistic self-sufficiency of the subject, a visible self-containment which can be consciously identified as happiness.[29] And what is the desire of *Herland*? Not, surely, parthenogenesis, or even an all-female community, but autonomy for women, which is to say an existence and an identity that is not merely differential, dependent or derivative.

William Morris's Nowhere is explicitly a dream, fulfilling the desires that were not gratified by life in the Socialist League or in Victorian Britain more generally, especially after Bloody Sunday in 1887.[30] The dream is 'An Epoch of Rest', as the text's subtitle indicates, a holiday, which is why the weather is continuously perfect and all the women are beautiful. But towards the end of the story Guest begins a holiday romance with the fascinating Ellen, and the desire depicted in the text is not fulfilled. Guest's last sight in Nowhere, while the dream fades, is of Ellen's sadness as she loses consciousness of his presence. 'I felt', he continues, 'lonely and sick at heart past the power of words to describe.'[31] In one sense Ellen represents emblematically everything that is desirable about this imagined future. As an object of desire, she is a personification of the new age, alluring, thrilling, and out of reach.[32] Infinitely precious, Ellen is always already lost, since Guest is no more than a ghost in her world,[33] and for him her place is Nowhere.

But it is surely not so much the figure of Ellen herself, but rather the story of an impossible love, that enlists the desire of the reader. Desire itself is paradoxically an object of desire. One of Freud's patients dreams that she wants to give a supper party, but with only a little smoked salmon in the house, she is obliged to renounce the idea. The context of the dream includes a thin woman friend, who would like to be plumper, and a husband who admires the thin friend, but prefers plump women. The thin friend offers to come to supper with the patient and her husband, which would almost certainly make her plumper . . .[34] In a witty sequence of increasingly outrageous extrapolations, Lacan reads this dream as evidence of the desire to have an unsatisfied desire, first on the part of the wife, who has everything and is not satisfied with that, but additionally on the part of the husband, who admires the thin friend when he prefers plump women. Desire is in a sense gratuitous, in excess of anything we could be said to need, and beyond what is spoken in the demand.[35] But at the same time desire itself is seductive.

Life without it, contentment, in other words, lacks motivation. Ursula Le Guin's *The Disposessed* shows what happens in a utopia when people's basic needs and demands are met. Anarres is a well-established anarchist community, and in order to prevent corruption it has kept the rest of the galaxy at bay. There is thus only minimal contact with other cultures. Meanwhile, the rules that are necessary even in an anarchist society have become coercive, preventing radical developments. The physicist Shevek, frustrated by the limitations a complacent culture imposes on his work, is compelled to leave for the corrupt, 'propertarian' Urras, in order, ironically, to follow the anarchist dream of pursuing knowledge and sharing it freely. *The Dispossessed* turns the utopian dream inside out to show how the realization of the ideal generates desire, precisely by satisfying every basic need and granting a good deal of what it is possible to formulate as demand.

News from Nowhere also acknowledges the problems that come with satisfaction, and indicates in the process a connection between desire and narrative. Nowhere has everything, it becomes clear, except stories. 'Peace and continuous plenty' seem to eliminate the need for history;[36] books are available, but not many people read them;[37] novels are largely an antiquarian pursuit; and in the absence of the events that would constitute news, people discuss the weather.[38] Even the idea of the future is not very exciting, since it will probably be much like the present. The happiness which is so constantly affirmed in Nowhere is sometimes barely distinguishable from indifference.

But there is unfulfilled desire in Nowhere, and the sorrow it generates, old Hammond tells Guest, has a purpose. Desire gives rise to stories:

> 'For this the Gods have fashioned man's grief and evil day
> That still for man hereafter might be the tale and the lay.'[39]

Hammond claims that he is quoting Homer from memory in one of the nineteenth-century translations.[40] The translation of *The Odyssey* in question, it turns out, is Morris's own, published three years before *News from Nowhere* in 1887, and the author's quotation from his own text is by no means accurate. At the end of Book VIII Alcinous sees Odysseus weep as the poet Demodocus tells the tale of the wooden horse. Alcinous interrupts the song and asks Odysseus to tell his own story, and also to explain,

> 'why thou wert grieving inly, and wherefore thou didst wail
> When the woe of the Argive Danaans, and of Ilios was the tale?
> But this thing the Gods have fashioned, and have spun the Deathful Day
> For men, that for men hereafter it might be the tale and the lay.'[41]

The apparent inference, both in Homer and in Morris's Homer, is that heroic events, even tragic ones, are made into stories which inspire heroism in future generations. The epic defines heroic values, and puts on display an ideal way of life as a model. In their context in *News from Nowhere*, however, and slightly modified as they are, the lines have a different implication. Here they come to indicate that stories themselves are an object of desire, and that what they affirm is not in the end moral values, but lack of satisfaction, dis-content.

Western culture tells stories everywhere: in novels, in newspapers, on television, in history books. Stories are narratives of a succession of events; they involve a difference between past and future; they indicate that things change. Stories involve enigmas, suspense, challenge, the risk that the wished-for future might in practice be worse, not better. They enlist the reader in danger. And paradoxically, they often leave us, I suggested in chapter 2, finally discontented, disappointed with happy endings, unsatisfied by sad ones. Stories are about desire. This need not be sexual desire: Odysseus wanted to get home; Captain Ahab wanted the whale. They also seek to elicit the desire of the reader, if only the desire for a closure that is finally withheld.

Conversely, desire transforms our own lives into narratives full of uncertainty, suspense and challenges. In its citationality, it turns us all into protagonists, heroic or legendary; it turns our objects of desire into figures from fiction, whether folktale or romance. Desire writes us 'like living stories'. Its narrative links our past with an imagined future which might possibly make up for an unnameable loss. Equally, the future might simply reaffirm the loss as irrevocable. Desire enlists us in this danger. And it is by definition unsatisfied.

It is easy to see how the sexual relation, where all the 'intervals of desire' are in play,[42] comes to occupy this field, but sexuality, nevertheless, is not its origin. Desire, which generates dreams, and constitutes their meaning, is no more than a dis-satisfaction whose names are all stand-ins, including 'love'. 'I have a dream,' reiterated Martin Luther King, and enlisted in the process a whole generation of Civil Rights workers. Utopian dreams are evidence of desire, and names for it too. But without stories, which is to say without desire, utopias are no longer desirable. The one desire that dreams themselves cannot finally satisfy is the desire to stay asleep,[43] to go on dreaming and so prolong the narrative. This is what *News from Nowhere* recognizes. The text represents a longing for a socialist utopia, but it also betrays a desire for stories.

VII

Happy or tragic, all stories are inscriptions of desire, but desire also writes stories. And so I end as I began – with writing and its relation to desire. Desire is in the end a question of writing; at the same time, desire is writing in question. The human being in love necessarily writes, inscribes desire in the hollows of enunciation, means passion in the physiology of sex. Nevertheless, desire remains finally uninscribed, in excess of its own performance.

We want what we don't have – and there is a good deal of that from any perspective. But desire is the metonym of a discontent which envisages utopia, a continuing restlessness that motivates change, whether for better or worse.

Notes

Chapter 1   Writing About Desire

1   For the 'oceanic' feeling see Sigmund Freud, *Civilization and its Discontents*, *Civilization, Society and Religion*, ed. Albert Dickson, Penguin Freud Library, vol. 12, London: Penguin Books, 1985, 243–340, pp. 251–60.

2   Monique Wittig, *The Straight Mind and Other Essays*, Hemel Hempstead: Harvester Wheatsheaf, 1992, p. 24.

3   Clare Richards, *Renaissance Summer*, New York: Silhouette Books, 1985, p. 36.

4   Plato, *The Phaedrus*, 237–7; 245–6; 253–6.

5   Arthur Marotti, ' "Love is not Love": Elizabethan Sonnet Sequences and the Social Order', *ELH* 49, 1982, pp. 396–428.

6   Jacques Derrida, 'Differance', *'Speech and Phenomena' and Other Essays on Husserl's Theory of Signs*, trans. David B. Allison, Evanston IL: Northwestern University Press, 1973, pp. 129–60. His translators and admirers do Derrida an injustice when they leave the word in 'French'. *Différance* is not a French word. In the essay Derrida emphatically makes the point that it is not possible to *hear* the difference between 'differance' and 'difference'. To differentiate orally it is necessary to invoke the spelling, the written form, to say 'differance with an a', thus demonstrating the invasion of writing into speech (pp. 132–3).

7   Harriett Hawkins, *Classics and Trash: Traditions and Taboos in High Literature and Popular Modern Genres*, London: Harvester Wheatsheaf, 1990.

8   Jacques Lacan, *Ecrits*, trans. Alan Sheridan, London: Tavistock, 1977, p. 265.

9   See Catherine Belsey, 'Desire's Excess and the English Renaissance Theatre: *Edward II, Troilus and Cressida, Othello*', *Erotic Politics: Desire on the English Renaissance Stage*, ed. Susan Zimmerman, London and New York: Routledge, 1992, pp. 84–102.

10 Malcolm Bowie, *Freud, Proust and Lacan: Theory as Fiction*, Cambridge: Cambridge University Press, 1987, pp. 105–6.

11 Barbara Cartland, *Riding to the Moon*, London: Arrow Books, 1983, pp. 163–4.

12 Roland Barthes, *A Lover's Discourse: Fragments*, trans. Richard Howard, London: Cape, 1979, p. 3.

13 Jacques Derrida, *The Post Card From Socrates to Freud and Beyond*, trans. Alan Bass, Chicago: University of Chicago Press, 1987.

14 Julia Kristeva, *Tales of Love*, trans. Leon S. Roudiez, New York: Columbia University Press, 1987.

15 Sarah Kofman, *Freud and Fiction*, trans. Sarah Wykes, Oxford: Polity Press, 1991, p. 6.

16 Julia Kristeva, *Revolution in Poetic Language*, trans. Margaret Waller, New York: Columbia University Press, 1984, pp. 21–106.

17 Jeanette Winterson, *The Passion*, London: Penguin, 1988, p. 13.

Chapter 2   Reading Love Stories

1 Carol Thurston, *The Romance Revolution: Erotic Novels for Women and the Quest for a New Sexual Identity*, Urbana: University of Illinois Press, 1987, p. 127.

2 Janice A. Radway, *Reading the Romance: Women, Patriarchy, and Popular Literature*, Chapel Hill: University of North Carolina Press, 1984, pp. 62–3.

3 Radway, *Reading the Romance*, p. 99. Peter Mann's British survey of Mills & Boon readers in 1968 elicited similar responses: 'They all leave one with a sense of pleasant and hopeful existence. I find them cheerful and relaxing.' Quoted in Rachel Anderson, *The Purple Heart Throbs: The Sub-literature of Love*, London: Hodder and Stoughton, 1974, p. 257.

4 Radway, *Reading the Romance*, pp. 99, 199–200. Bridget Fowler's later Scottish survey found that 53 per cent of readers of formula romance explicitly preferred happy endings (Bridget Fowler, *The Alienated Reader: Women and Romantic Literature in the Twentieth Century*, Hemel Hempstead: Harvester Wheatsheaf, 1991, p. 146). The comments Fowler records, however, reveal stronger parallels with the Smithton women (see pp. 167, 168, 181).

5 Radway, *Reading the Romance*, pp. 170, 74.

6 Ann Barr Snitow, 'Mass Market Romance: Pornography for Women is Different', *Powers of Desire: The Politics of Sexuality*, edited by Ann Barr Snitow, Christine Stansell and Sharon Thompson, New York: Monthly Review Press, 1983, pp. 259–61.

7 Patricia Wilson, *A Secret Understanding*, Richmond: Mills & Boon, 1989, p. 123.

8 Wilson, *A Secret Understanding*, pp. 17, 10.

9 Lynne Collins, *Surgeon in Disgrace*, London: Mills & Boon, 1985.

10 Judith Krantz, *Till We Meet Again*, London: Bantam Books, 1988, p. 40.

11 Collins, *Surgeon in Disgrace*, p. 181.

12 Jude Deveraux, *Lost Lady*, London: Arrow Books, 1986, p. 220.

13 Quoted in Anderson, *The Purple Heart Throbs*, p. 47.

14 Gustave Flaubert, *Madame Bovary: Provincial Lives*, trans. Geoffrey Wall, London: Penguin, 1992, p. 80.

15 Maurice Blanchot, *The Writing of the Disaster*, trans. Ann Smock, Lincoln: University of Nebraska Press, 1986, p. 5.

16 Margaret Mitchell, *Gone With the Wind*, London: Pan Books, 1974, p. 382.

17 Wilson, *A Secret Understanding*, p. 176.

18 Leigh Ellis, *Green Lady*, New York: Avon Books, 1981, p. 43. Quoted in Radway, *Reading the Romance*, p. 153.

19 Wilson, *A Secret Understanding*, p. 176.

20 Wilson, *A Secret Understanding*, p. 184.

21 Deveraux, *Lost Lady*, p. 271.

22 Collins, *Surgeon in Disgrace*, pp. 182–90.

23 Mitchell, *Gone With the Wind*, pp. 817–18.

24 Wendy Prentice, *Conditional Surrender*, Toronto: Harlequin, 1991, p. 163.

25 Helen Taylor, *Scarlett's Women: Gone With the Wind and its Female Fans*, London: Virago, 1989, p. 73.

26 'Was she beautiful or not beautiful? and what was the secret of form or expression which gave the dynamic quality to her glance?' (George Eliot, *Daniel Deronda*, London: Penguin, 1967); 'Scarlett O'Hara was not beautiful, but men seldom realized it.' (Mitchell, *Gone With the Wind*, p. 5). See Hawkins, *Classics and Trash*, pp. 153, 151–66.

27 Tom Henighan, quoted in Thurston, *The Romance Revolution*, pp. 114–15.

28 Blanchot, *The Writing of the Disaster*, p. 45.

29 Heartline Romances, published in Los Angeles and addressed to African-American readers, do not commonly reproduce the near-rape fantasies which characterize Harlequin and Silhouette romances. Sue Houchins pointed out to me that for a people with a memory of slavery, rape is anything but exciting. Eudora Carroll, *San Francisco Nights*, Los Angeles: Holloway House, 1983, is a best-selling instance. Here the protagonist's successful career is far more central than her romantic interests.

30 Radway, *Reading the Romance*, p. 60. Peter Mann's British survey also found high levels of consumption: 'My husband has had to build two cupboards to store my Mills & Boon books. I have about 500 or so.' Quoted in Anderson, *Purple Heart Throbs*, p. 257.

31 Tania Modleski interestingly attributes the disappointment and the repeated return to the genre to the precariousness of the characteristic romance resolution, which denies the reality of male hostility to women, calling it love (*Loving With a Vengeance: Mass-produced Fantasies for Women*, New York and London: Routledge, 1984, p. 111).

32 Radway is an exception here. She includes a brief discussion of the reader's activity (*Reading the Romance*, pp. 205–8). Tania Modleski also attends to the reader in *Loving With a Vengeance*, but she reads popular fiction for women as fantasy providing wish-fulfilment.

33 See, for instance, Roland Barthes, *The Pleasure of the Text*, trans. Richard Miller, London: Cape, 1976, pp. 10–12. Ross Chambers has written brilliantly about the ways that classical (or limit-case) nineteenth-century stories mobilize the desire of the reader for narrative itself (*Story and Situation: Narrative Seduction and the Power of Fiction*, Manchester: Manchester University Press, 1984). I have drawn on his

work in a general way, especially in chapters 7 and 8 below. But at this stage my argument is confined to the seductive power of the fictional world itself.

34　Krantz, *Till We Meet Again*, p. 52.

35　One of the Smithton women indicates that for her romances are a substitute for traditional Hollywood movies (Radway, *Reading the Romance*, p. 95).

36　Berthold Brecht, *Brecht on Theatre: The Development of an Aesthetic*, ed. and trans. John Willett, London: Eyre Methuen, 1964, p. 187.

37　Barthes, *Pleasure of the Text*, p. 10.

38　Blanchot, *The Writing of the Disaster*, p. 10

39　The alterity in question is the otherness of any object of desire: the difference is not necessarily one of sex, or sexual identity.

40　For a contrary view see Thurston, *The Romance Revolution*.

41　Helen Taylor, '*Gone With the Wind*: The Mammy of Them All', *The Progress of Romance: The Politics of Popular Fiction*, ed. Jean Radford, London: Routledge & Kegan Paul, 1986, pp. 113–36.

42　In *Critical Practice* I was much more confident that Barthes was right (London: Methuen, 1980, pp. 69–84).

43　*Intermezzo* (1939), with Ingrid Bergman and Leslie Howard, has a similar romantic structure, but has not achieved the same cult-status. I have not mentioned *The Third Man* (1949) here, though there are evident parallels, since the love story is complicated by a conflict between desire and friendship.

44　Denis de Rougemont, *Love in the Western World*, trans. Montgomery Belgion, Princeton: Princeton University Press, 1983, p. 15 and passim.

45　Taylor, *Scarlett's Women*, pp. 1–6.

46　Mitchell, *Gone With the Wind*, p. 1010.

47　Mitchell, *Gone With the Wind*, p. 117.

48　Mitchell, *Gone With the Wind*, pp. 914–16.

49　Taylor, *Scarlett's Women*, p. 145.

50　Taylor, *Scarlett's Women*, p. 141.

51　Taylor, *Scarlett's Women*, p. 143.

52　Ronald Haver, *David O. Selznick's Hollywood*, New York: Bonanza Books, 1985, p. 293. I owe this reference to Harriett Hawkins.

Chapter 3　Desire in Theory: Freud, Lacan, Derrida

1　Sigmund Freud, 'On the Universal Tendency to Debasement in the Sphere of Love', *On Sexuality*, ed. Angela Richards, Penguin Freud Library, vol. 7, London: Penguin Books, 1977, 243–60, p. 250. Subsequent page references are given in the text.

2　Sarah Kofman, *The Enigma of Woman: Woman in Freud's Writings*, trans Catherine Porter, Ithaca NY: Cornell University Press, 1985, pp. 85–6.

3　Sigmund Freud, *Three Essays on the Theory of Sexuality*, *On Sexuality*, ed. Angela Richards, Penguin Freud Library, vol. 7, London: Penguin Books, 1977, 31–169, p. 109.

4   Freud, *Three Essays*, p. 141 and n. 15. See also 'Female Sexuality', *On Sexuality*, 367–92, p. 388.

5   Sigmund Freud, '"Civilized" Sexual Morality and Modern Nervous Illness', *Civilization, Society and Religion*, ed. Albert Dickson, Penguin Freud Library, vol. 12, London: Penguin Books, 1985, pp. 27–55.

6   All these possibilities are also implicit in the earlier essay, '"Civilized" Sexual Morality and Modern Nervous Illness': 'the injurious influence of civilization reduces itself in the main to the harmful suppression of the sexual life of civilized peoples (or classes)' (p. 37).

7   The English translation is not quite right here. *Allgemeinste* is (unusually) a superlative: most general.

8   Jean Laplanche, *Life and Death in Psychoanalysis*, trans. Jeffrey Mehlman, Baltimore: Johns Hopkins University Press, 1976, p. 19.

9   Freud, *Three Essays*, p. 83.

10   'A child's intercourse with anyone responsible for his care affords him an unending source of sexual excitation and satisfaction from his erotogenic zones. This is especially so since the person in charge of him, who, after all, is as a rule his mother, herself regards him with feelings that are derived from her own sexual life: she strokes him, kisses him, rocks him and quite clearly treats him as a substitute for a complete sexual object. A mother would probably be horrified if she were made aware that all her marks of affection were rousing her child's sexual instinct and preparing for its later intensity.' (Freud, *Three Essays*, pp. 145–6).

11   Infantile auto-eroticism is parasitic on self-preservation, as the example of thumb-sucking demonstrates (Freud, *Three Essays*, pp. 95–9).

12   Freud, *Three Essays*, p. 146. It is tempting to attribute the male impulse towards a debased sexual object to the division of childcare in the nineteenth-century middle-class family between the mother and working-class nursemaids. But this would be to ignore the fact that little girls are similarly brought up but do not share the tendency to debasement. What they do share is a preference for the clandestine: the 'universal' component of the erotic as the essay analyses it is in practice prohibition, not debasement.

13   Laplanche, *Life and Death*, p. 20.

14   The terms are indistinguishable in Freud: 'Human civilization, by which I mean all those respects in which human life has raised itself above its animal status and differs from the life of beasts – and I scorn to distinguish between culture and civilization . . .' *The Future of an Illusion, Civilization, Society and Religion*, ed. Albert Dickson, Penguin Freud Library, vol. 12, London: Penguin Books, 1985, 179–241, p. 184. *The Future of an Illusion* was published in 1927. In *The Decline of the West* (1922) Spengler had differentiated between *Kultur* (the arts, philosophy, etc.) and *Zivilisation* (vulgar technological progress). I owe this point to Balz Engler.

15   Jacques Lacan, 'The Signification of the Phallus', *Ecrits*, trans. Alan Sheridan, London: Tavistock, 1977, 281–91, p. 281. Subsequent page references to this essay are given in the text.

16 Lacan, *Ecrits*, p. 65.

17 Lacan, *Ecrits*, p. 104.

18 Lacan, *Ecrits*, p. 263.

19 Lacan, *Ecrits*, p. 106.

20 Lacan, *Ecrits*, p. 86.

21 Lacan, *Ecrits*, p. 299.

22 Cf. Jacques Lacan, *The Four Fundamental Concepts of Psycho-analysis*, trans. Alan Sheridan, London: Penguin, 1979, pp. 103–5.

23 Sigmund Freud, *Beyond the Pleasure Principle, On Metapsychology: The Theory of Psychoanalysis*, ed. Angela Richards, Penguin Freud Library, vol. 11, London: Penguin Books, 1984, 269–338, p. 284.

24 Lacan, *Ecrits*, p. 234.

25 Lacan, *Ecrits*, pp. 103–4. For an expanded version of that discussion, see Jacques-Alain Miller (ed.), *The Seminar of Jacques Lacan*, Book I, trans. John Forrester, Cambridge: Cambridge University Press, 1988, pp. 173–4.

26 Lacan, *Four Fundamental Concepts*, p. 239.

27 Freud, *Beyond the Pleasure Principle*, pp. 285–6.

28 Lacan, *Ecrits*, p. 104.

29 Jacques Lacan, *Ecrits*, Paris: Seuil, 1966, p. 691 (hereafter referred to as *Ecrits* (Paris)) and Jacqueline Rose's translation in *Feminine Sexuality: Jacques Lacan and the Ecole Freudienne*, ed. Juliet Mitchell and Jacqueline Rose, trans. Jacqueline Rose, New York: Norton, 1985, p. 80.

30 'The fact that the Father may be regarded as the original representative of this authority of the Law requires us to specify by what privileged mode of presence he is sustained beyond the subject who is actually led to occupy the place of the Other, namely, the Mother.' The 'margin' between demand and need creates anxiety, and the 'whim' of the Other 'introduces the phantom of the Omnipotence, not of the subject, but of the Other in which his demand is installed . . . and with this phantom the need for it to be checked by the Law' (Lacan, *Ecrits*, p. 331).

31 For a discussion of this point see Charles Shepherdson, 'History and the Real', unpublished essay.

32 Lacan, *Ecrits*, p. 199.

33 Lacan, *Ecrits*, p. 197.

34 Lacan, *Ecrits*, p. 199.

35 Lacan, *Ecrits*, p. 263.

36 Lacan, *Ecrits*, p. 263.

37 Jacques-Alain Miller (ed.), *The Seminar of Jacques Lacan*, Book II, trans. Sylvana Tomaselli, Cambridge: Cambridge University Press, 1988, p. 223.

38 Lacan, *Ecrits*, p. 274.

39 Lacan, *Ecrits*, p. 166.

40 Jacques Lacan, 'Of Structure as an Inmixing of an Otherness Prerequisite to Any Subject Whatever', *The Structuralist Controversy: The Languages of Criticism and the Sciences of Man*, ed. Richard Macksey and Eugenio Donato, Baltimore: Johns

Hopkins University Press, 1970, 186–200, pp. 192–5.

41 Lacan, *Ecrits*, p. 24.

42 Miller (ed.), *The Seminar*, I, p. 184.

43 Lacan, *Ecrits*, p. 245.

44 Lacan, *Ecrits*, p. 311.

45 Miller (ed.), *The Seminar*, II, p. 223.

46 Lacan, *Ecrits* (Paris), p. 692.

47 Joan Riviere, 'Womanliness as a Masquerade', *Formations of Fantasy*, ed. Victor Burgin, James Donald and Cora Kaplan, London: Methuen, 1986, pp. 35–44. See also Stephen Heath, 'Joan Riviere and the Masquerade', *Formations of Fantasy*, 45–61.

48 For a discussion of the question see Jane Gallop, 'Reading the Phallus', *Reading Lacan*, Ithaca NY: Cornell University Press, 1985, pp. 133–56.

49 Cf. Lacan, *Ecrits*, pp. 197–8.

50 Charles Shepherdson, 'Image, Mother, Woman: Lacan and Kristeva', unpublished paper.

51 Elsewhere Lacan seems to attribute sexual difference to culture. The 'laws of urinary segregation' are palpably cultural, however widely shared, and in the case of the two children who see 'Ladies' and 'Gentlemen' from the window of the train, Lacan comments, 'For these children, Ladies and Gentlemen will be henceforth two countries towards which each of their souls will strive on divergent wings, and between which a truce will be the more impossible since *they are actually the same country . . .*' (my italics. *Ecrits*, pp. 151–2).

52 Jacques Derrida, '*Le Facteur de la vérité*', *The Post Card from Socrates to Freud and Beyond*, trans. Alan Bass, Chicago: University of Chicago Press, 1987, 411–96, p. 481.

53 Derrida, '*Le Facteur de la vérité*', pp. 414–15.

54 Derrida, '*Le Facteur de la vérité*', p. 472.

55 Derrida, '*Le Facteur de la vérité*', pp. 468–76.

56 Derrida, '*Le Facteur de la vérité*', p. 476, n. 54.

57 Derrida, '*Le Facteur de la vérité*', pp. 477–8.

58 Barbara Johnson, 'The Frame of Reference: Poe, Lacan, Derrida', *Literature and Psychoanalysis: The Question of Reading: Otherwise*, ed. Shoshana Felman, Baltimore: Johns Hopkins University Press, 1982, pp. 457–505.

59 Derrida, '*Le Facteur de la vérité*', p. 420.

60 Jacques Derrida, 'To Speculate – on "Freud"', *The Post Card*, 257–409, p. 293.

61 Derrida, 'To Speculate – on "Freud"', pp. 298–304.

62 Jacques Derrida, 'Envois', *The Post Card*, 1–256, p. 26. Subsequent page references are given in the text.

63 'In several places I will leave all kinds of references, names of persons and of places, authentifiable dates, identifiable events, they will rush in with eyes closed, finally believing to be there and to find us there when by means of a switch point I will send them elsewhere to see if we are there, with a stroke of the pen or the *grattoir* I will make everything derail . . .' (p. 177)

216

64 Lacan, *Ecrits*, p. 263.
65 Jacques Derrida, *La Carte postale: de Socrate à Freud et au-delà*, Paris: Flammarion, 1980, p. 196.
66 Jacques Derrida, *Of Grammatology*, trans. Gayatri Chakravorty Spivak, Baltimore: Johns Hopkins University Press, 1976, p. 143.

Chapter 4   Postmodern Love

1   Ferdinand de Saussure, *A Course in General Linguistics*, trans. Wade Baskin, London: Fontana, 1974, pp. 116–17.
2   Roland Barthes, *A Lover's Discourse: Fragments*, trans. Richard Howard, London: Cape, 1979, p. 151.
3   Barthes, *A Lover's Discourse*, p. 148.
4   Jean-François Lyotard, *The Differend: Phrases in Dispute*, trans. Georges Van Den Abbeele, Manchester: Manchester University Press, 1988, p. 13.
5   Lyotard, *The Differend*, p. 70.
6   Jeanette Winterson, *Written on the Body*, London: Cape, 1992, pp. 78–9.
7   Ludwig Wittgenstein, *Tractatus Logico-Philosophicus*, ed. and trans. D. F. Pears and B. F. McGuinness, London: Routledge & Kegan Paul, 1972, p. 151.
8   Derrida, *The Post Card*, p. 194.
9   Lyotard, *The Differend*, p. 13.
10 Winterson, *Written on the Body*, p. 9.
11 Linda Hutcheon, *A Poetics of Postmodernism: History, Theory, Fiction*, New York and London: Routledge, 1988, p. 5 and passim.
12 Barthes, *A Lover's Discourse*, p. 15.
13 Winterson, *The Passion*, p. 13.
14 Winterson, *The Passion*, p. 133.
15 Winterson, *The Passion*, p. 89.
16 Winterson, *The Passion*, pp. 5, 13; cf. p. 160.
17 Winterson, *The Passion*, p. 40.
18 Winterson, *The Passion*, p. 69.
19 Winterson, *The Passion*, pp. 157–8.
20 Julian Barnes, *Flaubert's Parrot*, London: Pan Books, 1985, pp. 12, 38, 65.
21 Barnes, *Flaubert's Parrot*, p. 81.
22 Barnes, *Flaubert's Parrot*, p. 18.
23 Julian Barnes, *Talking It Over*, London: Pan Books, 1992, p. 80.
24 Barnes, *Talking It Over*, p. 80.
25 Barnes, *Talking It Over*, p. 137.
26 Lyotard, *The Differend*, p. 151.
27 Winterson, *Written on the Body*, p. 89.
28 A. S. Byatt, *Possession: A Romance*, London: Vintage, 1991, pp. 267, 423.
29 Byatt, *Possession*, p. 425.
30 *Paradise Lost* IV, 271–2.

31 'Maud: A Monodrama', *The Poems of Tennyson*, ed. Christopher Ricks, London: Longmans, 1969, ll. 78–9.

32 W. B. Yeats, *Collected Poems*, London: Macmillan, 1958, p. 348.

33 Yeats, *Collected Poems*, p. 101

34 Byatt, *Possession*, p. 284.

35 Byatt, *Possession*, pp. 506–7.

36 Byatt, *Possession*, pp. 502, 506.

37 Byatt, *Possession*, p. 138; Lacan, *Ecrits*, p. 5.

38 The French renders the metaphoric topography marginally less obscure: *'la formation du* je *se symbolise oniriquement par un camp retranché, voire un stade, – distribuant de l'arène intérieure à son enceinte, à son portour de gravats et de marécages, deux champs de lutte opposés où le sujet s'empêtre dans la quête de l'altier et lointain château intérieur, dont la forme . . . symbolise le* ça . . .' (Lacan, *Ecrits* (Paris), p. 97).

39 Lacan, *Ecrits*, p. 4.

40 Byatt, *Possession*, pp. 140, 250

41 Byatt, *Possession*, p. 276.

42 Byatt, *Possession*, p. 507.

43 Byatt, *Possession*, p. 284.

44 Roland had to be made slightly more 'masculine' for the American edition (*Washington Post Book World* 22, no. 38, 20 September 1992). I am grateful to Lena Cowen Orlin for this information.

45 Lacan, *Ecrits*, pp. 245, 265. For a Hegelian reading of Lacan see Richard Boothby, *Death and Desire: Psychoanalytic Theory in Lacan's Return to Freud*, New York: Routledge, 1991.

46 Byatt, *Possession*, p. 289.

47 Byatt, *Possession*, p. 291.

48 Anne Rice, *Interview with the Vampire*, London: Futura, 1977, p. 97.

49 This characteristic is anticipated in 'Carmilla' (1872). 'The vampire is prone to be fascinated with an engrossing vehemence, resembling the passion of love, by particular persons. In pursuit of these it will exercise inexhaustible patience and stratagem, for access to a particular object may be obstructed in a hundred ways. It will never desist until it has satiated its passion, and drained the very life of its coveted victim . . . In these cases it seems to yearn for something like sympathy and consent. In ordinary ones it goes direct to its object, overpowers with violence, and strangles and exhausts often at a single feast.' Sheridan Le Fanu, 'Carmilla', *In a Glass Darkly*, Gloucester: Alan Sutton, 1990, 239-314, pp. 312–13.

50 Anne Rice, *The Queen of the Damned*, London: Futura, 1990, pp. 80-1.

51 Rice, *Queen of the Damned*, pp. 3-4.

52 Rice, *Queen of the Damned*, p. 528.

53 The film introduces elements from fairy-tale: for example, in Coppola's version Lucy's family is aristocratic, while Mina is a poor schoolteacher. Dracula, meanwhile, is identified as her 'prince'.

54 Barbara Johnson, '"Aesthetic" and "Rapport" in Toni Morrison's *Sula*', *Textual Practice* 7, 1993, pp. 165–72.

Chapter 5   Adultery in King Arthur's Court: Chrétien, Malory, Tennyson

1   C. S. Lewis, *The Allegory of Love: A Study in Medieval Tradition*, Oxford: Oxford University Press, 1936.

2   There are, of course, exceptions. F. Douglas Kelly, for instance, argues that Chrétien celebrates adultery (*Sens and Conjointure* in The Chevalier de la Charrette, The Hague: Mouton, 1966). For a more subtle, but still moralistic account, see Pamela Raabe, 'Chrétien's *Lancelot* and the Sublimity of Adultery', *University of Toronto Quarterly* 57, 1987–8, pp. 259–69.

3   John D. Sinclair (ed. and trans.), *The Divine Comedy of Dante Alighieri*, I, *Inferno*, Oxford: Oxford University Press, 1948, Canto v, lines 73–138.

4   Mario Roques (ed.), *Les Romans de Chrétien de Troyes*, III, *Le Chevalier de la charrete*, Paris: Champion, 1958. Subsequent line references are given in the text.

5   Georges Duby, 'Youth in Aristocratic Society', *The Chivalrous Society*, trans. Cynthia Postan, London: Edward Arnold, 1977, 112–22. See also Stephen Knight, *Arthurian Literature and Society*, London: Macmillan, 1983, p. 82. Knight's persuasive argument is that Chrétien's Arthurian romances were addressed to a knight-errant class seeking to gain independence of aristocratic landowners.

6   Hollywood heroes do their dreaming and suffering in private – 'round midnight'.

7   See, for example, L. T. Topsfield, *Chrétien de Troyes: A Study of the Arthurian Romances*, Cambridge: Cambridge University Press, 1981, p. 124; Peter S. Noble, *Love and Marriage in Chrétien de Troyes*, Cardiff: University of Wales Press, 1982, p. 67.

8   For a brilliant analysis of the rhetoric of paradox in Gottfried's *Tristan* see Robert Glendinning, 'Eros, Agape, and Rhetoric Around 1200: Gervase of Melkley's *Ars poetica* and Gottfried von Strassburg's *Tristan*', *Speculum* 67, 1992, 892–925.

9   Ovid, *The Art of Love* II, 235–6.

10   Thomas, *Le Roman de Tristan*, ed. Joseph Bédier, Paris: Firmin Didot, 1902–5, 2 vols, vol. 1, pp. 271–2. Subsequent references are to this edition.

11   Freud, *Beyond the Pleasure Principle*, p. 285; Lacan, *Ecrits*, pp. 103–4.

12   Lacan, *Ecrits*, p. 104.

13   In the thirteenth-century *Romance of the Rose*, Guillaume de Lorris's lover pays homage to the God of Love, and promises to obey his laws. But Reason, who is made by God himself in his own image, comes down out of her high tower to try to win him back. He is wasting his time, she argues, seeking his own suffering. In Chaucer's translation Reason urges:

> This is the yvell that love they call,
> Wherynne ther is but foly al;
> For love is foly everydell.

(*The Romaunt of the Rose, The Works of Geoffrey Chaucer*, ed. F. N. Robinson, London: Oxford University Press, 1957, lines 3269–71.) The lover, however, sends her away. In this instance, of course, Reason represents Christian morality and not just clear thinking.

14 Béroul does, however, raise the moral question. After three years the love potion suddenly wears off. The lovers then regret their love, though mainly, it appears, because they miss the luxurious life of the court. Ogrin the hermit urges repentance. The lovers agree and Yseut returns to King Mark – then resumes her relationship with Tristan, which continues to its tragic end. The text thus invokes the position of the Church and then goes on to ignore it. All our sympathy is with the lovers.

15 R. Howard Bloch argues that just as stories of marriage to an heiress resolved at the level of fantasy the discontents of the landless knights in the audience, so tales of rescue by handsome lovers offered women illusory compensation for the realities of aristocratic arranged marriages (*Medieval Misogyny and the Invention of Western Romantic Love*, Chicago: University of Chicago Press, 1991, pp. 165–73).

16 Georges Duby, *The Knight, The Lady and the Priest: The Making of Modern Marriage in Medieval France*, trans. Barbara Bray, London: Penguin, 1985.

17 I do not mean to take sides in the scholarly debate about whether Malory conceived the Arthurian stories as a set of separate Tales or a single unit. Clearly there are continuities between the Tales, but what the author had in mind is not now available and seems to me, moreover, a matter of some indifference. In quest of an account of desire, I shall not place the emphasis on the distinctions between separate Tales.

18 Eugène Vinaver (ed.), *Malory: Works*, London: Oxford University Press, 1971, p. 657. Subsequent page references are given in the text.

19 Something similar happens in Béroul's *Tristan*: see n. 14 above.

20 Homoeroticism is not apparently an option, at least explicitly. In one episode Lancelot wakes up to find himself embraced by a person with a rough beard. This turns out to be a case of mistaken identity, however, and nothing comes of it but comedy (p. 153).

21 Robert Merrill, *Sir Thomas Malory and the Cultural Crisis of the Late Middle Ages*, New York: Peter Lang, 1987.

22 Knight, *Arthurian Literature*, p. 107.

23 Christopher Ricks (ed.), *The Poems of Tennyson*, London: Longman, 1987, 3 vols, vol. 3. Subsequent references are to this edition.

24 Tony Tanner, *Adultery in the Novel: Contract and Transgression*, Baltimore MD: Johns Hopkins University Press, 1979, p. 15.

25 Charlotte Brontë, *Jane Eyre*, ed. Q. D. Leavis, London: Penguin, 1966, pp. 475–6.

26 Charles Dickens, *The Personal History of David Copperfield*, ed. Trevor Blount, London: Penguin, 1966, pp. 729, 733, 768.

27 George Eliot, *Middlemarch*, ed. W. J. Harvey, London: Penguin, 1965, p. 894.

28 William Makepeace Thackeray, *The Newcomes: Memoirs of a Most Respectable Family*, ed. George Saintsbury, London: Oxford University Press, n.d., p. 752.

29 Quoted in Erna Olafson Hellerstein et al. (ed.), *Victorian Women: A Documentary Account of Women's Lives in Nineteenth-century England, France, and the United States*, Stanford CA: Stanford University Press, 1981, p. 177.

30 Jeffrey Weeks, *Sex, Politics and Society: The Regulation of Sexuality Since 1800*, London: Longman, 1981, pp. 40–1. Sarah Austin was certainly not indifferent to sexual feeling in the 1830s: see Lotte Hamburger and Joseph Hamburger, *Contemplating Adultery: The Secret Life of a Victorian Woman*, New York: Ballantine, 1991.

31 For the Matrimonial Causes Act and the debates surrounding it, see Lawrence Stone, *Road to Divorce: England 1530–1987*, Oxford: Oxford University Press, 1990, pp. 368–82; and Roderick Phillips, *Putting Asunder: A History of Divorce in Western Society*, Cambridge: Cambridge University Press, 1988, pp. 479–515. Mary Poovey gives an excellent account of some of the implications in *Uneven Developments: The Ideological Work of Gender in Mid-Victorian England*, London: Virago, 1989, pp. 51–88.

32 William Morris, 'The Defence of Guenevere', *The Collected Works of William Morris*, vol. 1, London: Longmans Green, 1910, p. 3.

33 Morris, 'Defence', pp. 2, 5, 10. (The second line varies slightly each time.)

34 Lynda Nead, *Myths of Sexuality: Representations of Women in Victorian Britain*, Oxford: Basil Blackwell, 1988, p. 77.

35 Thackeray, *The Newcomes*, pp. 729, 733.

36 For examples see Nead, *Myths of Sexuality*, pp. 64, 66.

37 Anthony Trollope, *The Belton Estate*, London: Folio Society, 1991, p. 78.

38 Trollope, *The Belton Estate*, p. xiv.

39 John D. Jump (ed.), *Tennyson: The Critical Heritage*, London: Routledge & Kegan Paul, 1967, p. 258.

40 Ricks (ed.), *Poems* 3, p. 491.

Chapter 6 John Donne's Worlds of Desire

1 Henry James, *The Golden Bowl*, London: Penguin, 1966, p. 122. Subsequent page references are given in the text.

2 References to Donne's poems are to Helen Gardner (ed.), *The Elegies* and *The Songs and Sonnets*, Oxford: Clarendon Press, 1965.

3 Edmund Spenser, *Amoretti* 15, *Poetical Works*, ed. J. C. Smith and E. de Selincourt, London: Oxford University Press, 1912.

4 Lloyd A. Brown, *The Story of Maps*, London: Cresset Press, 1951, pp. 160–4.

5 See, for example, Andrew Marvell, 'Bermudas'. See also Stephen Greenblatt, *Renaissance Self-Fashioning: From More to Shakespeare*, Chicago: University of Chicago Press, 1980, pp. 180–1. These landscapes were commonly characterized as feminine: see Annette Kolodny, *The Lay of the Land: Metaphor as Experience and History in American Life and Letters*, Chapel Hill: University of North Carolina Press, 1975, pp. 4–25.

6 Antony Easthope, *Poetry and Phantasy*, Cambridge: Cambridge University Press, 1989, pp. 53–60. In Thomas Docherty's rather more blunt formulation, 'What is being sought by the poet is recognition of his maleness, recognition of his phallus, and an acknowledgement of the power which its potency is supposed to give him' (*John Donne, Undone*, London: Methuen, 1986, p. 82).

7 Easthope, *Poetry and Phantasy*, p. 58.

8 Sigmund Freud, 'On Narcissism: An Introduction', *On Metapsychology: The Theory of Psychoanalysis*, ed. Angela Richards, The Penguin Freud Library, vol. 11, London: Penguin Books, 1984, 59–97, pp. 81–3.

9 Lacan, *Ecrits*, p. 58.

10 Julia Kristeva, *Tales of Love*, trans. Leon S. Roudiez, New York: Columbia University Press, 1987, p. 33.

11 Easthope, *Poetry and Phantasy*, pp. 56–7.

12 Lacan, *Four Fundamental Concepts*, p. 81.

13 Lacan, *Four Fundamental Concepts*, p. 73. In the Seminar 'Of the Gaze as *Objet Petit a*' the gaze in question is always double: the gaze of the subject, which brings into being the imaginary world of objects, and the gaze of the world, which is constitutive for the subject.

14 'Julia Kristeva in Conversation with Rosalind Coward', *Desire*, ICA Document 1, London: Institute of Contemporary Arts, 1984, pp. 22, 23.

15 Kristeva, *Tales of Love*, p. 35.

16 Kristeva, *Tales of Love*, p. 34.

17 Kristeva, *Tales of Love*, p. 36.

18 Fredson Bowers (ed.), *The Complete Works of Christopher Marlowe*, Cambridge: Cambridge University Press, 2 vols, vol. 2.

19 Kristeva, *Tales of Love*, p. 5.

20 I owe this point to David Skilton.

21 Chaucer's version anticipates some of the comedy of Donne's. Troilus addresses the sun as follows:

> O fool, wel may men the dispise,
> That hast the dawyng al nyght by thi syde,
> And suffrest her so soone up fro the rise,
> For to disese loveris in this wyse.
> What! holde youre bed ther, thow, and eke thi Morwe!

(*Troilus and Criseyde*, lines 1465–9, F. N. Robinson (ed.), *The Works of Geoffrey Chaucer*, London: Oxford University Press, 1957.)

22 *Romeo and Juliet* 3. 5. 27–35, William Shakespeare, *The Complete Works*, ed. Peter Alexander, Glasgow: Collins, 1951.

23 Where Helen Gardner gives line 14 as 'Let us possesse our world, each hath one, and is one', most modern editors settle for the version of 1633: 'Let us possesse one world . . .' I have not thought it necessary to choose between them.

24 See Mary Jacobus, 'The Difference of View', *The Feminist Reader: Essays in Gender*

and the Politics of Literary Criticism, ed. Catherine Belsey and Jane Moore, London: Macmillan, 1989, 49–62, p. 57.

25 Helen Gardner (ed.), *The Elegies* and *The Songs and Sonnets*, p. 199.
26 Theodore Redpath (ed.), *The Songs and Sonets of John Donne*, London: Methuen, 1983, p. 231.
27 'The conceit that one's previous mistresses were only shadows or gleams of the lady one addresses is common in Renaissance lyrics, but "desir'd, and got" is not.' A. J. Smith (ed.), *John Donne: The Complete Poems*, London: Penguin, 1973, p. 378.
28 Lacan, *Four Fundamental Concepts*, p. 103.
29 H. M. Margoliouth (ed.), *The Poems and Letters of Andrew Marvell*, Oxford: Clarendon Press, 2 vols, vol. 1, 1971.
30 John Milton, *Paradise Lost* IV, 751–2, ed. John Carey and Alastair Fowler, *The Poems of John Milton*, London: Longman, 1968.
31 For a more detailed discussion of these issues, see Catherine Belsey, *The Subject of Tragedy: Identity and Difference in Renaissance Drama*, London: Routledge, 1985, pp. 129–221; and *John Milton: Language, Gender, Power*, Oxford: Blackwell, 1988, pp. 53–8.
32 See, for example, pp. 536–7. cf. pp. 318–19, 396.

Chapter 7 Demon Lovers

1 Ovid, *Metamorphoses*, XIV.
2 Edmund Spenser, *The Faerie Queene*, ed. A. C. Hamilton, London: Longman, 1977, II.12.83. Subsequent references are to this edition.
3 Lewis, *The Allegory of Love*, p. 298.
4 Lewis, *The Allegory of Love*, p. 360.
5 Lewis, *The Allegory of Love*, p. 340.
6 Lewis, *The Allegory of Love*, p. 332.
7 Lewis, *The Allegory of Love*, p. 332.
8 Lewis, *The Allegory of Love*, p. 326.
9 Greenblatt, *Renaissance Self-Fashioning*, pp. 171, 172.
10 Greenblatt, *Renaissance Self-Fashioning*, pp. 173–84.
11 Paul J. Alpers, *The Poetry of* The Faerie Queene, Princeton, NJ: Princeton University Press, 1967, p. 45.
12 Lacan, *Four Fundamental Concepts*, p. 112.
13 Lacan, *Four Fundamental Concepts*, p. 103.
14 This holds even when the fiction in question is an allegory. 'Allegory' (other speaking) points to a duality of meaning within the text, not a truth outside it.
15 Lacan, *Four Fundamental Concepts*, pp. 111, 116.
16 Spenser, *The Faerie Queene*, p. 737. In Greenblatt's account this fashioning process slides into 'self-fashioning', the ultimate dream of individualism, as if, like Coriolanus, 'a man were author of himself', independent of textuality or culture (Greenblatt, *Renaissance Self-Fashioning*, p. 177).

17 *Amoretti*, Sonnet 65. See Scott Wilson, *Elizabethan Subjectivity and Sonnet Sequences*, unpublished doctoral dissertation, University of Wales, 1990, pp. 182–3.

18 See Richard Gordon, 'Lucan's Erictho', *Homo Viator: Classical Essays for John Bramble*, ed. Michael Whitby, Philip Hardie and Mary Whitby, Bristol: Bristol Classical Press, 1987, 231–41, p. 240. I owe this reference to Cynthia Dessen.

19 *Lamia, The Poems of John Keats*, ed. Miriam Allott, London: Longman, 1975, I, 115. Subsequent line references are given in the text.

20 Riviere, 'Womanliness as a Masquerade', p. 38.

21 Lacan, *Four Fundamental Concepts*, p. 75.

22 Jacques Lacan, *Le Séminaire, livre XI: Les Quatre Concepts fondamenteaux de la psychanalyse*, Paris: Seuil, 1973, p. 72.

23 Lacan, *Four Fundamental Concepts*, pp. 75–6.

24 Lacan, *Four Fundamental Concepts*, p. 107.

25 Lacan, *Four Fundamental Concepts*, p. 76.

26 Lacan, *Four Fundamental Concepts*, p. 81. It could be argued, of course, that Descartes was *more* sceptical than Berkeley, since Berkeley did not share Descartes's distrust of the senses. Lacan's point is not offered, however, as a contribution to philosophical debate within the Enlightenment tradition.

27 'Ode to a Nightingale', line 70.

28 Sigmund Freud, *The Interpretation of Dreams*, ed. Angela Richards, Penguin Freud Library, vol. 4, London: Penguin, 1976, p. 429.

29 'The philosopher, as philosopher, is a secret accomplice of the phallocrat. For philosophy is not just any discipline. It is the search for a constituting order that gives meaning to the world, society and discourse. Philosophy is the West's madness and never ceases to underwrite its quests for knowledge and politics in the name of Truth and the Good.' (Jean-François Lyotard, 'One of the Things at Stake in Women's Struggles', trans. Deborah J. Clarke, *SubStance* 20, 1978, 9–17, p. 14.

30 Derrida mentions the power of the *trompe-l'oeil* to overthrow the system of truth implied by mimesis (*Acts of Literature*, ed. Derek Attridge, New York: Routledge, 1992, p. 152).

31 Jacques Derrida, *Spurs: Nietzsche's Styles*, trans. Barbara Harlow, Chicago: University of Chicago Press, 1979, pp. 51, 53. For a sympathetic feminist reading of *Spurs* see Jane Moore, 'Unseating the Philosopher-Knight', *Political Gender: Texts and Contexts*, ed. Sally Ledger, Josephine McDonagh and Jane Spencer, Hemel Hempstead: Harvester Wheatsheaf, 1994, 72–84.

32 Mario Praz, *The Romantic Agony* [1931], trans. Angus Davidson, London: Oxford University Press, 1970. Praz was primarily concerned with the erotic fascination of beauty in combination with horror. His categories are in consequence much broader, of course, than my 'demon lovers'.

33 Edgar Allan Poe, 'Ligeia', *Selected Writings*, ed. David Galloway, London: Penguin, 1967, 110–26, p. 116. Subsequent line references are given in the text.

34 Sigmund Freud, 'The "Uncanny"', *Art and Literature*, ed. Albert Dickson, Penguin Freud Library 14, London: Penguin, 1985, 335–76, p. 364.

35 In practice the first meaning is rare: the usual meaning of *heimlich* is 'secret'.

36 For an extremely sophisticated reading which settles, in the end, for the view that the revenant is an illusion, see Elisabeth Bronfen, *Over Her Dead Body: Death, Femininity, and the Aesthetic*, Manchester: Manchester University Press, 1992, pp. 324–36.

37 Freud, 'The "Uncanny"', p. 374. For the importance of generic indeterminacy in Freud's essay see Kofman, *Freud and Fiction*, pp. 119–62; and Lis Møller, *The Freudian Reading: Analytical and Fictional Constructions*, Philadelphia: University of Pennsylvania Press, 1991, pp. 111–39.

38 It is also, and perhaps more recognizably, Miltonic (*Paradise Lost*, IV. 301).

39 Walter Pater, *The Renaissance: Studies in Art and Poetry*, ed. Donald L. Hill, Berkeley: University of California Press, 1980, pp. 98–9.

40 W. B. Yeats (ed.), *The Oxford Book of Modern Verse, 1892–35*, Oxford: Clarendon Press, 1936, p. 1.

41 'The Great Silkie of Sule Skerry', *The English and Scottish Popular Ballads*, ed. Francis James Child, New York: Dover Publications, 1965, 5 vols, vol. 2, p. 494.

42 See Milan V. Dimic, 'Vampiromania in the Eighteenth Century: The Other Side of the Enlightenment', *Man and Nature: Proceedings of the Canadian Society for Eighteenth-century Studies* 3, ed. Robert James Merrett, Edmonton, Alberta: Academic Printing and Publishing, 1984, 1–22; Christopher Frayling, *Vampyres: Lord Byron to Count Dracula*, London: Faber & Faber, 1992, pp. 19–36.

43 Transylvania: on the other side of the forest. Bram Stoker had access to Emily Gerard's travel book, *The Land Beyond the Forest*, New York: Harper and Bros, 1888 (see Leonard Wolf, *The Annotated Dracula*, New York: Clarkson N. Potter, 1975, xiii–xiv).

44 Thomas Laqueur, *Making Sex: Body and Gender from the Greeks to Freud*, Cambridge MA: Harvard University Press, 1990.

45 For a brilliant textual analysis of the dissolution of gender in *Dracula* see Christopher Craft, '"Kiss Me with Those Red Lips": Gender and Inversion in Bram Stoker's *Dracula*', *Representations*, 8, 1984, pp. 107–33.

46 Katharina M. Wilson, 'The History of the Word '"Vampire"', *Journal of the History of Ideas* 46, 1985, 577–83, p. 580.

47 Wilson, 'History', pp. 581–2.

48 John William Polidori, *The Vampyre: A Tale*, London: Sherwood, Neely and Jones, 1819, pp. xix–xx.

49 Bram Stoker, *Dracula*, ed. Maurice Hindle, London: Penguin, 1993, p. 475. Subsequent page references are given in the text.

50 Derrida, *Spurs*, p. 101.

51 Derrida, *Spurs*, p. 54. My translation. (*Spurs* is full of puns and *double entendres*, instances of linguistic *trompe-l'oeil*, which make it particularly difficult to translate satisfactorily. I have diverged from the translator here in order to bring out the sexual implications of Derrida's *prendre*: take/capture.

52 In 'La Double Séance' it is specifically the hymen, 'the fine, invisible veil', which represents the undecidability of meaning (Derrida, *Acts of Literature*, p. 165), but in *Spurs* the veil is less determinate.

53 Derrida, *Spurs*, p. 61.

54 In 'Sex and Repression in Civilized Societies', a paper delivered at the ESSE Conference in 1993, Maria Cândida Zamith Silva draws attention to the great number of fictional women who refuse or challenge the Law.

55 Derrida, *Spurs*, p. 107.

56 Derrida, *Spurs*, p. 133.

57 Mary Ann Doane discusses *Spurs* and Lacan's account of the gaze in relation to cinematic images of women, and concludes that the poststructuralist 'envy' of woman is an idealization that reduces her to a symptom of the lack which haunts theory ('Veiling Over Desire: Close-ups of the Woman', *Femmes Fatales: Feminism, Film Theory, Psychoanalysis*, New York: Routledge, 1991, pp. 44–75). The problem with the debate about whether poststructuralism is 'for' or 'against' women is that it tends to essentialize the theory. My concern is rather what we might do with a cultural meaning which is certainly patriarchal, but which points to the limits of patriarchal control. Since poststructuralist theory proposes that 'man' is no more than a symptom of the desire for plenitude, the question is where we might (all) go from here.

Chapter 8   Desire in Utopia

1 Joanna Russ, *The Female Man*, Boston, MA: Beacon Press, 1986, p. 76.

2 Russ, *The Female Man*, pp. 75–6.

3 Russ, *The Female Man*, p. 77.

4 Russ, *The Female Man*, p. 79.

5 For a historical account of utopian writing see Frank E. Manuel and Fritzie P. Manuel, *Utopian Thought in the Western World*, Oxford: Basil Blackwell, 1979.

6 Thomas More, *Utopia*, trans. Raphe Robynson, ed. Robert Steele, London: Dent, 1898, p. 103.

7 More, *Utopia*, p. 114.

8 Charlotte Perkins Gilman, *Herland*, London: The Women's Press, 1979, p. 127.

9 William Morris, *News from Nowhere*, *News from Nowhere and Other Writings*, ed. Clive Wilmer, London: Penguin, 1993, p. 92.

10 Morris, *News from Nowhere*, p. 189.

11 Fay Weldon, *Darcy's Utopia*, London: William Collins, 1990, p. 114.

12 Ursula Le Guin, *The Dispossessed*, London: Granada, 1975, p. 154.

13 Sarah Scott, *A Description of Millenium Hall and the Country Adjacent*, London: Virago, 1986, p. 115.

14 Scott, *Millenium Hall*, p. 179.

15 Divorce is available in Utopia on the basis of the consent of both parties, as well as the magistrate and his wife.

16 Greenblatt, *Renaissance Self-Fashioning*, pp. 43–4.

17 Marge Piercy, *Woman on the Edge of Time*, London: The Women's Press, 1979, p. 125.

18 Monique Wittig, *Les Guérillères*, trans. David Le Vay, Boston: Beacon Press, 1985, p. 108.

19 More, *Utopia*, p. 84.

20 Northrop Frye, 'Varieties of Literary Utopias', *Utopias and Utopian Thought*, ed. Frank E. Manuel, London: Souvenir Press, 1973, 25–49, p. 36.

21 Darko Suvin, *Metamorphoses of Science Fiction: On the Poetics and History of a Literary Genre*, New Haven: Yale University Press, 1979, p. 4.

22 Russ, *The Female Man*, p. 22.

23 Le Guin, *The Dispossessed*, p. 51.

24 Wittig, *Les Guérillères*, p. 134.

25 Roland Barthes, 'Textual Analysis of Poe's *Valdemar*', *Untying the Text: A Post-Structuralist Reader*, ed. Robert Young, London: Routledge & Kegan Paul, 1981, p. 142.

26 Piercy, *Woman*, p. 9.

27 Russ, *The Female Man*, p. 160.

28 Lacan, *Ecrits*, p. 260.

29 Michèle le Doeuff, *Recherches sur l'imaginaire philosophique*, Paris: Payot, 1980, pp. 35–42.

30 E. P. Thompson, *William Morris: Romantic to Revolutionary*, London: Merlin, 1977, pp. 692–8.

31 Morris, *News from Nowhere*, p. 227.

32 Jan Marsh, 'Concerning Love: *News from Nowhere* and Gender', *William Morris and News from Nowhere: A Vision for Our Time*, ed. Stephen Coleman and Paddy O'Sullivan, Bideford: Green Books, 1990, 107–25, p. 124.

33 Patrick Parrinder, 'News from the Land of No News', *Foundation* 51, 1991, 29–37.

34 Freud, *The Interpretation of Dreams*, pp. 229–33.

35 Lacan, *Ecrits*, pp. 261–3.

36 Morris, *News from Nowhere*, p. 89.

37 Morris, *News from Nowhere*, p. 166.

38 Morris, *News from Nowhere*, p. 193.

39 Morris, *News from Nowhere*, p. 92.

40 Morris, *News from Nowhere*, p. 91.

41 *The Collected Works of William Morris, vol. XIII, The Odyssey of Homer Done into English Verse*, London: Longmans Green, 1912, p. 117.

42 Lacan, *Four Fundamental Concepts*, p. 192.

43 Freud, *The Interpretation of Dreams*, pp. 330–1.

Index